Acquisition
and Corporate
Development

Arthur D. Little Books

A series of books on management and other scientific and technical subjects by senior professional staff members of Arthur D. Little, Inc., the international consulting and research organization. The series also includes selected nonproprietary case studies.

Acquisition and Corporate Development
   James W. Bradley and Donald H. Korn

Bankruptcy Risk in Financial Depository Intermediaries: Assessing Regulatory Effects
   Michael F. Koehn

Board Compass: What It Means to Be a Director in a Changing World
   Robert Kirk Mueller

Career Conflict: Management's Inelegant Dysfunction
   Robert Kirk Mueller

The Corporate Development Process
   Anthony J. Marolda

Corporate Responsibilities and Opportunities to 1990
   Ellen T. Curtiss and Philip A. Untersee

The Dynamics of Industrial Location: Microeconometric Modeling for Policy Analysis
   Kirkor Bozdogan and David Wheeler

Systems Methods for Socioeconomic and Environmental Impact Analysis
   Glenn R. De Souza

The Incompleat Board: The Unfolding of Corporate Governance
   Robert Kirk Mueller

Energy Policy and Forecasting
   Glenn R. De Souza

Communications Network Analysis
   Howard Cravis

Board Score: How to Judge Boardworthiness
   Robert Kirk Mueller

International Telecommunications: User Requirements and Supplier Strategies
   Edited by Kathleen Landis Lancaster

New Dimensions of Project Management
   Edited by Albert J. Kelley

Wind Power for the Electric-Utility Industry: Policy Incentives for Fuel Conservation
   Frederic March

Acquisition and Corporate Development

A Contemporary Perspective for the Manager

James W. Bradley
Donald H. Korn
Arthur D. Little, Inc.

An Arthur D. Little Book

LexingtonBooks
D.C. Heath and Company
Lexington, Massachusetts
Toronto

Library of Congress Cataloging in Publication Data

Bradley, James W
    Acquisition and corporate development.

    Includes bibliographies.
    Includes index.
1. Consolidation and merger of corporations. 2. Corporations—Growth.
I. Korn, Donald H., joint author. II. Title.
HD2746.5.B7   658.1′6   79-7719
ISBN 0-669-03170-4   AACR2

Third printing, June 1982

Published simultaneously in Canada

Printed in the United States of America

International Standard Book Number: 0-669-03170-4

Library of Congress Catalog Card Number: 79-7719

Contents

List of Figures

List of Tables

Preface

This book is designed to provide managers with a unifying conceptual and analytical framework from which to plan for, develop, and carry out an acquisition program as part of the overall corporate-development process. In focusing on these objectives, we have integrated certain basic economic forces and principles underlying the acquisition versus internal-development decision, as well as the broad questions of acquisition strategy and value creation. These have been tied into a discussion of issues of antitrust; industry/candidate selection and evaluation; accounting, financial, and valuation issues; and the functions, roles, and organization of the acquisition process itself. Finally, we comment on the reasons that completed acquisitions succeed or fail and also discuss the buy-back of one's own stock as a possible alternative to both acquisition and internal development.

The idea for this book grew out of our experience in consulting for a number of corporations, domestic and foreign. We were often asked to define the basis and rationale for the acquisition activity in the United States of recent years and to relate these to a particular company's interests, strategic growth options, and specific acquisition opportunities.

Our hope is that this overall treatment of acquisitions will be useful to business managers and others and will complement the extensive material readily available, which for the most part deals with specific aspects of the acquisition process. We also hope that this book will fill a niche between some of the excellent work on general strategic planning and acquisition strategy, on the one hand, and the more-practical how-to material, on the other. Although it is directed toward acquisition, it should also be of value to those concerned with sale or divestiture.

A highly detailed treatment was neither intended nor possible in an overview of this kind. A list of selected references is given at the end of most chapters, however, to provide guidance for those who wish to pursue individual topics further.

Some of the concepts and material here have been updated and adapted from that of the authors that appeared earlier in *Sloan Management Review, Financial Analysts Journal,* and *Management Review.* We are grateful to the publishers for permission to use this material.

Finally, we acknowledge the help and assistance of our colleagues at Arthur D. Little, Inc., particularly Robert K. Mueller, chairman of the board, and George B. Rockwell, vice-president and director of financial industries, both of whom have been heavily involved in our firm's acquisition practice. Our thanks also go to Martin L. Ernst, Gail V. Ferreira, Allen H. Seed III, and Karl M. Wiig, who contributed chapters, and to Edda Faro and Mary Melican, who typed the manuscript and generally assisted in its preparation. Most of all, we express our appreciation to our wives, Helen Bradley and Lyndalee Korn, for their continual encouragement and support.

Achieving sales, earnings, and asset growth with attendant increased value to the stockholders remains a nearly universal corporate objective. We take full responsibility for the views and conclusions of this book and hope they will be helpful to managers in seeking to achieve this objective.

Part I
Contemporary Forces
and Strategies

1 Introduction and Historical Perspective

Scope

As stated in the preface, this book is designed to provide managers with a unifying conceptual and analytical framework from which to plan, develop, and carry out an acquisition program as part of the overall corporate-development process. To address these objectives, the book has been divided into three sections.

Part I (chapters 1-4) focuses on a historical perspective and the general principles of business combinations. Drawing heavily on contemporary applied economic concepts, these chapters discuss overall aquisition strategy and objectives, including the important issues of the economic basis for mergers, value creation, and diversification. They also cover the antitrust, legal, and other impediments to mergers.

Part II (chapters 5-9) further develops the concepts and analytical tools we consider appropriate in mounting an acquisition program. Here we address analysis and selection of industries of interest, as well as candidate identification and selection. This is followed by an introduction to the new tool of alternative-futures procedures. Covered next are the key issues of company evaluation/valuation, as well as general accounting, financial, and deal-structuring questions. Finally, decision-analysis and financial-modeling techniques are addressed, including methods of handling risk/return and multiple-objective tradeoffs.

Part III (chapters 10-12) reviews the organization, functions, and roles in the acquisition process, including the fact that elements of personality, fad, and whim, as well as the actions and views of peers and competitors, are often significant and sometimes controlling factors. This is followed by a discussion of the reasons that business combinations succeed or fail. Finally, chapter 12 deals with buying back one's own stock as a possible alternative to acquisition.

Acquisition has been and will continue to be a part of the growth strategy of corporations. Only the degree to which businesses emphasize this form of corporate development has varied over time. A number of economic and other forces help account for the cyclical nature of merger activities. These forces make this approach, rather than internal development or joint ventures, more appropriate for more companies at certain times. However, acquisition is a viable strategy for many firms under any particular set of prevailing economic conditions. Therefore, it is an approach that should always be viewed as a corporate-development alternative.

Although the emphasis in this book is clearly on acquisitions and their role in the corporate-development process, much of the material is also applicable to the sale of companies, including divestitures. In fact, a substantial part of today's merger activity relates to the acquisition of parts of other firms that are themselves being divested.

The Merger Movement in Perspective

Although mergers have continually been a part of the corporate scene, major surges of activity have occurred at three earlier periods of our economic history.[1] Each period of heightened activity has been followed or terminated by depression or recession. Furthermore, the antitrust and regulatory environment has changed and matured either during or after each period of activity, thus affecting the type and trend of later acquisitions.

The first major spurt of mergers occurred around the 1895-1905 period and primarily involved horizontal mergers. In this period a number of major and (at that time) single-industry firms evolved. Examples include U.S. Steel, DuPont, and others. A significant percentage of total U.S. manufacturing assets and employees were involved.

In the 1920s a second burst of merger activity occurred. The focus here was on vertical integration of industrial firms and the formation of utility holding companies. The number of mergers was then sharply reduced by the depression of 1929.

The third period occurred after World War II, particularly between 1960 and 1969, although activity began to pick up in the 1950s. In 1969, the all-time peak occurred in terms of numbers—more than 6,000 transactions.[2] Whereas earlier periods were characterized by horizontal mergers and vertical integration, the 1950s and 1960s were unique in that the emphasis was on diversifying acquisitions and the growth of conglomerates. Examples of the latter include LTV Corporation; Fuqua Industries, Inc.; and Textron, Inc. For the most part, the largest U.S. corporations were not heavily involved with acquisitions during this period.

Following the recession of 1973-1975, a new round of mergers began, which differentiated itself from that of the postwar period by a distinct set of conditions, characteristics, and "players."

In summary, the development of the typical large U.S. corporation parallels that of the various merger eras: horizontal mergers and market/product growth, followed by vertical integration and, finally, the evolution of broader-based firms. Members of this last group, although not necessarily highly diversified companies, for the most part no longer represent single-business or single-market companies. This is in keeping with current strategic-planning philosophy, including product- and market-portfolio concepts and the balancing of activities between units with both different maturities and different financial characteristics. Concurrently there has evolved more of a useful, coherent economic basis for considering, carrying out, and managing acquisitions. In addition, the inherent difficulties, time lags, and risks of failure in de novo internal-development projects have become better appreciated.

The 1960s versus the Present

An understanding of the activity of the late 1960s compared to that of today is important in developing a framework for considering the acquisition and overall corporate-development decision facing the corporation. It is necessary as well in order to understand the economic forces behind merger activity.

General

Between 1966 and 1979, the number of acquisition and merger transactions grew, reached a peak, waned, and then leveled off (figure 1-1). These data are based on W.T. Grimm statistics, which record the *number* of reported mergers and acquisitions, both large and small. The numbers are dominated by small acquisitions. Although large transactions are important and their significance has been increasing, the bulk of transactions are relatively small. In 1979 about 39 percent of mergers and acquisitions represented transactions of $5 million or less, 28 percent between $5 million and $15 million, and 33 percent over $15 million (table 1-1). For 1969, the all-time peak of activity, Grimm's data show 6,100 mergers and acquisitions announced with a total value of $24 billion. For 1979, when 2,128 announcements were made, the total dollar volume was about $44 billion. Not only was the size of the typical transaction larger than in the earlier period, but there was also a far greater number of major corporations participating as buyers. Twenty of the largest acquisitions are shown in table 1-2; the majority of these was announced during 1979. The indications for 1980, based on six months' data only, is that the number of transactions will decline somewhat. However, the total dollar value appears to be up. The largest transaction announced in the first half of 1980, Sun Company's acquisition of Texas Pacific Oil Company from Seagram Company Ltd. for $2.3 billion, dwarfs most earlier transactions.

The business combinations of the late 1960s, typified by conglomerates, were often oriented toward short-term-earnings reporting objectives, and

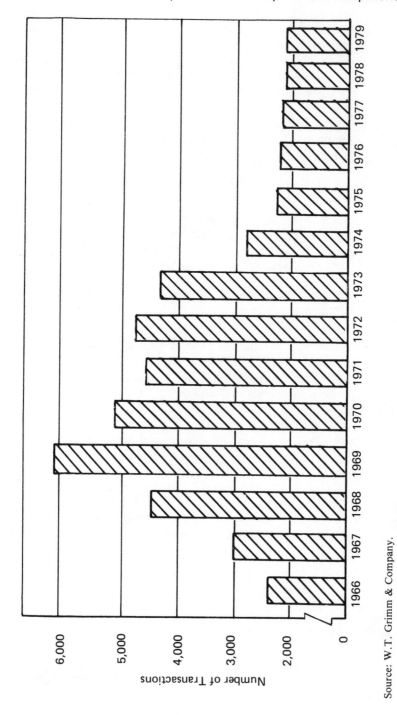

Figure 1-1. Number of U.S. Mergers and Acquisitions, 1966-1979

Source: W.T. Grimm & Company.

Table 1-1
Merger Activity, by Price Paid for Company Acquired, 1979

Price	Approximate Number of Transactions	Percentage
$1 million or less	192	9
$1.1-$2.0 million	170	8
$2.1-$3.0 million	192	9
$3.1-$4.0 million	150	7
$4.1-$5.0 million	128	6
$5.1-$7.0 million	192	9
$7.1-$15.0 million	404	19
Over $15 million	700	33
Total	2,128	100

Source: Based on data from W.T. Grimm & Company, Chicago.
Note: Approximately 50 percent of the total number of transactions represented closely held sellers.

were also often characterized by the lack of well-conceived longer-term financial and diversification goals. Many acquisitions in this period were done on a "pooling" basis because of favorable accounting treatment. Because of a more optimistic and speculative stock-market environment, sellers often accepted an exchange of equity securities and/or unsecured debt rather than cash.

In many instances growth in earnings per share following the earlier acquisitions proved to be of short duration, and sometimes the increases were related only to the financial mechanisms of the transactions. Although most acquirers in the late 1960s sought more than simply a short-term earnings boost, many did not place enough emphasis on prospective future earnings and their quality. Corporate executives also found it difficult to manage the assets of unrelated businesses. The merger movement was further tarnished by the poor performance of several highly leveraged conglomerates when they faced unfavorable business conditions and/or a sharply declining stock market in the recession period of 1974-1975.

Opinion nos. 16 and 17 of the Accounting Principles Board (APB), which became effective in 1970, contributed in a major way to the reduction of the number of acquisitions after 1969 and to the encouragement of more soundly conceived ones. These Opinions severely restricted the conditions under which acquisitions could be accounted for by pooling, and mandated the write-off of goodwill against after-tax earnings in purchase transactions. In combination, APB nos. 16 and 17 had the effect of requiring purchase transactions in many instances—sometimes significantly reducing reported earnings from acquisitions and creating a "soft" goodwill item on

Table 1-2
The Largest Acquisitions, 1968-1979

Buyer/Seller	Approximate Price Paid (Millions)	Year Announced
Shell Oil Co./Belridge Oil Co.	$3,653.0	1979
General Electric Co./Utah International, Inc.	1,906.5	1975
Mobil Oil Corp./Marcor, Inc.	1,687.2	1974 and 1976[a]
Schering Corp./Plough, Inc.	1,428.6	1970
RCA Corp/C.I.T. Financial Corp.	1,350.0	1979
Newmont Mining Corp., Williams Cos., et al./ Kennecott Copper Corp. (Peabody Coal Co.)	1,200.0	1976
Exxon Corp./Reliance Electric Co.	1,160.0	1979
Chessie Systems, Inc./Seaboard Coast Line Industries, Inc.	1,037.5	1978
Xerox Corp./Scientific Data Systems, Inc.	999.9	1969
United Technologies Corp./Carrier Corp.	821.7	1978 and 1979[b]
International Paper Co./Bodcaw Co.	805.0	1979
Mobil Corp./International Paper Co. (oil and gas operations of General Crude Co.)	800.0	1979
J. Ray McDermott & Co./Babcock & Wilcox Co.	758.5	1977
Tenneco, Inc./Southwestern Life Corp.	757.3	1979
McGraw-Edison Co./Studebaker-Worthington, Inc.	727.8	1979
Kohlberg, Kravis, Roberts & Co./Foremost-McKesson, Inc.	648.0	1979
Cooper Industries, Inc./Gardner-Denver Co.	629.3	1979
Imperial Group Ltd.—Britain/Howard Johnson Co.	618.5	1979
Boise Cascade Corp./Ebasco Industries, Inc.	598.4	1969
Allied Chemical Corp./Eltra Corp.	587.7	1979

Source: W.T. Grimm & Company, Chicago.
[a]Mobil acquired 54 percent in 1974 and purchased the remaining interest in 1976.
[b]United acquired 49 percent in 1978 and purchased the remaining interest in 1979.

the balance sheet. (It should be noted that in many cases the assets and liabilities of the acquired company can be restated to higher levels based on fair market value so that little or no goodwill is created. See chapter 8.)

At the same time that overall merger activity was decreasing after 1969, a high proportion of the transactions that did occur represented divestitures—further evidence of problems among the earlier mergers. In 1967, for example, W.T. Grimm data showed divestitures accounting for only about 11 percent of all mergers and acquisitions; in 1977, however, divestitures accounted for an estimated 45 percent of acquisition transactions. The comparable 1979 figure was 35 percent. The point is that divestitures, often of operations acquired earlier, have become an increasingly important part of total acquisition transactions. For buyers, acquisition terms have been and should continue to be somewhat more favorable and more related to assets and earning power than they were in the late 1960s. Published W.T. Grimm data for 1979 (based on 333 transactions) indicate that the average price paid was 14.3 times earnings, compared with, for example, over 26 times earnings in 1969. (For comparison, the average price-to-earnings ratio for a broad list of stocks, as measured by the Standard & Poor's Industrial Index, was about 7.5 for 1979, and 17.5 for 1969.) However, in 1979 the average premium paid was about 50 percent over market, compared to 25 percent ten years earlier.

More than 70 percent of the total number of transactions in 1979 were for cash or a combination of cash and securities. Although interest in stock deals may be increasing on both sides, there has not yet been any major movement toward entirely noncash deals, as were prevalent in 1969.

Acquisitions or Mergers versus
Internal Development

Reliance on internal development as the preferred route to corporate growth has been a recent rule for many firms—both large, technically sophisticated corporations and smaller, more traditional firms. Now, however, companies increasingly weigh the costs and risks of internal-development programs against renewed opportunities for acquisitions, which can often provide more rapid, stepwise, and predictable results for corporate growth. Recent research indicates, for example, that on average eight years are required before new ventures of major U.S. corporations become profitable.[3]

In today's uncertain business environment, many corporations have come to favor acquisitions over internal development as the preferred path to corporate growth. Table 1-3 illustrates some of the external financial and economic conditions that influence corporate-management attitudes toward the choice between acquisition and internal development. These conditions are cyclical in nature and, to a large extent, account for the type and level of corporate development. In the early 1970s, for example, low liquidity, moderate price-to-earnings (*P/E*) ratios, conservative accounting rules, and major political and economic uncertainties—Watergate, the oil embargo by the Organization of Petroleum Exporting Countries (OPEC), wage and price controls—were factors conducive to internal development. Today it appears that cash acquisition deals are supported by relatively low *P/E* ratios, conservative accounting rules, high (but selective) liquidity, and expectations about inflation. The possibility exists that a rising stock market, high interest rates, and the economic uncertainties of 1981 may begin to reduce near-term acquisition activity and to favor more stock transactions rather than all-cash deals.

Table 1-3

External Financial Conditions Influencing Type of Growth Strategy and Means of Acquisition

| | Sources of Corporate Growth | | Form of Transaction | |
	External Acquisition	Internal Development	Cash	Stock
Late 1960s				
Moderate liquidity				
High P/E ratios				
Liberal accounting rules				
Buoyant economy	+	−	−	+
Early 1970s				
Low liquidity				
Moderate P/E ratios				
Conservative accounting				
Major political and economic				
uncertainties (Watergate,				
oil embargo, wage and				
price controls)	−	+	+	−
Today				
Relatively low P/E ratios				
Conservative accounting				
Relatively high liquidity				
(selective)				
Inflation concerns	+	−	+	−

Source: Reprinted by permission of the publisher from James W. Bradley and Donald H. Korn, "Acquisitions and Mergers: A Shifting Route to Corporate Growth," *Management Review*, March 1979, © 1979 by AMACOM, a Division of American Management Associations, p. 47. All rights reserved.

Present Forces and Incentives on Buyers and Sellers

At the same time that buyers are becoming more active, forces within the business environment are encouraging some companies to become potential sellers. The contemporary forces acting on corporations that encourage acquisitions and mergers, other than normal diversification considerations, are shown in figure 1-2. They can be classified as internal or external, positive or negative, controllable or uncontrollable. For example, those forces opposing acquisition or merger are shown in figure 1-2 as arrows pointing away from the company.

Founders and principal stockholders of most privately held or closely held corporations are not finding the hoped-for opportunities to capitalize on their entrepreneurial success via public offerings. The sharp decline in the number of initial public offerings in 1975-1978 compared with earlier years is indicative of these difficulties (table 1-4). It is significant, however, that public offerings increased substantially in 1979 over recent prior years.

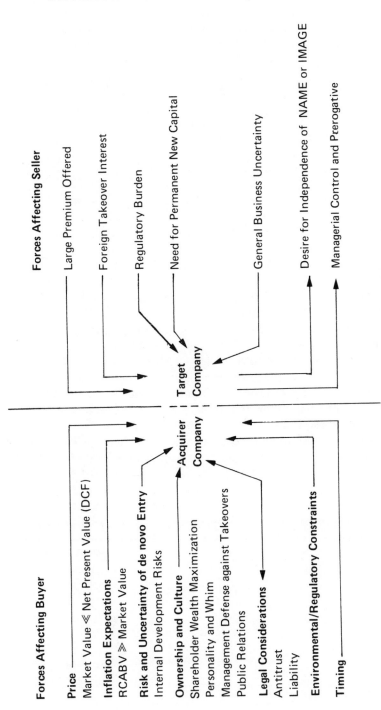

Figure 1-2. Contemporary Acquisition Forces Acting on Corporations

Source: J.W. Bradley and D.H. Korn, "Bargains in Valuation Disparities: Corporate Acquirer Versus Passive Investor," *Sloan Management Review* Winter 1979. Reprinted by permission.

Except for those active in recognized growth areas or with other unusual characteristics, small companies typically have trouble going public. Moreover, companies in the $30- to $50-million sales range and above often have problems. These capital-market forces increase pressures on some firms to consider acquisition or joint-venture overtures in order to increase their financial resources and support growth. This route may, in fact, be the best possible way for some of these firms to continue to grow and prosper, unless capital markets improve substantially.

These factors, added to present economic uncertainties, help explain why small companies, both publicly and privately held, have recently been receptive to selling out at a premium. Many takeover candidates simply believe that large, diversified corporations are better equipped to manage today's business and economic risks.

The availability of foreign capital seeking direct investment in the United States represents an important current stimulus to the rate of merger and acquisition activity—one that was not a major factor in the 1960s. Acquisition of U.S. companies by foreign companies began to be important in 1973-1974, and this trend has continued through the first half of 1981. Prospective foreign buyers are now competing with domestic ones for attractive takeover candidates, greatly enhancing the bargaining positions of the prospective sellers.

The U.S. market offers a number of characteristics that attract foreign capital. These include lower perceived economic and political risk, larger markets, higher profits, faster growth, and more advantageous manufacturing and labor costs than in the home countries. The strength of foreign currencies relative to the dollar is also a major influence.

The number and magnitude of transactions by foreign corporations continue to increase. The largest numbers of acquisitions in recent years

Table 1-4
Common-Stock Offerings for which No Prior Market Existed, 1970-1979

Year	Number of Issues
1970	566
1971	446
1972	646
1973	177
1974	55
1975	24
1976	46
1977	46
1978	58
1979	144

Source: *Investment Dealers Digest*. Reprinted with permission.

have been by corporations in West Germany, the United Kingdom, Canada, and Japan, although corporations in other countries have also been active. Swiss-based Sandoz acquired Northrup King for $197 million in cash in late 1976. Unilever offered $482 million for National Starch and Chemical. In 1979 Imperial Group Ltd. of Great Britain offered $618.5 million for Howard Johnson Company, and Allianz Versicherungs AG of West Germany offered over $350 million for Fidelity Union Life Insurance Company.

The business and securities-market climate also affect acquisitions by making the managements and stockholders of selling companies more receptive to offers above current market value. Indicative of the changed valuations is the *Value Line Investment Survey* of all stocks with earnings; it showed that the median P/E ratio was 4.8 at the time of the recent market low (27 December 1974), compared to 8.1 on 31 December 1976, 7.4 on 31 December 1977, 7.0 on 31 December 1978, and 7.1 on 31 December 1979.

The cost of acquisition compared to that of internal development, value creation through acquisition, and the issue of valuation disparities are discussed in detail in chapter 2.

The Lessons of the 1960s: Prospects
for Recent Acquisitions

Many acquisitions during the period ending in 1969 proved unsuccessful. Will history repeat itself—are we in store for a new wave of divestitures? Some of today's acquisitions will not work out, and some divestitures will take place; but we believe that today's activity is more soundly based than were earlier acquisitions.

Today's merger activity is distinguished from that of the 1960s in several important respects:

A more sophisticated corporate view, with far more intensive and realistic planning by management.

Diversification that is related more to present activities than to entirely new fields.

More consideration by internal staff of long-term strategic objectives, alternative acquisition possibilities, and postmerger management issues.

In evaluating possible acquirees, for example, buyers are more commonly using capital-budgeting techniques that use several sets of cash-flow estimates to establish a range of values based on earning power over a period of years. Earlier, reliance was primarily on short-term earnings-per-share effects, which, however important, are not the whole story. This deeper and longer-range consideration contributes to more soundly conceived transactions. Required accounting changes indicated previously have also added conservatism. Furthermore, because of their experience with federal antitrust and antitakeover laws, corporations are now better able to judge what acquisitions will be allowable and what tender offer and other strategies and tactics are most effective.

Industries of Interest and the Outlook for the Future

As discussed, acquisitions occur for a variety of reasons. Some situations represent genuine efforts of buyers to establish a position in areas of high growth and unusually favorable future prospects outside their own current fields. Many other business combinations, of course, do not represent a major departure from a firm's major business thrust but are, rather, part of the firm's strategy for growth in related areas. Some occur because sellers have poor prospects on their own and must seek a buyer.

Buyers in the first category, who seek longer-term growth, higher returns, and diversification, typically look for certain characteristics among industries and companies. Current criteria often sought include both high sales-growth potential plus above-average profitability or profit potential, with high growth often defined as 1.5-2.0 times the growth rate of the gross national product (GNP); and favorable environmental and regulatory outlook, coupled with a high societal need for and acceptance of the product or service.

In many cases, an industry can present attractive acquisition opportunities and meet the preceding criteria largely because of new economic, societal, technological, or legislative and regulatory trends affecting the fortunes of the industry, plus changes in investors' perceptions about the level and uncertainty surrounding company earnings in that industry as a result of such developments. Tax considerations sometimes enter the picture; for example, the Tax Reform Act of 1976 had favorable features for insurance companies being acquired.

On the basis of our review of corporate acquisition behavior, industry financial characteristics, and trends in the business environment, we have identified a number of attractive industry areas for acquisition. These are outlined in table 1-5 as areas of current and continuing interest, and several others are suggested as future possibilities.

In addition, negative forces acting on an industry because of market, regulatory, or other reasons may produce acquisition candidates attractive to larger buyers. Small banks and savings-and-loan institutions may fall in

Table 1-5
Industries Favorably Positioned for Acquisition Activity[a]

Current and Continuing Areas of Interest
  Specialized sectors of agribusiness
  Coal producers
  Energy services and energy conservation
  Chemical specialities, including drugs
  Communications
  Specialized areas of electronics
  Products and services related to the environment, fire protection, and safety
  Medical instruments
  Oil-company diversification (including nonferrous mining, mining machinery, and services)
  Financial services
  Automation, including computer-aided design (CAD) and manufacturing (CAM)

Other Likely Future Areas
  Equipment and services related to public transport
  Equipment and services for maintenance/reliability/productivity improvement
  Nonconventional energy sources and services
  Precious metals, gems, and other capital-preservation forms
  Recreation/leisure
  Bioengineering

[a]In addition to overall, general acquisition activity

this category. Deregulation can also have its effect and can cause a con-solidation within an industry. Although industries "favored" for acquisi-tion change over time, acquisitions will continue as an important mode of corporate growth. Subsequent chapters outline the processes and steps necessary to the development of a sound acquisition program.

Notes

1. This material in part draws on a fuller but still concise and highly readable summary in Salter and Weinhold, *Diversification Through Ac-quisition*.
2. W.T. Grimm & Company, Chicago.
3. Biggadike, "The Risky Business of Diversification."

References

Biggadike, Ralph. "The Risky Business of Diversification." *Harvard Busi-ness Review*, May-June 1979.
Bradley, James W., and Korn, Donald H. "Acquisition and Merger Trends Affecting the Portfolio Manager." *Financial Analysts Journal*, November-December 1977.

_____ . "Bargains in Valuation Disparities: Corporate Acquirer vs. Passive Investor." *Sloan Management Review*, Winter 1979.

_____ . "Acquisitions and Mergers: A Shifting Route to Corporate Growth." *Management Review*, March 1979.

Bureau of Economics, Federal Trade Commission. *Statistical Report of Mergers & Acquisitions* (annual).

Leavitt, Theodore F. "Dinosaurs Among the Bears and Bulls." *Harvard Business Review*, January-February 1975.

Merger Summary, W.T. Grimm & Company, Chicago (annual and midyear reports).

Salter, Malcolm S., and Weinhold, Wolf A. *Diversification Through Acquisition*. New York, N.Y.: Free Press, 1979. (see esp. chap. 1, pp. 3-35).

Wasserstein, Bruce. *Corporate Finance Law*. New York: McGraw-Hill Book Company, 1978. (See esp. pp. 183-184.)

2 General Principles

Introduction

This chapter presents material from the several fields and disciplines dealing with acquisitions and corporate development: law, accounting, economics, management, finance, and government. It is in contrast to chapter 8, which, although building on material here, emphasizes the factors to be examined in considering and structuring individual transactions.

The ordering of the material that follows is somewhat arbitrary. We begin with definitions that are general and nontechnical, but with emphasis on a legal and regulatory framework. However, the reader will find additional versions of the definitions of certain terms under the accounting framework. A common denominator is the requirement of the U.S Internal Revenue Code (and any similar or analogous feature of non-U.S. jurisdictions), which defines the types of acquisition transactions that either qualify as exchanges exempt from income tax, or else present some immediate tax liability to the parties concerned.[1] The real common denominator is the economic substance of a business combination. The legal, tax, managerial, and accounting treatments are, fortunately, often consistent. In some cases, however, the tax treatment may be at odds with economic theory and the economic presumptions at odds with the sociopolitical trends.

In this chapter we present the principles behind the general thrust of acquisition and corporate-development activity. As will be seen, many different aspects and points of view are involved. The corporation, through its management and board of directors, may see its opportunities and its role in a different light than do economists, regulators, or even investors. Hence, each acquisition must be evaluated on its own merits, given the circumstances at hand. Simply stated, the objective from the acquirer's point of view is to improve his lot, subject to diverse constraints. Later chapters will discuss the strategies and techniques associated with a successful acquisition and corporate-development program.

Legal and Regulatory Framework

Types of Acquisitions: Definitions

Acquisitions may involve purchase of a going business, including all or a part of a corporation's assets; or they may involve acquisitions of stock

17

from the stockholders of a corporation. Each type of acquisition will usually involve areas of corporate law, tax law, and securities law. The definitions that follow involve terms used in discussing acquisitions generally in a legal or regulatory sense.[2]

Acquisition. The term *acquisition* is used to describe any transaction in which a buyer acquires all or part of the assets and business of a seller, or all or part of the stock or other securities of the seller, where the transaction is closed between a willing buyer and a willing seller, that is, a seller whose management agrees to the acquisition and helps negotiate its terms. The element of willingness on the part of both buyer and seller distinguishes an acquisition from a takeover. Provided the element of willingness is present, the mechanics for accomplishing a transaction will not affect its status as an acquisition. Included within the general term *acquisition* are more specific forms of transactions such as: (1) a merger, (2) a consolidation, (3) an asset acquisition, and (4) a stock acquisition.

Statutory Merger. A *statutory merger* is a combination of two corporations pursuant to the requirements and procedures set forth in the corporation laws of the states of incorporation. Generally, merger statutes require that the boards of directors of both corporations approve and recommend the merger to the stockholders, and that the stockholders of each corporation approve the merger by a required favorable vote—normally two-thirds. In a statutory merger, one of the two corporations is merged into the other corporation, the latter generally being referred to as the *surviving corporation*. Under state laws, the surviving corporation becomes the owner of all of the assets, business, and liabilities of the merged corporation by operation of law—that is, automatically—at the time the necessary statutory-merger certificate is filed with the secretary of state of the state in which the surviving corporation is located. Specific title-transfer documents are not required to transfer title to the business to the surviving corporation. Upon completion of a statutory merger, one of the two corporations involved falls heir to the combined assets and business, as well as to all of the liabilities, of the two parties to the merger; the other corporation disappears, and the disappearing corporation's stockholders normally substitute an equity interest in the surviving corporation for their equity interest in the disappearing corporation. Since a statutory merger requires the approval of the boards of directors and stockholders of both corporations, the statutory merger is an acquisition, as opposed to a takeover.

Statutory Consolidation. A *consolidation* is also an acquisition that involves a combination of two corporations pursuant to state corporation laws. However, unlike a statutory merger, a consolidation causes both of the merged corporations to disappear. A third corporation is formed, into which both of the corporations to be consolidated are merged. The new corporation becomes the survivor corporation and the heir to the combined assets and business, as well as to all the liabilities, of the two corporations that are consolidated into it, both of which thereupon cease to exist. As is the case in a statutory merger, a consolidation requires the approval of the boards of directors and the stockholders of both corporations.

Asset Acquisition. An *asset acquisition* is an acquisition in which the buyer acquires all or a part of the assets and business of the seller, pursuant to a contract entered into between buyer and seller. The asset acquisition may require the approval of the seller's stockholders, but generally not that of the buyer's. It is distinguishable from a stock acquisition in that assets of a seller are acquired—not stock of a seller's stockholders. It is distinguished from a statutory merger and from a consolidation in that the transfer of title to the seller's assets is not effected by operation of law; rather, specific instruments of title must be delivered from the seller to transfer legal title to the buyer. The consideration paid by the buyer may be in any form, including cash; property; common or preferred stock; or bonds, debentures, or other securities. The corporate structure of the seller remains intact, and ownership of stock by the stockholders of the seller is not affected. However, the seller may subsequently be liquidated; and the stockholders of the seller, upon such liquidation, will receive the cash and securities paid for the assets of the seller as well as any other assets of the seller that were not sold to the buyer. Generally, where substantially all of the assets and business of a seller are sold, the second step—that is, a liquidation of the seller—follows.

Stock Acquisition. A *stock acquisition* is an acquisition in which all or a part of the outstanding stock of the seller is acquired from the stockholders of the seller. As in the case of an asset acquisition, the stock of the seller may be bought for any property, including cash, common or preferred stocks, debt securities, or any combination of such property. A stock acquisition does not require the consent of the management of the seller, but involves a direct contractual relationship between the buyer and the stockholders of the seller.

Takeover Bid. Management of the seller may be opposed to an offer to purchase the assets or the stock of the seller, or may be an unwilling partner to the combination of corporate entities. In such instances, the acquisition offer is a *takeover bid*.

Tender Offer. A *tender offer* is a takeover bid in which the buyer offers to acquire stock for cash. The distinguishing feature of a tender offer is that the takeover bid made by the buyer is made for cash. Tender offers are subject to the requirements contained in the Securities and Exchange Act of 1934, as amended by the Williams Act, and to more recent filing requirements.

Registered Exchange Offer. A *registered exchange offer* is a takeover bid in which the buyer offers to acquire the stock of the seller in exchange for stock or other securities of the buyer. The distinguishing feature of a registered exchange offer, as opposed to a tender offer, is that the offer of the buyer is made in the form of stock or securities of the buyer, rather than for cash. The registered exchange offer is not subject to the requirements of the Williams Act but is subject to the general Securities and Exchange Commission (SEC) registration requirements.

Target Company. A *target company* or *target* is a seller that is the subject of a takeover bid, whether such bid is in the form of a tender offer or a registered exchange offer. The term is also applied to a company under study for possible acquisition.

Nonpublic Corporation. A *nonpublic corporation* involves a distinction between a closely held corporation and a public corporation. The dividing line between the two may be shadowy. Generally, a closely held corporation is one in which the stockholders of 100 percent of the stock are relatively few—for our purposes, no more than twenty-five individuals—whereas the public corporation is one whose shares are more widely held. The distinction between the two types of corporations may be of significant importance in connection with SEC rules and regulations relative to proposed acquisition transactions.

Summary of Key Features

In summary, purchases of businesses may be made with the approval of the management of the seller, or over the objections or the management of the seller. Where the seller's management approves of the transaction, it is generally referred to as an acquisition; where the management disapproves, as a takeover. Acquisitions may be divided into three basic types: mergers, stock acquisitions, and asset acquisitions. Takeovers may be divided into two types: tender offers and registered exchange offers. From an income-tax point of view, both acquisitions and takeovers may be classified as taxable or taxfree; and from an SEC viewpoint, both acquisitions and takeovers may require the filing of a registration statement, or may be exempt from such filing requirements.

Accounting Framework

Influence of Objectives of Financial Statements

We draw on the excellent materials prepared by the Financial Accounting Standards Board (FASB), which address the purpose and objectives of corporation financial statements.[3] Existing conclusions about the purpose and objectives of financial statements include the following.

Purpose. The basic purpose of financial accounting and financial statements is to provide quantitative financial information about a business enterprise that is useful to statement users, particularly owners and creditors, in making economic decisions. This purpose includes providing information that can be used in evaluating management's effectiveness in fulfilling its stewardship and other managerial responsibilities.

Objectives. The basic objective of financial statements is to provide information useful for making economic decisions. This basic objective requires that every accounting objective, standard, principle, procedure, and practice should serve users' needs.

The Report of the American Institute of Certified Public Accountants (AICPA) Study Group on the Objectives of Financial Statements states that "users' needs for information, however, are not known with any degree of certainty." It sets forth the following assumptions about those needs and users' decision processes:

Users of financial statements seek to predict, compare, and evaluate the cash consequences of their economic decisions.

Information about the cash consequences of decisions made by the enterprise is useful for predicting, comparing, and evaluating cash flows to users.

Financial statements are more useful if they include information that is primarily factual, and that therefore can be measured objectively, and distinguish such information from information that is primarily interpretative.

Scope

The subject of this book treats acquisitions in the context of business enterprises organized for profit, rather than other entities such as religious, charitable, scientific, educational, and similar not-for-profit institutions, and governmental and quasigovernmental units.

Definitions Applicable to General
Business-Acquisition Transactions

Business Combinations. The term *business combination* or *combination* is defined, in general, in the accounting sense, as an event or transaction in which two or more business enterprises, or their net assets, are brought under common control and into one accounting entity.[4] In this definition, control of an enterprise means ownership of over 50 percent of the outstanding voting stock (ownership interests) of that enterprise. A combination may be effected in various ways, for example, if one enterprise merges into, becomes a subsidiary of, or transfers its net assets to another enterprise; or if two enterprises merge into, become subisidiaries of, or transfer their net assets to a newly formed enterprise.

Business Enterprises. The Accounting Principles Board (APB) issued APB Statement no. 4, "Basic Concepts and Accounting Principles Underlying Financial Statements of Business Enterprises," which defined business enterprises to be

> individuals or associations of individuals that control and use resources for a variety of purposes including the purpose of yielding a return to the owners of the enterprise. They produce for sale rather than their own consumption and generally engage in market exchanges to acquire inputs for the production process and to dispose of goods and services produced.

The term *business enterprises* includes subsidiaries, divisions, and other components. Although most discussion focuses on combinations of incorporated business enterprises, the term *business combination* or *combination* encompasses combinations of unicorporated ones as well, including proprietorships, partnerships, and special forms used in certain industries (for example, mutual companies, associations, investment trusts, and cooperative organizations).

Accounting for a combination may be affected by the organizational structures of the enterprises entering into the combination.

Combined Enterprise. This is the accounting entity that results from a combination.

Combined Companies. These are the business enterprises that enter into a combination.

Combinor. This is a constituent company entering into a combination whose stockholders (owners) as a group end up with control of the voting stock (ownership interests) in the combined enterprise. For combinations involving more than two constituent companies, the combinor is the company whose stockholders (owners) end up with the largest portion, but not necessarily the majority, of the voting stock (ownership interests) in the combined enterprise. In certain combinations, a "combinor" may not be identifiable.

Combinee. This is a constituent company other than the combinor.

Purchased Intangibles. These encompass intangibles purchased either singly, as part of a group of economic resources, or as part of a company acquired in a business combination in which a new accounting basis is recognized. The term *intangibles* connotes the same set of attributes that the term *intangible assets* ordinarily implies in accounting usage, but does not predetermine the accounting treatment that may be appropriate for the costs incurred to purchase those intangibles. Intangibles are economic resources having no physical existence, their value being determined by the rights and other future benefits that possession confers. (Monetary resources, such as cash, receivables, and investments, are not considered to be intangibles.)

Goodwill. *Goodwill* is the excess of investment cost over the net tangible assets and net identifiable intangible assets (such as patents) acquired through purchase of another company. This excess investment cost is an asset that could not have been recorded in the accounts of the acquired company.

Goodwill cannot be amortized as an expense or loss for income-tax purposes, for as long as the company is not resold or abandoned. Thus, to the extent that can be justified, the acquiring company assigns as much of the purchase price as possible to both tangible assets and identifiable intangible assets, which later can be accounted for as expenses, amortized, or depreciated for income-tax purposes. The APB has expressed the opinion that goodwill should be amortized in a systematic manner over its estimated useful life, which should not, however, exceed forty years.[5].

Special Situations

Combinations involving nonoperating companies, as well as operating companies.

Transactions giving rise to joint ventures and other intercorporate investments, but not resulting in an investor owning more than 50 percent of the investee's ownership interests.

Combinations involving companies that have significant interrelated investments, but that are not already under common control.

Accounting for minority interests.

Managerial Framework: The Economic Substance of Business Combinations

The FASB has presented four possible descriptions of the economic substance of various combinations. These are as follows and are referred to throughout the subsequent discussions.

1. The constituent companies are united to carry on together their previous operations (Type 1).
2. One company acquires a controlling interest in the net assets of another company or other companies (Type 2).
3. A new economic entity results that is significantly different in nature or scope of operations from any of the constituent companies (Type 3).
4. All other.

The "determinants of economic substance" have been categorized by the FASB as follows:

1. Motivations and expectations of the parties entering into a combination.
2. Type of consideration given in exchange.
3. Income-tax treatment of a combination.
4. Effect of a combination on the ownership interests of a combinee's stockholders.
5. Ability or inability to identify a dominant constituent company.
6. Other.[6]

We shall now present the salient points with regard to selected items.

Motivations and Expectations

Possible Relevance of Motivations and Expectations to Economic Substance. As previously indicated, the parties to a combination usually include the combinor's board of directors and management, and possibly also its stockholders; and the combinee's stockholders, board of directors, and management—each with somewhat different motivations and expectations.

Within each category are individuals who may also have differing motivations and expectations. FASB used two examples to illustrate how differences might exist for the same combination:

> First, the combinor's board of directors and management and the combinee's management may view a combination as being Type 1; whereas, the combinee's stockholders, because they will receive cash and no longer will be associated with the combinee, may view the same combination as Type 2. Second, the combinor's board of directors and management may enter into a combination primarily to acquire vast real estate holdings of the combinee on which to build new plants for expanded operations of the combinor (Type 2), but be willing to accept the combinee's present operations in another industry and management/stockholders. The combinee's management/stockholders on the other hand, may view this combination as Type 1 because they will continue to be associated with the combinee's operations.[7]

The motivations and expectations of the parties in various circumstances are elaborated on in the next two sections.

Motivations and Expectations of Combinors. Accounting Research Study no. 5 describes four general motivating factors for combinors to enter into combinations: *growth or expansion*, *diversification*, *financial considerations*, and *competitive pressures*.[8] The results of a questionnaire on combination policies sent to 700 major companies in the early 1960s indicated that, during that period, diversification was one of the most important motives for a combinor to enter into a combination.[9]

Another questionnaire, sent to 412 combinors that had effected combinations during the period 1946-1965, asked respondents to rate the importance of various reasons for entering into combinations by assigning each reason a weight ranging from 0 to 5. The ten reasons that were indicated by the ninety-three respondents as being the most important were as follows.[10]

Reason	*Points*
1. To complete product lines.	159
2. To increase market share.	102
3. To utilize fully existing marketing capabilities, contracts, or channels.	73
4. To offset unsatisfactory sales growth in present market.	70
5. To capitalize on distinctive technological expertise.	64
6. To obtain patents, licenses, or technological knowhow.	53
7. To meet demand of diversified customers.	45
8. To fully utilize existing production capacity.	43
9. To increase control of sales outlets.	39
10. To reduce dependence on suppliers.	38

Recently, more emphasis has been placed on the effects that potential combinations will have on the availability of adequate funds for carrying out existing operations or for expansion. Also, recent low market prices for securities have motivated combinors to take advantage of the availability of numerous companies' securities at prices believed to provide excellent investments in their existing assets. Based on FASB staff interviews, the combinor typically focuses on the combinee's operations rather than on its separable economic resources and obligations in assessing the merits of a potential combination. The combinee's existing and projected operations are evaluated from standpoints such as the potential earnings contribution to the combined enterprise, working capital and other requirements, and capability with other operations of the combined enterprise. The usual expectation is that the combinee's existing operations will continue. In some cases, however, the combinor may plan to change substantially the combinee's operations. In some cases, the attraction to the combinor may be a specific resource (for example, mineral deposits, proven technology, a license, or talented individuals), rather than the combinee's existing operations. That resource may or may not be used in those existing operations. Also, potential income-tax benefits to be derived from utilization of the combinee's operating loss or other income-tax carryforwards may be a signficant motivation in certain circumstances.

The most important qualitative factor about a combination indicated by the financial users surveyed was management's capability to supervise the combinee's operations. The product or market compatibility of the constituent companies was also rated as important. (Combinors responding to the study by Ansoff et al. placed the most emphasis on product or market compatibility and considerably less emphasis on management capability.[11])

Several of those interviewed agreed that most publicly held combinors have as their most important negotiating factor the projected effect of particular combination on earnings per share. Typically, such a company is reluctant to enter into a combination that will dilute earnings per share in the next fiscal year, although it may be willing to accept some short-term dilution if this is merited by the combination's projected long-term contribution to earnings per share. A privately held combinor also has earnings-per-share expectations but, typically, is less concerned with the earnings levels over the next year or two than is a public company. Accordingly, such a company may be more inclined to enter into a combination with a combinee that has low, or no, present earnings but that has good long-term earnings potential.

The projected effect of a combination on liquidity and net worth may also be important factors, particularly if a combinor has limited liquidity or must maintain certain financial ratios under credit agreements. The projected effects of a combination on total cash flows may be considered closely. In that connection, the combinor will typically make assumptions about the borrowing potential of the underleveraged combinee or the additional cash requirements of the overleveraged combinee.

Motivations and Expectations of Combinees and Their Stockholders. An understanding of the motivations and expectations of the combinee and its stockholders is important in determining a combination's economic substance. Those motivations vary considerably, particularly depending on variables such as whether the combinee is privately or publicly held and whether it is autonomous or is a subsidiary, division, or other component being divested. Wyatt and Kiesco indicated that at least one of the following business or personal reasons is usually influential when an autonomous combinee enters into a combination.

Business Reasons.

Financial anemia. A company may have extended itself beyond its financial means—insufficient working capital and inability to extend its credit, either short or long term—and yet not nearly have attained its potential growth. Merger with a firm having excess funds available or borrowing ability may aid a financially anemic but product-sound company realize its potential.

Inadequate distribution or too short a product line. A firm selling only regionally may quickly attain national distribution by merging with a firm which already has a national sales force, warehouse system, and promotional program. A firm with a quality product but an incomplete product line may only invite slow growth and imitation by competitors unless it merges with a company possessing a complete product line, engineering, and repair services.

Technological or marketing changes. Sensing the prospects of technological or marketing changes that will adversely affect the future operations of the company frequently motivates management to sell rather than take the risk of change.

Attractive offers. The increased competition among the large companies for desirable medium-sized and smaller companies as merger candidates has produced attractive purchase and exchange offers. . . .

Lack of qualified managers. Firms too small to afford a well-rounded management team but too large to be run efficiently by one or two men are frequently merged with companies having strong management. . .

Personal Reasons.

Retirement. The major management stockholders may wish to retire but may not have developed understudies capable of continuing the business profitably.

Marketable versus unmarketable stock. The owners of a closely held corporation may wish to make liquid their equity, and the best way is to convert it into marketable securities of an acquiring company. . .

Diversification of personal holdings. A prime target for acquisition or merger is a closely held firm the owner of which would like to exchange his holdings in a small specialty firm for stock in a large diversified corporation.

Estate-tax inducement. It is commonly contended that one of the greatest single inducements to sell out or merge an established business is the pressure of anticipated heavy estate taxes that the owner sooner or later must face.[12]

As indicated elsewhere, in recent years increasing numbers of subsidiaries, divisions, and other components have been divested. The motivations for divestitures are as varied as those discussed here, but include also the factor of antitrust divestiture, which is discussed in chapter 4.

Stockholders. A combinee's stockholders who do not anticipate being associated with that company after the combination typically view the combination primarily as a vehicle to carry out their investment objectives. The motivating factor might be their desire to relinquish control over the combinee, or it might be an attractive tender offer. It is important to note that they are selling the company and that its future therefore is probably not of ongoing concern to them.

Management. Managers of the combinee will be particularly interested in the degree of autonomy to be retained for the combinee's operations. At one extreme, operations may be virtually unchanged, with the same senior management remaining in charge of those operations. At the other extreme, operations and management ranks may be substantially changed.

Type of Consideration

The FASB discussed the type of consideration with the following example (from a press release).[13]

The Burroughs Corporation announced—that it had reached an agreement in principle to acquire Graphic Sciences, Inc., of Danbury, Conn., for stock worth $30-million. . . . Under terms of the agreement, Burroughs . . . will exchange one-eighth of one share of its common shares of Graphic Sciences outstanding.

Burroughs stock closed on the New York Stock Exchange at 79¼.

If the common stock declines to less than $67.95, the agreement provides that, immediately prior to the execution of the definitive agreement, the Graphic Sciences board can elect to have Burroughs acquire Graphic Sciences for $9.44 a share of Graphic Sciences common stock instead of Burroughs stock.[14]

The FASB posed the following question:

> Would the economic substance of that proposed combination differ depending on whether Burroughs Corporation were to give its common stock or cash to effect the combination? If so, how would it differ? To generalize, does the type of consideration given in a combination affect its economic substance? If so, how should differences in economic substance based on the type of consideration be identified and described?

Those believing that the type of consideration is a determinant of economic substance make a distinction generally as follows:

> a. Combinations effected by all, or certain, types of equity securities, and possibly meeting other conditions, represent the *uniting of the constituent companies* to carry on their previous operations (Type 1).
>
> b. Other combinations represent the *acquisition of* a controlling interest in the asset of another company or other companies (Type 2) [emphasis added].

The background information presented in APB Opinion no. 16 sets forth the following arguments for concluding that a combination's substance is largely determined by whether common stock is given to effect the combination:

> . . . a business combination effected by issuing common stock is different from a purchase in that no corporate assets are disbursed to stockholders and the net assets of the issuing corporation are enlarged by the net assets of the corporation whose stockholders accept common stock of the combined corporation. There is no newly invested capital nor have owners withdrawn assets from the group since the stock of a corporation is not one of its assets. Accordingly, the net assets of the constituents remain intact but combined; the stockholder groups remain intact but combined. Aggregate income is not changed since the total resources are not changed. . . . In a business combination effected by exchanging stock, groups of stockholders combine their resources, talents, and risks to form a new entity to carry on in combination the previous businesses and to continue their earnings streams. The sharing of risks by the constituent stockholder groups is an important element in a business combination effected by exchanging stock. By pooling equity interests, each group continues to maintain risk elements of its former investment and they mutually exchange risks and benefits.[15]

A number of writers have supported the view that one combination is fundamentally different from another because of differing types of consideration, generally based on a rationale similar to that just described. Some have stressed the exchange of "risks and benefits" referred to previously, sometimes described as the sharing-of-rights-and-risks concept. According to that concept, the effect on the constituent companies' stockholders, particularly those of the combinee, is important in assessing a combination's substance. Paragraph 45 of APB Opinion no. 16 indicates that where voting common stock is given, the ". . . stockholder groups neither withdraw nor invest assets but in effect exchange voting common stock in a ratio that determines their respective interests in the combined corporation." There are divergent views about the conditions necessary for a sharing of rights and risks by those stockholders. According to some, the type of consideration is only one of several conditions in evaluating the effect of a combination on the combinee's ownership interests.

Some, in supporting a type-of-consideration distinction, have stressed that, where equity securities are given, the combinor neither sacrifices economic resources nor incurs economic obligations. According to them, the substance of a combination effected by equity securities is merely the uniting of resources that continue to be utilized in the same operating environments, whereas a combination otherwise effected involves the sacrifice of resources—either immediately or subsequently to liquidate obligations incurred to effect the combination.

A number of writers have expressed theoretical and pragmatic reasons for rejecting the view that the type of consideration is a determinant of economic substance. Some have contended that, regardless of the type of consideration, combinations are basically similar to the variety of other transactions of an enterprise in which resources are acquired. Wyatt, for example, concluded that most combinations effected through an exchange of stock represent "exchange transactions" and are the same for accounting purposes as combinations effected through an exchange of assets. Proponents of this view contend, that (1) the resources acquired have become part of a different accounting entity, which formerly had no direct financial interest in those assets; and (2) any equity securities used to effect the combination are mere substitutes, without substantive difference, for cash, other assets, or debt securities. Foster emphasized that cash and common stock, for example, are freely interchangeable: cash can be used to acquire common stock; common stock can be sold for cash.[16]

Others, although contending that the substance of combinations is not affected by the type of consideration, have stressed the need to focus on whether the constituent companies' operations are to be continued substantially unchanged. Still others have urged rejecting a distinction based on type of consideration because it would require arbitrary criteria that are difficult to apply.

Income-Tax Treatment

Some have suggested that the income-tax laws pertaining to combinations provide meaningful information about the economic substance of various types of combinations.[17] They have contended that the tax treatment of a combination is, or should be used as a surrogate for, the primary determinant of economic substance; they have advocated the following conclusions:

1. In a nontaxable combination, the constituent companies are united to carry on together their previous operations (Type 1).
2. In a taxable combination, one company acquires a controlling interest in the assets of another company or other companies (Type 2).

Those proponents have indicated that conformity of accounting and tax requirements for assessing economic substance would simplify planning for and carrying out combinations. Also, in their view, a substantive difference resulting from present income-tax laws is that a taxable combination causes direct changes in cash flows related to the combinee (recognition of certain gains and losses and assignment of new tax bases to assets and liabilities), whereas a nontaxable combination does not.

In contrast, others assert that the objectives of income taxation are fundamentally different from those for financial reporting and that the distinctions between taxable and nontaxable combinations are not relevant in determining their economic substance.

Because some have suggested income-tax treatment as a possible determinant and because a general understanding of tax requirements related to business combinations provides a helpful background, excerpts follow from a nontechnical overview by Wright and Helpern of the pertinent basic tax rules. We shall come back to these rules in the context of acquisition strategy and implementation tactics in chapter 8.

> A business combination may be completely tax-free, partly tax-free, or completely taxable to the seller. Generally, a tax-free acquisition of one corporate entity by another is accomplished through an exchange of stock with a continuity of ownership, in contrast to a taxable acquisition which is usually accomplished by an exchange of cash or other property for stock or assets of the acquired company and where there is often little or no continuity of ownership by shareholders of the acquired company. Partly tax-free transactions result when consideration other than stock is given in an otherwise tax-free transaction.
>
> There are three basic methods available to accomplish a nontaxable combination. These three methods are referred to as "statutory merger or consolidation", "stock-for-stock" acquisitions and "stock-for-assets" acquisitions.

Statutory Merger or Consolidation. A nontaxable merger or consolidation is a merger or consolidation which has been effected pursuant to a state or Federal merger or consolidation statute. The selling shareholders as a group must retain a continuing common or preferred stock interest in the acquiring corporation. As in the case of the two other primary tax-free methods, the acquisition may be accomplished by a subsidiary using its parent's stock.

The statutory merger is the most flexible tax-free method because the use of nonvoting stock is permitted and because combinations of stock and cash or other property (i.e., warrants, debentures, etc.) may be used. . . .

Stock-For-Stock. A stock-for-stock exchange occurs when one corporation exchanges solely voting common or preferred stock for the stock of another corporation. The acquiring corporation must obtain control of the acquired corporation which is defined as 80% of the total combined voting power and 80% of the total number of shares of each class of nonvoting stock.

A difficulty in a stock-for-stock exchange is the restriction on the use of cash or other property. Nevertheless, a number of important planning possibilities involving cash or other property are available. For example, unwanted assets may be used to redeem shares of minority or dissenting shareholders, provided, under current Treasury guidelines, the total shares redeemed do not exceed 50% of all shares outstanding prior to the redemption. As in the case of the statutory merger, it may be possible to spin off or split off assets to the shareholders tax-free prior to the exchange. Selling shareholders may sell up to 50% of the shares received in the exchange, as a part of a prearranged plan, for cash and not upset the tax-free nature of the combination. . . .

Stock-For-Assets. A tax-free stock-for-assets acquisition occurs when the acquiring corporation exchanges voting stock for substantially all of the assets of a corporation. . . .

According to present IRS guidelines [for advanced ruling purposes on proposed transactions], "substantially all of the assets" means 90% of the fair market value of the net assets *and* 70% of the fair market value of the gross assets. This limits the use of the redemption technique for disposing of unwanted assets or buying out dissenting shareholders that is available in the other two tax-free methods. . . .[19]

There are certain pervasive rules common to the three nontaxable methods that must be satisfied to have a nontaxable combination. Examination of three of those rules—continuity of interest, business purpose, and the so-called step-transaction doctrine—provides some insight about the rationale for the distinction between taxable and nontaxable combinations.

Continuity of Interest. The continuity of interest doctrine requires that selling shareholders retain a sufficient stock interest (either preferred or common, voting and nonvoting) in the combined corporation. With respect to the three primary tax-free methods, the current IRS guidelines [for advanced ruling purposes on proposed transactions] specify that the consideration (determined by fair market values on the exchange date) received by the selling shareholders as a group must be at least 50% of the value of all the formerly outstanding stock of the acquired company. Since the total consideration is considered in determining whether the requisite continuity of interest exists, all of the shareholders of the acquired corporation need not receive stock in the exchange.

Business Purpose. Overriding the literal compliance with the statutory requirements in qualifying an acquisition as tax-free is the time-honored nonstatutory requirement that the transaction must be motivated by a business purpose other than the avoidance of tax. Where a transaction has as its only purpose the avoidance of tax, it will be disregarded as a "sham", and the IRS will look through the formalities and treat the transaction in accordance with its economic substance.

The "Step Transaction" Doctrine . . . . The "step transaction" doctrine causes the separate steps of each transaction to be telescoped in order to view the transaction as a whole for tax purposes. In connection with non-taxable mergers and acquisitions, this doctrine is frequently applied to determine whether or not the continuity of interest, control and solely for voting stock tests have been satisfied.[20]

As can be seen from the preceding extracts, some of the tests to determine whether a combination is taxable or nontaxable are essentially those discussed previously as possible determinants of economic substance.

Tender Offers

The economic substance of a specialized type of combination that has become increasingly popular—the tender offer—is of great interest.[21] As we saw earlier, the term is sometimes used more narrowly to refer to an offer in which the consideration is cash; the term *exchange offer* is then used to refer to tender-type offers in which the consideration is securities.

Guardino provides the following description of a tender offer in which the consideration is cash.

A corporation makes an offer in the newspapers to stockholders of another corporation at a price substantially in excess of the current market value . . . with the condition that the offer must be accepted within a certain specific period of time. . . . The tendering or acquiring corporation only wishes to acquire a specific number of shares necessary to effectuate control. The tendering corporation usually reserves the option to reject when more or less than the specific number of shares is tendered. Another condition is that the . . . corporation can terminate its offer if there should occur conditions which will adversely affect the acquisition.

The key feature of such an acquisition is that no violation of any Securities Act is involved. The reason for this is that the Securities Act only applies to sales and not the purchase of securities.[22]

The SEC has completed several studies that have led to new regulations providing investors with more information about the identity of individuals and companies involved in both foreign and domestic takeovers. These studies and related regulations are referred to or alluded to in several places in this and other chapters.

The market prices of the securities of a number of companies have been so low in recent years that an unfriendly company could obtain control of such a company and, if it desired, be able to use the combinee's cash or other liquid assets to repay most of the borrowing possibly undertaken to finance the takeover. Market prices approached unprecedented lows in relation to net asset values based on historical cost. For example, in July 1974, of 2,700 listed and unlisted industrial stocks, more than 40 percent were selling at or lower than the carrying amounts of the underlying assets, including 81 companies with market value of $300 million or more and 16 of the 30 listed in the Dow Jones Industrial Average.[23]

As pointed out in the FASB discussion on tender offers, a usual crucial element of an unfriendly tender offer is that the target company is previously unaware of the offer. Accordingly, the offering company must rely substantially on public information to analyze the target company's merits. For a number of companies, filings with the SEC, investment-research reports, and other sources provide a wealth of public information that can be analyzed comprehensively. One result of the SEC's increased disclosure requirements for various filings is that an outsider can know more about a public company and assume less risk in making a tender offer than was previously possible.

The factors considered by an offering company in making a tender offer are essentially the same as those considered by a combinor: primarily, an emphasis on the anticipated effect on earnings per share and cash flows.

A difference that may be pertinent in accounting for the identifiable assets at the time of a combination is that, particularly in depressed general market conditions, the price offered may be significantly less than either the offering company's or the target company's estimate of the target company's intrinsic value. The price offered publicly must be only high enough to persuade the target company's stockholders to tender their share. Much emphasis is placed on how those stockholders will perceive an unfriendly tender offer. That difference may primarily be one of form rather than substance, however, for at least two reasons.[24] First, even in a friendly combination the negotiating parties may offer and counteroffer various prices that differ from their estimates of the combinee's intrinsic value. Second, in many cases involving an unfriendly tender offer, another company has subsequently made an offer for the same target company's stock, so that two or more offering companies have competed for the same shares. One result has been that, in a number of cases, the offer finally accepted by the target company's stockholders has substantially exceeded the original offer.[25]

For example, in the well-publicized tender offers in 1974 for the common stock of ESB, Inc., International Nickel Company of Canada initially offered $28 per share. After a hectic battle with United Aircraft Corporation (now United Technologies Corporation) for control, however International Nickel finally successfully offered $41 per share—a 46-percent increase from its initial offer.[26] As another example, in 1975, Alaska Interstate Company's offer of $17 per share for the common stock of Apco Oil led to an eventual $25-per-share offer by Northwest Energy Company—almost a 50-percent increase.[27] As a third example, in 1980, McDermott Inc. was vying with Wheelabrator-Frye, Inc., in a cash tender offer for the stock of Pullman, Inc., which had been trading at a price of $20-25 per share when McDermott made its first offer. The Wheelabrator-Frye and Pullman boards approved a merger, and then a revised merger plan, valuing Pullman shares at over $50 per share, with the intention of blocking an unfriendly tender for a block of Pullman shares by McDermott, at $28 per share (see figures 2-1 through 2-5). It seemed clear that the result would see Pullman's stockholders receiving approximately a 150-percent increase in the value of their holdings as a consequence of the McDermott tender offer; and, in fact, shareholders of Pullman, Inc., and Wheelabrator-Frye, Inc., approved Wheelabrator's acquisition of Pullman in early November 1980. The nearly $600-million cash and stock transaction was finally consummated on 12 November 1980.

The efforts of Pullman to find a "white-knight" suitor to overcome McDermott's bid, and the generous offer from Wheelabrator-Frye (whose price was ultimately nearly three times the value at which Pullman's shares were traded on the New York Stock Exchange several months earlier—a period during which the general market-price levels experienced no such upward valuation) illustrate that emotional factors can be pivotal. Indeed, this was how the *Wall Street Journal* described the situation in a long article on the subject.[28] The *Wall Street Journal* article also suggested that the pride and ambition of the chief executive officers (chairmen) concerned, and the "tense struggle for prestige and fees among blue ribbon Wall Street investment banking firms" (Pullman—First Boston; McDermott—Smith Barney; Wheelabrator—Lazard Frères) was very much involved, and that "until the current bidding war, Pullman hardly looked worth fighting for." (The *Journal* article, on the other hand, did present the serious arguments that Pullman's intrinsic value might be worth even more than was offered, based on future potential, and so forth.)

OFFER TO PURCHASE FOR CASH

Up to 2,000,000 Shares of Common Stock

of

Pullman Incorporated

at

$28 Per Share Net

by

J. Ray McDermott & Co., Inc.

THE OFFER EXPIRES ON AUGUST 11, 1980, AT
12:00 MIDNIGHT, NEW YORK CITY TIME, UNLESS EXTENDED.

IMPORTANT

Any stockholder desiring to accept this Offer to Purchase should either (1) request his broker, dealer, commercial bank, trust company or nominee to effect the transaction for him or (2) complete and sign the Letter of Transmittal or a facsimile thereof, have his signature thereon guaranteed if required by Instructions (1) or (5) of the Letter of Transmittal and forward the Letter of Transmittal, together with his stock certificate(s) and any other required documents to the Forwarding Agent or the Depositary. Stockholders having Shares registered in the name of a broker, dealer, commercial bank, trust company or other nominee are urged to contact such person if they desire to tender the Shares so registered.

Questions and requests for assistance may be directed to the Dealer Manager or the Information Agent at their respective addresses and telephone numbers set forth at the end of this Offer to Purchase. Requests for additional copies of this Offer to Purchase and the Letter of Transmittal may be directed to the Information Agent, the Dealer Manager or to brokers, dealers, commercial banks or trust companies.

The Dealer Manager for the Offer is:

Smith Barney, Harris Upham & Co.
Incorporated

July 3, 1980

Figure 2-1. Offer to Purchase for Cash Up to 2,000,000 Shares of Common Stock

Such activity often reflects what we have called the "vital role of personality and whim" (see chapter 10). However, one additional and important point deserves mentioning: in these corporate bidding contests, often the "losers" and the selling stockholders are in reality the big winners.[29] This is because the selling stockholders "take the big premium

Pullman Incorporated   200 South Michigan Avenue
                                                 Chicago, Illinois 60604

                                                 Clark P. Lattin, Jr.
                                                 President and
                                                 Chief Executive Officer

Dear Fellow Pullman Stockholders:

At a meeting of your Board of Directors it was unanimously determined that the tender offer made on July 3, 1980 by J. Ray McDermott & Co., Inc. to purchase up to 2 million shares of Pullman common stock at a price of $28.00 per share is inadequate as to price and not in the best interests of the Company or its stockholders and should be rejected.

In arriving at its decision, the Board of Directors gave careful consideration to a number of factors described in the enclosed Schedule 14D-9 and certain exhibits appended to it filed with the Securities and Exchange Commission. The Board of Directors was advised by The First Boston Corporation, a major investment banking firm, that, after consideration of the matters referred to in their opinion ". . . the tender offer by McDermott for up to 2,000,000 shares of common stock of Pullman is inadequate as to price and that the acquisition by McDermott of 2,000,000 shares of common stock of Pullman would be disadvantageous to Pullman from a financial point of view." The First Boston opinion letter is enclosed with the Schedule 14D-9.

Moreover, your Board has determined that the tender offer raises serious questions under federal antitrust and securities laws. Accordingly, litigation has been instituted seeking to enjoin the offer.

We urge you to read the documents carefully. They will help you to understand why the Board is convinced that the offer should be resisted by your Company.

We can assure you that we will act in the manner which we believe will be in the interests of Pullman's stockholders as a whole and we will take all action to protect the interests of our stockholders.

                        Very truly yours,

                        Clark P. Lattin, Jr.
                        President and Chief Executive Officer

Figure 2-2. Pullman Incorporated—Letter to Stockholders

and run," whereas the losing corporate bidder is left with a block of stock that can be disposed of at a substantial profit. Besides McDermott's experience with Pullman, there are more colorful examples—for example, separate situations in which Crane Company (Anaconda), Esmark (Inmont), Gulf & Western Industries, Teledyne, and other corporate conglomerates were involved, finally disposing of their stockholdings at a very large profit to their respective shareholders. Meanwhile, the returns may be substantially lower to the shareholders of the acquiring corporation if the target company was overvalued.

SECURITIES AND EXCHANGE COMMISSION
Washington, D.C. 20549

SCHEDULE 14D-9

SOLICITATION/RECOMMENDATION STATEMENT
PURSUANT TO SECTION 14(D)(4)
OF THE SECURITIES EXCHANGE ACT OF 1934

Pullman Incorporated
(Name of Subject Company)

Pullman Incorporated
(Name of Person(s) Filing Statement)

Common Stock without nominal or par value
(Title of Class of Securities)

745791 10 3
(CUSIP Number of Class of Securities)

John J. McLean, Esq.
Senior Vice President, General
Counsel and Secretary
Pullman Incorporated
200 South Michigan Avenue
Chicago, Illinois 60604
(312) 322-7070

(Name, address and telephone number of person authorized to receive
notice and communications on behalf of the person(s) filing statement)

Copy to:

Figure 2-3. SEC Solicitation/Recommendation Statement

Major Accounting Principles Affecting
Acquisition and Merger Transactions

The concepts resulting from discussion of the types and economic substance
of, and the motivations for, business combinations, underlie the accounting
principles used subsequent to a transaction. There are two major alternatives: the acquisition or merger can be structured either as a purchase or

Announcement of Amended Offer to Purchase for Cash
6,300,000 Shares of Common Stock
of
Pullman Incorporated
at
$43.50 Per Share Net
by
McDermott Incorporated

McDermott Incorporated has amended its Offer for Common Stock of Pullman Incorporated and is now offering to pay $43.50 per Share net in cash for up to 6,300,000 Shares of Pullman Incorporated. McDermott's Offer has been extended until 12:00 Midnight, New York City Time, on September 12, 1980, and will be on a pro rata basis until 12:00 Midnight, New York City Time, on September 8. Stockholders who tender after the time of this announcement will have the right to withdraw any Shares not accepted for payment at any time. (Through August 29, McDermott has received tenders of 3,367 shares and has purchased 2,355 Shares under the Offer.)

THE AMENDED OFFER IS CONDITIONED UPON A MINIMUM OF CERTIFICATES FOR 5,400,000 SHARES BEING VALIDLY TENDERED IN FORM FOR TRANSFER INTO THE NAME OF McDERMOTT AND NOT WITHDRAWN ON THE EXPIRATION DATE.

Subject to the satisfaction of the conditions of the Offer, the earliest time for the acceptance for payment of Shares properly tendered and not withdrawn under the amended Offer will be after the later of September 8 or the expiration of a second waiting period under Section 7A of the Clayton Act.

If the Offer is successful, McDermott will own 61% of the Shares, which is more than the amount required to approve a business combination or to take any other permitted action by vote or consent of stockholders. In such event, although no plan has been formulated, McDermott presently intends to seek to accomplish a business combination of McDermott and Pullman under which remaining stockholders of Pullman would receive securities of McDermott. McDermott believes that the consideration to be received by remaining stockholders of Pullman would have to approximate the price paid pursuant to this Offer, subject to there not having been any material misstatements in published financial statements of Pullman and there not being any material adverse change in the business or financial condition of Pullman after June 30, 1980 and prior to the proposal and to the closing of such business combination. Any such transaction would probably be taxable to remaining stockholders of Pullman.

Funds required by McDermott to purchase the 6,300,000 Shares of Pullman pursuant to the amended Offer will be approximately $276,000,000 inclusive of related expenses. In addition to the $75,000,000 to be obtained as described in Section 10 of the Offer, $200,000,000 will be obtained under a revolving and term loan arrangement with a group of four banks, including the bank referred to in Section 10 of the Offer. Such arrangement provides for revolving three-year borrowings, convertible to two-year term borrowings at the election of McDermott payable in eight equal quarterly installments. Interest payable on revolving credit borrowings will be, at the election of McDermott, at the prime lending rate of the lead bank or ½ of 1% over LIBOR (London InterBank Offered Rate). Interest payable on the term loans will be, at McDermott's election, at ¼ of 1% over the prime lending rate of the lead bank or ⅜ of 1% over LIBOR. In addition, McDermott is obliged to pay a commitment fee on the unused portion of the revolving and term loan arrangement. McDermott has not made any plan for repayment of such additional borrowings. The balance of the funds required to purchase the Shares will be derived from McDermott's general corporate funds.

THE AMENDED OFFER EXPIRES AT 12:00 MIDNIGHT, NEW YORK CITY
TIME, ON SEPTEMBER 12, 1980, UNLESS EXTENDED, AND WILL BE
ON A PRO RATA BASIS UNTIL SEPTEMBER 8, 1980.

The Offer may be extended from time to time by oral or written notice to the Depositary of such extension, which extension will be promptly announced.

McDermott filed under Section 7A of the Clayton Act with respect to the amended Offer (which would increase McDermott's holdings of Pullman to more than 50%) on August 29, 1980 and the waiting period is scheduled to expire at 10:00 A.M., New York City Time, on September 15, 1980, subject to early termination or to extension. (See Section 3 of the Offer.)

After giving effect to all of the above, all other terms and conditions of the Offer to Purchase dated July 3, 1980 remain the same, except that McDermott reserves the right not to purchase Shares under the amended Offer if Wheelabrator-Frye Inc. shall have varied the terms of its present Offer at $43 a Share for up to 2,000,000 Shares. Also, in addition to other conditions of the Offer, McDermott specifically reserves the right not to purchase Shares under the amended Offer if, prior to McDermott's acceptance for payment of tendered Shares, the New York Stock Exchange shall have authorized the listing of up to 1,800,000 new Shares purportedly issuable by Pullman to Wheelabrator-Frye Inc. under an option at $36⅞ a Share, or any of such Shares shall have been issued; or if Wheelabrator-Frye Inc. shall have given notice of exercise of an option to purchase Pullman's construction and engineering division purported to have been granted by Pullman management on behalf of Pullman. Wheelabrator-Frye Inc.'s Offer to Purchase stock of Pullman, dated August 22, 1980 and mailed to Pullman stockholders, purports to describe the foregoing options and other merger arrangements between Wheelabrator-Frye Inc. and Pullman. McDermott takes no responsibility for the completeness or accuracy of such document. Stockholders are urged to consult their broker or financial advisor.

McDermott has announced that revenues for the three months ended June 30, 1980 were $730,894,000 and net income was $12,423,000. Revenues and net income for the three months ended June 30, 1979 were $710,037,000 and $19,810,000, respectively.

Requests for copies of the Offer to Purchase and the Letter of Transmittal forms may be directed to the Information Agent or the Dealer Manager as set forth below, and will be furnished promptly at McDermott's expense.

The Information Agent is:

Morrow & Co.

345 Hudson Street   39 South La Salle Street
New York, New York 10014   Chicago, Illinois 60603
(212) 255-7400   (312) 236-8600
(Call Collect)   (Call Collect)

The Dealer Manager for the Offer is:

Smith Barney, Harris Upham & Co.

Incorporated

1345 Avenue of the Americas
New York, New York 10105
(212) 399-6409

August 29, 1980

Source: *The Wall Street Journal*, 2 September 1980.

Figure 2-4. Pullman Incorporated at $43.50 per Share Net by McDermott

as a pooling of interests. The accounting treatment is governed in large part by Opinions nos. 16 and 17 of the Accounting Principles Board of the AICPA. For technical details, the reader is referred to these and other accounting references, such as those listed at the end of this chapter. The point here is that the accounting treatment affects the assets and capital structure reported for the surviving corporation. When purchase account-

Notice of Supplement to Offer to Purchase for Cash
3,000,000 Shares of Common Stock of

PULLMAN INCORPORATED

at

$52.50 Per Share Net

by

WHEELABRATOR-FRYE INC.

The Offer will expire at 12:00 midnight, New York City time, on Friday, September 19, 1980, unless extended.

Wheelabrator-Frye Inc., a Delaware corporation (the "Purchaser"), is offering to purchase 3,000,000 outstanding shares of Common Stock, without nominal or par value (the "Shares"), of Pullman Incorporated, a Delaware corporation (the "Company"), at $52.50 per Share, net to the seller in cash, upon the terms and conditions set forth in the Offer to Purchase dated August 22, 1980, including the Supplement thereto dated September 3, 1980, and in the related Letter of Transmittal (which together constitute the "Offer").

The Offer is not conditioned upon any minimum number of Shares being tendered.

The Purchaser and the Company entered into an Agreement of Merger, dated August 20, 1980, as amended on September 3, 1980, which contemplates the Offer and the subsequent merger (the "Merger") of the Company into a wholly owned subsidiary of the Purchaser, pursuant to which each Share not purchased by the Purchaser pursuant to the Offer will be exchanged, in a transaction intended to be tax-free, for 1.1 shares of the Purchaser's Common Stock. Cash will be provided in lieu of fractional interests of the Purchaser's Common Stock. The Offer is, therefore, the first step in the acquisition of the Company by the Purchaser, and one of the purposes of the Offer may be deemed to be the acquisition of control of the Company by the Purchaser.

The Board of Directors of the Company has unanimously approved the Offer and the Merger and has recommended that the Company's stockholders who wish to receive cash for their Shares at this time accept the Offer.

Upon the terms and subject to the conditions of the Offer, the Purchaser will purchase up to 3,000,000 Shares properly tendered (and not withdrawn) by 12:00 midnight, New York City time, on September 19, 1980, or the latest time and date, if any, to which the Offer is extended. The Purchaser reserves the right from time to time to extend the Offer by oral or written notice of such extension to Mellon Bank, N.A. (the "Depositary"). The Purchaser shall be deemed to have purchased tendered Shares when, as and if it gives oral or written notice to the Depositary of its acceptance of the tender of such Shares. The Purchaser also reserves the right (i) to terminate the Offer and not purchase or pay for any Shares not theretofore purchased upon the occurrence of any of the conditions set forth in the Offer and (ii) to amend or supplement the Offer.

If more than 3,000,000 Shares (or any greater number of Shares to be purchased pursuant to the Offer) are properly tendered and not withdrawn prior to 12:00 midnight, New York City time, on September 19, 1980, purchases of Shares will be made on a pro rata basis (with appropriate adjustments to avoid purchases of fractional Shares). If the Offer is extended, all Shares properly tendered (and not withdrawn) by 12:00 midnight, New York City time, on September 19, 1980, will be purchased before any Shares tendered during any extension are purchased. Shares tendered during any extension will be purchased in the order tendered until 3,000,000 Shares (or any greater number of Shares to be purchased pursuant to the Offer) have been purchased. The Purchaser has reserved the right to purchase up to 1,000,000 additional Shares upon the terms and subject to the conditions of the Offer.

Tenders of Shares shall be irrevocable, except that Shares may be withdrawn prior to 12:00 midnight, New York City time, on September 15, 1980, and unless theretofore purchased by the Purchaser as provided in the Offer, may also be withdrawn after October 20, 1980. In addition, if a tender offer by another bidder is made for some or all of the Shares, Shares not yet accepted for payment may be withdrawn on the date of, and for 10 business days after, the formal commencement of such other offer, provided that the Purchaser has received notice or otherwise has knowledge of the commencement of such other offer. To be effective, a written, telegraphic, telex or facsimile transmission notice of withdrawal must be timely received by the Depositary and must specify the name of the person who executed the particular Letter of Transmittal and the number of Shares to be withdrawn. If certificates have been delivered or otherwise identified to the Depositary, the name of the registered holder and the serial numbers shown on the stock certificates evidencing the Shares to be withdrawn must be furnished to the Depositary.

The information required to be disclosed by Rule 14d-6(e)(1)(vii) of the General Rules and Regulations under the Securities Exchange Act of 1934 is contained in the Offer to Purchase, including the Supplement thereto, and is incorporated herein by reference.

The Purchaser will not pay any fee or commission to any broker, dealer, or other person (other than the Dealer Manager and the Information Agent) in connection with the solicitation of tenders of Shares pursuant to the Offer.

The Offer to Purchase, including the Supplement thereto, and the Letter of Transmittal, which are being mailed to stockholders of the Company, contain important information which should be read before any decision is made with respect to the Offer.

Requests for copies of the Offer to Purchase, including the Supplement thereto, and the Letter of Transmittal may be directed to the Information Agent or the Dealer Manager as set forth below, and will be furnished promptly at the Purchaser's expense.

The Information Agent is:

GEORGESON & CO., INC.

150 South Wacker Drive	Wall Street Plaza	606 South Olive Street
Chicago, Illinois 60606	New York, New York 10005	Los Angeles, California 90014
(312) 346-7161 (Collect)	(212) 440-9800 (Collect)	(213) 489-7000 (Collect)

The Dealer Manager for the Offer is:

LAZARD FRÈRES & CO.

Attention: Syndicate Department
One Rockefeller Plaza
New York, New York 10020
(212) 489-6600, Extensions 345-350
(Collect)

September 4, 1980

Source: *The Wall Street Journal*, 4 September 1980.

Figure 2-5. Pullman Incorporated at $52.50 per Share Net by Wheelabrator-Frye, Inc.

ing is called for, a new basis of cost accountability arises for the assets acquired, based on the value of consideration paid. The amount of future depreciation and amortization expenses shown for financial-accounting and reporting purposes will depend in part on the particular accounting treatment used.

The recognition of goodwill arises under a purchase, but not under pooling-of-interest accounting. In the latter case (pooling), a new basis of asset accountability is not called for, since it is deemed to represent a continuation of existing ownership. Since the introduction of any new cost basis of accountability has an influence on the future reported earnings, managements and stockholders will be concerned about the accounting rationale, other things being equal. On the other hand, modern financial economics places little, if any, emphasis on the financial-accounting treatment; it focuses rather on the *investment merits* of the transaction in terms of the expected present value of cash flow received in return for the financial consideration given (cash, securities, and so on).

Both pooling and purchase accounting have been "abused" in the past in that they have been used by management to create favorable earnings-per-share comparisons under various circumstances.

As discussed elsewhere (see, for example, chapters 1 and 8), APB Opinions nos. 16 and 17, which became effective in 1970, contributed in a major way to the reduction in the number of acquisitions after 1969 and to the encouragement of more soundly conceived ones. These Opinions severely restricted the conditions under which pooling could be used, and mandated the write-off of goodwill in purchase transactions.

Specific considerations arising in structuring and implementing acquisitions and merger transactions are discussed and illustrated in chapter 8.

Sociopolitical Framework

The sociopolitical framework refers to the macrocultural setting in which acquisitions take place, as distinguished from the microeconomic and corporate-culture considerations discussed elsewhere. The basic context of corporate development is profit-seeking enterprise. Shareholder-wealth maximization is presumed to be the central driving force. However, in the United States—and, to a greater extent, elsewhere in the world—constituencies other than private stockholders are increasingly influential: organized labor, environmental protectionists, government entities representing financial backing and/or employee rights and benefits.

These influences manifest themselves through various mechanisms. Three of the most important are corporate-taxation policies, antitrust laws, and pension legislation. All constrain corporate financial behavior, and can influence the attractiveness of various acquisitions and alter the balance between acquisition and internal research and development (R&D). U.S. tax policy, for example, did not allow the write-off of R&D as a deductible business expense until the Internal Revenue Code was revised after the Korean War (1954). U.S. tax policy presently prohibits expensing goodwill arising from an acquisition transaction. In the antitrust area (discussed in chapter 4), with each merger wave new legislation is proposed that would institute various barriers or disincentives, particularly for conglomerate mergers—precisely the kind that may make sense from the portfolio-theory standpoint of diversification to spread corporate risk. Granted, there is some controversy over whether the individual investor could better effect such diversification by holding shares in a variety of industries (for example, a mutual fund) than in the corporate acquirer. Whether or not this is true, and whether or not conglomeration that leads to very large corporations is good or bad, the manager of a single-line business in the U.S. sociopolitical framework is under pressure to show competitive financial performance. This is usually measured by annual comparisons of sales, earnings, and profitability growth. Growth is central to the culture, since only through real growth can the economy promise more for the future in return for today's investment of labor and capital. Acquisitions offer management an opportunity to demonstrate corporate growth. However, acquisitions in and of themselves do not necessarily produce more real output for the economy as a whole—and that is the rub. But the aggressive manager seeks to achieve growth.

The politics of social security and pension funds also rest on the presumption of real, long-term growth. However, the salaries and bonuses of most managers rest on demonstrated short-run performance: A year of sales or earnings decline is usually intolerable—although it need not be. The point is that the cultural setting puts pressure on U.S. managements to show stable and growing earnings, and that certain businesses do not enjoy the outlook for either, without acquisitions. Many shareholders may stick with such a company through its ups and downs (for example, Chrysler, Bethlehem Steel); but management cannot stand put. However, it may take many years for such corporations to afford the necessary diversification through new product developments and/or acquisitions. Such companies are thus often accorded pessimistic valuations, and may themselves become targets for their basic assets alone.

These particular examples also illustrate the case in which labor unions have a significant employment and pension stake in the corporation, and therefore will cooperate, in their own self-interest, to improve company fortunes.

The environmental-protection and occupational-health and -safety movements are parts of the macroculture that bring other pressures and opportunities to businesses, the outcome of which is likely to be additional acquisition activity.

Outside the United States, particularly in Japan and West Germany, corporate growth has been robust in the last decade; and the combination of good cash flow, strong currency vis-à-vis the dollar, and a quest for more opportunities has brought such foreign capital increasingly into investments and joint ventures in the United States. The cultural forces are not identical, nor are the financial constraints. Thus there are likely to be many disparities in the value attached to various acquisitions. Foreign investors typically have a longer planning and investment horizon than do U.S. investors (corporate or individual) when it comes to equity investments. This may be traced not to any difference in individual risk aversion, but rather to differences (in the case of foreign investments) in government incentives of one form or another.

Financial Framework

Return on Investment and Costs of Capital

Acquisitions are usually evaluated against financial criteria, the most important of which, in practice, include investment magnitude, expected return on investment, minimum acceptable return commensurate with the risk (the so-called hurdle rate), and cash-payback period.

An investment is financially attractive if its expected rate of return exceeds the cost of capital associated with the investment. This criterion is usually set in the framework of discounted cash flow and net present value, where the discount rate is taken as the opportunity cost of capital for the type of investment under consideration. One of the most troublesome issues is the determination of this cost of capital. We have witnessed many situations in which corporate staff and boards of directors have acted on acquisition proposals that have probably incorporated a misspecified discount rate. Since this is equivalent to compounding at the wrong rate of interest, the perceived value of an acquisition can thereby be dramatically overstated or understated.

A related problem is the economic theory and assumptions behind the notion of the cost of capital. Financial economists often deal with the theory of the shareholder-wealth-maximizing firm under equilibrium conditions in the capital markets, and approximate the cost of capital—a value that may often be derived analytically—in this setting. The Gordon-Shapiro growth model of the firm, the cost of capital studies by Modigliani and Miller, and other well-known studies available in the literature are eloquent and powerful pieces of work along these lines. More recently, S.C. Myers, as well as several other investigators, has incorporated the results of modern capital-market theory and the capital-asset pricing model (CAPM) of Sharpe and others. The issues here are far from resolved, however, at either the theoretical or the operational level. The apparent cost of capital that may be associated with an acquisition under equilibrium conditions is not necessarily the same as or even close to the one that may be appropriate for the time frame of acquisition. Moreover, the perception of the acquiring corporation of what cost of capital should be used in discounting the incremental cash flows projected from an acquisition investment often differs markedly in concept from the theory itself. Some would view an acquisition financed entirely with bank debt as requiring the use of the current cost of short-term bank debt (net of tax) as the cost of capital in evaluating a long-term acquisition. Some would view exchange of stock as having no "cash" investment cost to the acquirer. Neither of these views is correct, and either can lead to valuation error. Valuation techniques are discussed in chapter 7, where the cost-of-capital problem may be seen in proper focus. A helpful benefit/cost framework is presented later in this chapter.

Portfolio Theory and Diversification

Developments in portfolio theory have occurred rapidly since the seminal work of Markowitz in the 1950s. However, most of this development has focused on the application to common stocks and the management of portfolios of stocks, bonds, cash, and cash equivalents. See Hagin for a review of modern portfolio theory (MPT).[30]

In the 1960s the application to government R&D and corporate-development programs was studied with some limited success. As will be seen, this is an even more difficult area for application, since one needs knowledge about and estimates of the statistical means and variances and covariances among many different investments or projects. Unlike common stocks, new R&D projects have no history of financial performance. Moreover, the population of R&D projects is very heterogeneous; and such projects often are not amenable to measurement of the realized rates of return. There are many other important distinctions between R&D projects and investments in common stock or in operating assets such as new plant and equipment, such as machine tools. These will be obvious to the reader. Acquisitions, in contrast to R&D, are analogous to investments in stocks, with the important exception that a corporate acquisition or merger can change the operating basis of the assets acquired, something that passive investment does not do. As an oversimplified illustration, let us look first at an internal-development program limited to new R&D projects.

Insurance-Benefit and Portfolio-Risk
Aspects of a Corporate R&D Program

The notion here is that increasing the number, N, of projects in the funded R&D program "portfolio" decreases the risk that the outcome will differ substantially from that expected, and increases the benefit per unit of risk, as $\sqrt{N}$. An insurance benefit of an N-project R&D program can be expressed in terms of its failure probabilities and an assumed catastrophic loss.

The point is that there is an analogy between sponsorship of mission-oriented research and development and the purchase of insurance, and that this insurance analogy may ultimately be quantified. Similarly, there is an analogy between designing a portfolio of risky securities (that is, ownership of stocks or other assets whose rates of return are uncertain) and designing a portfolio of research projects. Such an analogy is based on the application of statistics and portfolio theory to the management of diversifiable risk. This analogy can also be drawn in quantitative terms.

The following examination is an illustration taken from an Arthur D. Little, Inc., study for the U.S. Energy Research and Development Administration.[31] The illustration is for a hypothetical case. A more elaborate analysis would be required in the real case, where project costs and parameters may differ widely from project to project.

In brief, the insurance benefits can be expressed in terms of an incremental expected benefit (or loss avoided) per unit of incremental research cost; the treatment of the insurance benefit carries with it the notion of an optimal number of research projects, which is a function of the size of a "catastrophic loss" (for example, in a corporate-survival sense) assumed to be possible in the absence of any research or if all research projects fail. Similarly, the optimal number of research projects depends on the project-failure probabilities—the higher the failure probability, the larger must be the research program.

The word *risk* can have various meanings. For the purposes of this section, we will define *failure risk* as *the probability that all research projects in a research program will fail to achieve a given purpose.*

If we use this definition of risk, then it is appropriate to ask: *How does failure risk vary with the number of research projects in a research program?* We cannot quantify an answer to this broad question in this study. However, it is useful to consider the following idealized example: If one has the opportunity to fund some number of projects, all of which have the same probability P_F of failure, and all of which are independent in the sense that the success of any one does not depend on the success of the others, then

$$\left.\begin{array}{l}\text{The probability that all } N \\ \text{projects fail}\end{array}\right\} = (P_F)^N$$

Therefore:

$$P_0 = \left.\begin{array}{l}\text{The probability that at least} \\ \text{one project will succeed}\end{array}\right\} = 1 - (P_F)^N$$

and we can call P_0 the *certainty of success.* We might then ask: *How many projects should be supported if the certainty of one success must exceed some given amount?* (See table 2-1.)

The portfolio effect is based on the statistical properties of variances and covariances among project outcomes and the combinatorial properties of the variance (that is, the square of the standard deviation). In general, *if there is little or no covariance (correlation) associated with the outcome of projects in a research program, then the variability (a measure of risk)*

Table 2-1
Number of Projects Required

Probability of Success of the Individual Research Project (Percentage)	*Percentage Certainty of Success of Research Program Must be at Least:*		
	99	*99.9*	*99.99*
10	44	66	88
20	21	31	41
50	7	10	14
90	2	3	4

associated with the outcome of the overall program will be reduced as the number of projects is increased. This is analogous to the concept of diversification in a portfolio of securities where the diversifiable risk (non-market-related risk) can be reduced by increasing the number of holdings.

A somewhat more general concept of risk than that used up to this point is *variability risk*, which can be defined as *the probability that the outcome of a research program will differ substantially from what is expected*. One way to measure the variability risk is by the ratio of the standard deviation of the possible outcome to the average value of the outcome; the larger this ratio, the greater the variability risk. It is then appropriate to ask: *How does the variability risk of a research program vary with the number of research projects?* Variability risk in this case is affected by the number of projects that one has the opportunity to fund, all of which have an uncertain outcome. If the expected value of the outcome of each one is μ, the standard deviation of the outcome of each is σ, the projects are independent, and the outcome of the program is the sum of the outcomes of the projects, the variability risk of an N-project program is then given by:

$$\frac{\sigma}{\mu\sqrt{N}}$$

and so decreases with the number of projects. This reduction occurs because the larger the number of projects, the better the chances of an unusually good outcome occurring to compensate for an unusually bad outcome. This is the simplest type of "portfolio effect."

Increasing the number of R&D projects is a way of buying insurance against the risk of failure. It is necessary to consider how much of such insurance is cost effective; appendix 2A contains a methodology for appraising the relative benefits of success and costs of failure in an R&D program for which there are insurance benefits.

Extension to Acquisitions

With the foregoing in mind, we may consider two elementary principles of portfolio theory, in the context of corporate acquisitions. Here, we consider the business as a portfolio of various assets:

1. True diversification reduces risk.
2. For a given set of risk/return preferences or tradeoffs (the corporate investor's utility curve), there is an "efficient" or optimal portfolio of assets that should be held.

With respect to the first point, Myers has argued that usually corporate diversification is redundant from the investor's point of view, since the investor can accomplish the same thing, in theory, by buying a mutual fund.[32]

Salter and Weinhold, on the other hand, indicate the nature of diversification through acquisition, which may create economic value.[33]

With respect to the second point, such a portfolio would produce the highest expected return for a given risk exposure (taken, for example, as the standard deviation in mean rate of return, or the annual variability of cash flow); or the lowest risk for a given expected rate of return.

Benefits and Costs of an Acquisition

Although corporate diversification by means of acquisition may be a redundant service to a shareholder, as S.C. Myers has argued ("he can buy a mutual fund and spread his investment over most of the economy"),[34] it is a means of reducing the personal risk and/or increasing the earnings available to corporate management. Conglomerate mergers "place the eggs in more baskets"; vertical mergers may "produce more eggs" through integration and efficiencies than would be produced otherwise. The point is that, for the acquiring firm, corporate earnings are usually expected by management to be higher and/or more stable than otherwise. True, in economic theory, if conglomerate mergers were banned, the shareholder might receive as great or greater benefits through mutual-fund investment. However, the other benefits of acquisitions—for example, acquisitions that allow operating and/or financial efficiencies, or acquisitions that provide synergies—cannot be duplicated by means of mutual-fund holdings.

It is well known that mergers can increase reported earnings *per share in the short run*, even if there are no real economic benefits, no real increase in total earnings of the merged businesses or assets. This phenomenon occurs when the price-to-earnings (*P/E*) ratio of the acquiring firm is greater than that of the acquired or merging firm. The literature abounds with such examples. And most corporate executives prefer transactions that, although they promise significant long-term benefits to the firm, can also boost—or at least not dilute—short-term earnings as well.

Myers has presented a concise notation and treatment of the concept of measuring the *benefits* (value) and *financial costs* of an acquisition. Salter and Weinhold have presented a three-element framework with which to attempt to create value through acquisitions as a means of diversification, with an emphasis on assessing the various types of risks associated with different levels of corporate activity and relations with the external environment, and the notion of receiving returns commensurate with risk. The elements incorporated are known independently in the management and finance literature, and are the so-called strategy model (for operation-level, single-business enterprise), the product/market portfolio model (for corporate-level cash flows), and the risk/return model (for capital-market-level risk, associated with changing share valuations, and cost of capital).[35]

It is helpful to think about the corporate transaction first in the mensuration framework of Myers (which here implicitly, and elsewhere explicitly, recognizes the risk-return tradeoffs emphasized by Salter and Weinhold, among others), from whom the following is taken.[36]

Benefits of an Acquisition or Merger. The *benefit* can be defined as the difference between (1) the total present value (that is, the discounted cash-flow value as seen by investors) of the merged firms and (2) the sum of their values if they do not merge. If V represents present value, then

$$\text{BENEFIT} \equiv \Delta V \equiv V_{AB} - V_A - V_B \qquad (2.1)$$

where V_A is the present value of firm A, which is analyzing the possible acquisition of firm B. The framework for analysis presented here could just as well be applied from firm B's viewpoint.

The implied question is: What aspects of the proposed merger make the two firms worth more together than apart?

If this definition of benefit is accepted, then *cost* must be defined as the *difference* between the amount paid for the acquired firm and the amount it is worth as a separate entity. If B's owners receive cash for their shares, for example, then

$$\text{COST} = \text{CASH} - V_B \qquad (2.2)$$

Defining benefits in this way focuses attention on the economic value of the merger. Estimating this value is indeed "just like a capital budgeting problem." Estimating cost, however, requires consideration of how the merger benefits are shared between the owners of A and B. As we will see later in this section, cost can depend on how the merger is financed.

Firm A should go ahead with acquisitions or mergers for which benefit exceeds cost. If the merger is financed by cash, this requires that

$$\text{BENEFIT} - \text{COST} = \Delta V - (\text{CASH} - V_B) > 0. \qquad (2.3)$$

It may not be obvious that A's stockholders gain when equation 2.3 holds. If not, consider the following: if there is no merger, then the aggregate value of their shares is V_A. If the merger goes through, then their position is $V_{AB} - \text{CASH}$. Their net gain is exactly as given by equation 2.3:

$$\begin{aligned} \text{NET GAIN} &= V_{AB} - \text{CASH} - V_A \\ &= \Delta V + V_A + V_B - \text{CASH} - V_A \\ &= \Delta V - (\text{CASH} - V_B) \end{aligned}$$

Costs of Achieving Merger Benefits. Merger benefits should be calculated net of the costs of achieving them. Managers should be careful not to overlook these costs, which can be substantial. They fall into two categories. First, there is the transaction cost of arranging the merger: the management time spent, in search for suitable merger candidates, negotiation, and so forth; fees for legal advice and other services; and costs of paperwork. Second, there are the organizational costs of integrating two organizations, each with its own customs and standard operating and accounting procedures. At least at first, it seems to take more management talent to run two merged firms than to run them separately.

Estimating the Cost. *Cost* is the difference between the amount paid for the acquired firm and what it is worth as a separate entity. Estimating cost is straightforward as long as the merger is financed by cash. However, it is useful to distinguish between V_B, the "intrinsic" value of the acquired firm as a separate entity, and MV_B, the aggregate market value of the firm as observed around the time of the merger, since MV_B may be affected by information about the merger.

We can rewrite equation 2.2 as

$$\text{COST} = (\text{CASH} - MV_B) + (MV_B - V_B)$$

$$= \begin{array}{l}\text{Premium paid over}\\ \text{observed market}\\ \text{value of } B\end{array} + \begin{array}{l}\text{Difference between observed}\\ \text{market value of } B \text{ and what}\\ \text{it is worth on its own}\end{array}$$

For example, suppose that on the day before the merger of A and B is announced, we observed the following:

	Company A	Company B
Market price per share	$50	$20
Number of shares	1,000,000	500,000
Market value of firm	$MV_A = \$50$ million	$MV_B = \$10$ million

Firm A intends to pay $12.5 million in cash for B. If MV_B reflects only B's separate value, then

$$\text{COST} = (\text{CASH} - MV_B) + (MV_B - V_B)$$

$$= \$2.5 \text{ million} + 0 = +\$2.5 \text{ million}$$

On the other hand, suppose B's price had risen $2.00 per share because of rumors about the merger. (We have indicated that sellers are almost always paid a premium over the market value of their shares; consequently, a merger rumor is good news for the seller.) Then,

$$\text{COST} = (\text{CASH} - MV_B) + (MV_B - V_B)$$

$$= \$2.5 \text{ million} + \$1 \text{ million} = \$3.5 \text{ million}$$

It is also conceivable that A's management has inside information that leads it to believe that B's real value is 20 percent higher than MV_B. If they are right, B is a *bargain*, and the cost is reduced:

COST = \$2.5 million − (\$10 million − \$12 million) = +\$500,000

Estimating Cost When the Acquisition is Financed by Common Stock. Estimating cost is more complicated when mergers are financed by an exchange of shares. Suppose that company A offers 250,000 shares worth \$50 per share before the merger announcement, instead of \$12.5 million cash; MV_B is \$10 million, as before. The apparent cost of the merger is:

APPARENT COST = \$50(250,000) − \$10,000,000 = +\$2.5 million

However, this is not likely to be the true cost, for three reasons. First, company B's final value may not be \$10 million. Second, A's share may not be valued correctly at \$50. Third, and most important, a portion of the benefits generated by the merger will accrue to B's shareholders, who *will be partners of the merged firm*.

The true cost is therefore

$$\text{COST} = \phi V_{AB} - V_B \qquad (2.5)$$

where ϕ is the proportion of the merged firm that B's shareholders end up owning.

Continuing with our example, consider again A's 250,000-share offer. B's shareholders will end up with one-fifth of the merged firm:

$$\phi = \frac{250,000}{1,000,000 + 250,000} = \frac{1}{5}$$

Suppose the market values observed before the merger announcement accurately reflect the firm's separate values. Also, the merger generates benefits worth \$5 million, so

$$V_{AB} = V_A + V_B + \Delta V = \$60 \text{ million} + \$5 \text{ million} = \$65 \text{ million}.$$

Then the merger's true cost to A's shareholders is $1/5\ V_{AB} - V_B$, or

COST = 1/5 (\$65 million) − \$10 million = \$3 million.

The implication is that A's shareholders are as well off offering \$13 million in cash as they are offering stock worth \$12.5 million before the merger announcement. *The larger the benefits generated by the merger, the greater the true cost of the 250,000-share offer.*

In making these calculations, management is essentially attempting to estimate what B's share will be worth *after* the merger agreement is sealed and announced. When this happens, the price of the 500,000 shares of company B will immediately jump to $26.00, a $6.00 capital gain over their initial $20.00 price. (This assumes that the market agrees with the $5-million estimate of merger benefits.) If A's management could wait until the merger terms were announced, estimating cost would be easy:

$$\text{COST} = (MV_V - V_B) = 26(\$500,000) - \$10,000,000 = +\$3 \text{ million}$$

Myers asks, rhetorically: "Why not just announce tentative merger terms, and then sit back to see how the market reacts before completing the merger negotiations? Would that not avoid these somewhat complicated calculations? He points out that the flaw in this strategy is that observed market prices will be extremely difficult to interpret if the market knows that the announced terms are tentative and that further negotiations are pending.

Cash versus Stock for Financing Mergers. *The key distinction between cash and stock as means of financing mergers is that, if cash is offered, the ultimate payoff to B's stockholders is independent of the success or failure of the merger.* Cost can be estimated without reference to the merger's benefits. *If stock is offered, cost depends on benefits, because they must be shared with B's owners.*

It is hard to generalize about whether other financing instruments should be treated like cash or stock. For practical purposes, bonds or preferred stock issued by A will probably be treated like cash. The value of the bonds given to B's stockholders will be essentially independent of the success or failure of the merger, providing A is a good credit risk to start with. *Convertible* bonds (or convertible preferred stock) introduce the same problems that common stock does: the option to convert gives B's shareholders the chance to share in merger benefits. In order to estimate cost, A's management must estimate the bond issue's value once the final merger terms and benefits are known to the market.

It is impossible here to catalog or analyze the many ways of financing mergers. Instead, we return to the simple question of stock versus cash, remembering that the qualitative conclusions apply to more complex packages also. We are indebted to Myers for this succinct summary:

> What are the consequences of financing mergers with stock rather than cash? Other things being equal, the greater the merger benefits, the greater the cost of stock financing. Also, stock financing mitigates the effect of over- or undervaluation of the acquired firm. If, for example, A's management mistakenly offers more shares for B than that firm is really worth, then the inevitable bad news will land partly on B's shareholders'

shoulders. Finally, stock financing is less advantageous than cash if A's stock is undervalued by the market. If it is overvalued then stock financing is cheap. Note, however, there is no necessary connection between high or low price-earnings ratio and over- or undervaluation.

A high price-earnings ratio does NOT mean that stock financing is cheap. . . .

Mergers can be explained only by assuming DIFFERENCES in valuation errors made by the market AND by assuming that the errors are perceived by buyers and not sellers. No doubt hindsight can supply some instances where this has happened, but it is a weak theory for explaining merger cycles. Unfortunately, other theories are weak also, which means that responsible management must approach mergers on a case-by-case basis, without any presumption that "the odds are with us."

We shall focus considerable attention in this book on determining V_B, that is, the "intrinsic" value of a potential acquisition candidate as a separate entity, as well as the estimation of the benefit of an acquisition. As seen previously, the perceived benefit must be greater than the cost. It may also be noted that V_B and COST may be dealt with quantitatively in relatively straightforward fashion. However, BENEFIT involves considerable judgment about many qualitative factors, which often tip the scales when the decision is made.

Reasons for Disparities in Valuation

A point related to the preceding was presented independently by the authors in an article entitled "Bargains in Valuation Disparities: Corporate Acquirer Versus Passive Investor" (*Sloan Management Review*, Winter 1979).

The issue of disparity in asset valuation, which is most important, may be addressed with the following question: Why are certain companies attractive to a corporate investor at substantial premiums over the stock market value established in trading among informed investors in the well-developed securities markets of the United States?

The answer, we believe, must reflect the recognition of different perceptions of risk as well as differing time horizons, motivations, and the wealth/welfare-maximizing behavior of the corporate manager versus the behavior of the typical investor during the present period of nonequilibrium conditions in the economy.[37] Historically, premiums have been paid over current market levels in order to obtain control. However, we are currently witnessing premiums far above the 20-25 percent range normally associated with control.[38] There are several explanations for this phenomenon.

1. Aggressive growth-oriented firms are less risk averse than the typical institutional investor—especially today, under evolving Employee Retire-

ment Income Security Act (ERISA) policy regarding the "prudent man rule" and fiduciary responsibility.

2. Many major industrial corporations have achieved and expect to continue to earn rates of return, with "normal business risk," greater than the inflation-adjusted risk-free rate of interest; they do not find "safe" investments an appropriate alternative vis-à-vis investment in operating businesses. Moreover, they are attracted by the availability of good plant and equipment by way of acquisition, at a fraction of the cost of building the same capacity today. In other words, the "Replacement Cost Adjusted Book Value (RCABV)" exceeds the acquired company's market value.[40]

3. Most large corporations evaluate alternatives using discounted-cash-flow (DCF) methods. This analytical framework is similar to that employed in contemporary security-valuation models used by many institutional investors. Other things being equal, the present value is sensitive to both the discount rate and the time horizon. As Malkiel has shown, the *P/E* ratio of a stock is also sensitive to investors' time horizons.[39] Thus the conditions exist for large valuation disparities. Apparently, corporations are now willing to discount and/or truncate the projected future returns from an acquired firm *less* (that is, they may risk more) than other investors. An investment horizon in perpetuity, or the equivalent (say, a fifteen-year mineral-recovery venture with a high discount rate for opportunity cost of capital), is in fact more often appropriate for the corporation, chartered in perpetuity, than for the portfolio of an investor/client with specific short-term anxieties and performance targets.

4. The capital-asset pricing model (CAPM), which is increasingly significant in modern portfolio management, links the expected returns from holding risky assets to returns on the market portfolio. CAPM is only a one-period rate-of-return model, and it assumes equilibrium in the capital markets. Recent attempts have been made to reconcile and link CAPM with long-term corporate capital-budgeting decisions.[41] Progress has been made, especially by Myers and his associates; but more work is needed along these lines, particularly to take into account the heterogeneity of uncertain decision makers under nonequilibrium conditions.

Acquisitions are dynamic—that is, nonequilibrium—in nature. Corporations that acquire other corporate businesses and assets can actively intervene in the operations of the acquired firm and change its earnings potential, through management and efficiency improvements and/or through changes in the capital structure of the enterprise (for example, adding financial leverage by increasing debt, or decreasing the cost of capital by improving the accounting practices and hence the "quality of earnings"). To use an often abused word, there may be "synergy," resulting in an increment of future earnings and cash flow that other investors were not anticipating prior to the merger.

Whether the whole, indeed, becomes greater than the sum of its parts by corporate actions is a controversial matter, both theoretically and in practice. Nevertheless, most corporate acquisitors behave as if they believe they can create and benefit from synergistic effects in a merger.

Appendix 2A:
A Methodology for
Appraising Benefits
and Costs in Corporate-
Development/R&D
Programs

Increasing the number of corporate-development research projects is a way of "buying insurance" against the risk of failure. It is necessary to consider how much insurance of this type it is wise to buy, by considering the relative benefits of success and costs of failure. The following example illustrates this: suppose that each of the research projects requires a cost C, and that only one of the successful projects will be implemented to produce a benefit B. One approach to selecting the number of projects might be to attempt to maximize the expected value of net benefits. If at least one project is successful, then the net benefit will be:

$$B - NC \Big\} \text{benefit less cost of research program,}$$

whereas if no project succeeds, then the net benefit will be:

$$- NC \text{ cost of research program}$$

the *expected* net benefit of an N-project program will then be

$$\left\langle B_{\text{Net}} \right\rangle = B [1 - (P_F)^N] - NC$$

and the expected net benefit is maximized when

$$N = \frac{\log\left(\frac{B}{C}\right) + \log\ (-\log P_F)}{(-\log P_F)}$$

The values of N for several project benefit/cost ratios and failure probabilities are illustrated in table 2A-1. It is important to remember that (1) the number of projects would be changed if the cost of program failure were greater than the simple loss of the research budget, and (2) maximizing expected net benefits is not the only way to choose the number of projects

Arthur D. Little, Inc., *The National Benefits/Costs of Enhanced Oil Recovery Research*, Report to the United States Energy Research and Development Administration, under Contract no. E(49-18)-2021, August 1976. Springfield, Va.: National Technical Information Service, FE-2021-4, Dist. Cat. UC-92.

Table 2A-1
Number of Projects that Maximize Expected Net Benefits

Probability of Successful Implementation of Any Project (Percentage)	Benefit/Cost Ratio for Implementation of Any Successful Project	
	100	1,000
10	22	44
50	6	9
90	2	3

and the concomitant certainty of success. The expression for the expected net benefits is written on a probabilistic basis using only monetary rewards (such as savings), B, net of research program costs, NC, where N is the number of projects.

We can expand and modify the resulting expression to include two additional factors:

1. $V = N\Omega$: the estimated total societal value of the research program, in monetary equivalents, assuming a standard value Ω per project. The net cost per project is then $C' = C - \Omega$.
2. $K =$ an additional (say, catastrophic) loss that could be assumed to occur if no R&D project succeeds.

Substituting in the derivation in terms of probabilities, its expected value is then

$$\left\langle B_{Net} \right\rangle = B\left(1 - P_F^N\right) - NC' - KP_F^N$$

The change in this expected value with each additional project may be expressed as the first difference $B(N + 1) - B(N)$ and divided by the net cost of an incremental project, C',

$$\frac{\Delta \text{ Benefit}}{\Delta \text{ Cost}} = \frac{\Delta E}{C'} = \left[\frac{(B + K)}{C'} \cdot (P_F)^N \cdot (1 - P_F)\right] - 1$$

The optimal N gets very large as the "catastrophic" loss K gets large. The quantity $\Delta E/C'$ will have a positive value until this optimum N is reached.

As an example, suppose that $N = 10$, $P_F = 0.8$, $B = \$200$ million (discounted) and $C' = \$50$ million (discounted).

$\dfrac{\Delta E}{C'}$	If $K = 0$ $= -0.6$	$K = \$500$ million $= +0.3$	$K = \$1$ billion $= +1.3$

Thus, with $K = 0$ and no loss other than the R&D costs from failure, 10 programs represent more than the optimum number to maximize net benefits; similarly, with a large catastrophic-loss possibility, 10 is less than the optimum—in this idealized example.

The cost of each additional project up to $N = N_o$ (o = optimum) results in additional expected net benefits; this cost may be thought of as buying additional insurance against a loss K.

Notes

1. The emphasis in this book is primarily on acquisitions in the United States, or foreign acquisitions by corporations governed in large measure by U.S. income-tax regulations.

2. These definitions are based on the presentation in Charles A. Sharf, *Acquisitions, Mergers, Sales, and Takeovers.* (Englewood Cliffs, N.J.: Prentice-Hall, Inc., 1971). Reprinted with permission.

3. See FASB, *Discussion Memorandum.*

4. Ibid., pp. 2-4.

5. Nickerson, *Accounting Handbook for Non-Accountants.*

6. FASB, *Discussion Memorandum*, app. C, p. C-1.

7. Ibid., pp. C-2-C-7. Financial Accounting Standards Board, High Ridge Park, Stamford, Conn. 06905 U.S.A. Reprinted with permission. Copies of the complete document are available from the FASB.

8. Wyatt, *Accounting Research Study No. 5.*

9. "Mergers Keep Growing."

10. Ansoff, et al., *Acquisition Behavior.*

11. FASB, op. cit., pp. C-4, C-5.

12. Wyat and Kiesco, *Business Combinations*, as quoted in FASB, *Discussion Memorandum.*

13. FASB, *Discussion Memorandum*, C-8-C-10.

14. Koshetz, "Burroughs to Buy Graphic Sciences."

15. The type-of-consideration discussion is abstracted from FASB, op. cit., app. C, pp. C-9-C-10.

16. See Wyatt, *Accounting Research Study No. 5*; and Foster, "Does Pooling Present Fairly?"

17. The discussion of income-tax treatment is taken from FASB, *Discussion Memorandum*, C-23-C-25.

18. Wright and Helpern, "Corporate Business Combinations." *The CPA Journal* May 1973.

19. References in support of this are *Accounting, Legal and Tax Aspects*; Guardino, Wright and Helpern, "Corporate Business Combinations;" Hagendorf, "Tax-Free Reorganizations"; and Wyatt and Kiesco, *Business Combinations.*

20. Wright and Helpern, "Corporate Business Combinations."

21. FASB, *Discussion Memorandum*, pp. C-27, C-28.

22. Guardino, *Accounting, Legal and Tax Aspects.*

23. Gaskill, "Are You Ready?"

24. FASB, *Discussion Memorandum*, p. C-29.

25. "Tender Offers and Stock Prices," pp. 70-71.

26. "ESB, in Switch."

27. "Tender Offers and Stock Prices."

28. "Bidding for Pullman Indicates Pressures from Emotional Factors May Be Pivotal," *Wall Street Journal*, 9 September 1980, p. 6.

29. Empirical evidence to this effect has been analyzed by Shad, "Financial Realities of Mergers"; by Mandelker, "Risk and Return"; and by Dodd and Ruback, "Tender Offers and Stockholder Returns," among others. See also "Corporations Loaded With Cash," *Dun's Review*, January 1978, pp. 54-55.

30. Robert Hagin's *Modern Portfolio Theory* reviews the research leading to today's concepts. Hagin includes some 300 selected references.

31. The concepts of R&D as insurance and of portfolio-diversification benefits of R&D were advanced in a 1974 Arthur D. Little, Inc., study for a predecessor agency, then part of the U.S. Bureau of Mines. These concepts were refined and presented in a 1976 report to the Energy Research and Development Administration (ERDA), and reaffirmed, in principle, in a 1978 update for the successor agency, the Department of Energy (DOE).

32. See Myers, *Modern Developments in Financial Management*, pt. VI.

33. See Salter and Weinhold, *Diversification Through Acquisition.*

34. Myers, *Modern Developments in Financial Management.*

35. Salter and Weinhold, *Diversification Through Acquisition.*

36. Myers, *Modern Developments in Financial Management.*

37. Treatment of the subject of wealth-maximization behavior is beyond the scope of this chapter. Some important theorems are explored in Michael C. Jensen and John B. Long, Jr., "Corporate Investment Under Uncertainty and Pareto Optimality in the Capital Markets," *Bell Journal of Economics and Management Science*, Spring 1972; in Modigliani and Miller's classic work, "Dividend Policy, Growth and the Valuation of Shares," *Journal of Business* 34, no. 4 (October 1961):411-433; and in Findlay and Whitmore, "Beyond Shareholder Wealth Maximization."

38. For example, see *Mergers and Acquisitions.*

39. See Malkiel's brilliant paper, "Equity Yields, Growth and the Structure of Share Prices," for the mathematical illustration.

40. The application of the RCABV concept is similar to that of the "Q" ratio developed by James Tobin of Yale University. For a discussion of the RCABV concept, see the authors' "Acquisition and Merger Trends Affecting the Portfolio Manager," *Financial Analysts Journal*, November-December 1977.

41. See Myers and Turnbull, "Capital Budgeting and the Capital Asset Pricing Model"; and Treynor and Black, "Corporate Investment Decisions." Also see Williams, "Capital Asset Prices with Heterogeneous Beliefs."

References

"Accounting Principles for Pooling of Interests: A Panel Discussion, Sponsored by the Section on Taxation, American Bar Association, in May 1971." *Tax Lawyer*, Fall 1971.

Ansoff, Igor H.; Brandenburg, Richard G.; Portner, Fred E.; and Radosevich, Raymond. *Acquisition Behavior of U.S. Manufacturing Firms, 1946-1965*. Nashville, Tenn.: Vanderbilt University Press, 1971. (See p. 30.)

Bradley, James W., and Korn, Donald H. "Acquisition and Merger Trends Affecting the Portfolio Manager." *Financial Analysts Journal*, November-December 1977.

Brealey, R.A., and Myers, S.C. *Principles of Corporate Finance*. New York: McGraw-Hill, 1981.

Dodd, P., and Ruback, R. "Tender Offers and Stockholder Returns: An Empirical Analysis." Working Paper no. 7801, University of Rochester, Graduate School of Management, January 1978.

"ESB, in Switch, Decides to Back Inco's Tender Bid." *Wall Street Journal*, 30 July 1974.

Financial Accounting Standards Board (FASB). *Discussion Memorandum: An Analysis of Issues Related to Accounting for Business Combinations and Purchased Intangibles*. Stamford, Conn.: Financial Accounting Standards Board, 19 August 1976.

Findlay, M. Chapman, and Whitmore, G.A. "Beyond Shareholder Wealth Maximization." *Financial Management*, Winter 1974.

Foster, William C. "Does Pooling Present Fairly?" *The CPA Journal*, December 1974, p. 37.

Gaskill, William J. "Are You Ready for the New Merger Boom?" *Financial Executive*, September 1974, p. 38.

Guardino, Joseph R. *Accounting, Legal and Tax Aspects of Corporate Acquisitions*. Englewood Cliffs, N.J.: Prentice-Hall, 1973.

Hagendorf, Stanley. "A Study of Tax-Free Reorganizations." *Mergers and Acquisitions*, March-April 1970, pp. 5-25.

Hagin, Robert. *Modern Portfolio Theory*. Homewood, Ill.: Dow Jones-Irwin, 1979.

Jensen, Michael C. "Take-Over Study Started by S.E.C." *New York Times*, 10 September 1974, p. 53.

Koshetz, Herbert. "Burroughs to buy Graphic Sciences in 30 Million Deal."
   New York Times, 23 October 1974, p. 67.
Malkiel, Burton. "Equity Yields, Growth and the Structure of Share Prices."
   American Economic Review 53, no. 5 (December 1963):1004-1031.
Mandelker, G. "Risk and Return: The Case of Merging Firms." In Modern
   Developments in Financial Mnagement, edited by S.C. Myers, chap.
   33. New York: Praeger, 1978.
Mergers and Acquisitions: Planning and Action. New York: Financial
   Executives Research Foundation, 1963.
"Mergers Keep Growing—With a Difference." *Management Review*, June
   1964, p. 27.
Myers, S.C., ed. Introduction to part VI. *Modern Developments in Finan-
   cial Management*. New York: Praeger, 1976. Reprinted with permis-
   sion.
Myers, S.C., and Turnbull, S.M. "Capital Budgeting and the Capital Asset
   Pricing Model: Good News and Bad News." *Journal of Finance* 32
   (May 1977):321-333.
Nickerson, Clarence B. *Accounting Handbook for Non-Accountants*, 2d
   ed. Boston: CBI Publishing Company, 1979.
Salter, Malcolm S., and Weinhold, Wolf A. *Diversification Through Ac-
   quisition*. New York: Free Press, 1979.
Scharf, Charles A. *Acquisitions, Mergers, Sales and Takeovers: A Hand-
   book With Forms*. Englewood Cliffs, N.J.: Prentice-Hall, 1971.
Shad, John R. "The Financial Realities of Mergers." *Harvard Business
   Review*, November-December 1969, pp. 133-146.
"Take the Money and Run." *Barron's*, 8 December 1975, p. 11.
"Tender Offers and Stock Prices." *Barron's*, 8 December 1975, p. 70.
Treynor, Jack L., and Black, Fischer. "Corporate Investment Decisions."
   in S.C. Myers, ed., *Modern Developments in Financial Management*,
   New York: Praeger, 1976, pp. 310-327.
Weston, J. Fred, and Brigham, Eugene. *Managerial Finance*, 3d ed. New
   York: Holt, Rinehart & Winston, 1969.
Williams, Joseph T. "Capital Asset Prices with Heterogeneous Beliefs."
   Journal of Financial Economics 5 (1977):219-239.
Wright, Robert F., and Helpern, Stephen R. "Corporate Business Com-
   binations—A New Look at the Basic Tax and Accounting Considera-
   tions." The *CPA Journal*, May 1973, pp. 362-363.
Wyatt, Arthur R. *Accounting Research Study No. 5: A Critical Study of
   Accounting for Business Combinations*. New York: AICPA, 1963. (See
   pp. 7-8, 73.)
Wyatt, Arthur R., and Kiesco, Donald E. *Business Combinations: Planning
   and Action*. Scranton, Penn.: International Textbook Company, 1969.
   (See pp. 20-21, chap. 5.)

3 Acquisition Strategies

Introduction

Acquisition activity should be viewed in the context of corporate strategy and the corporate-development process. Corporate strategy, of course, refers to the process of establishing and achieving the firm's goals and objectives, a process for which the board of directors and chief executive(s) of a business are responsible. Corporate development is a part of this process; however, the term *corporate development* is vague and often misused. Sometimes it is applied broadly to external growth (acquisitions, joint ventures), as well as to internal growth of all kinds. The concept of *strategic planning* is closely related to that of corporate development. Both strategic-planning and corporate-development functions may be performed by one department or may report to the same individual.

Definition of Corporate Development and the Corporate-Development Process

In the context of this book, the term *corporate development* relates to the corporate activity responsible for programs and plans concerning the implementation of the corporation's overall strategic growth plan, as it specifically applies both to acquisition (and divestiture), and to those internal new ventures not carried out by operating units in the normal evolution of their respective businesses. We call this activity the corporate-development process.

The internal corporate-research and product/process-development (R&D) program is also closely related to corporate strategy, and hence to strategic planning. Although in theory R&D is also related to corporate development, corporate practice varies widely with respect to which activities are classified as corporate R&D, as opposed to operating-unit R&D, and which relate to overall corporate development. More firms are now recognizing R&D as an investment in the future of the business, and find it difficult to evaluate the tradeoffs involved in spending an incremental sum on R&D as opposed to acquisition plans and programs, or a de novo enterprise development.

Most large corporations budget funds to conduct all three types of activity—acquisition, de novo enterprises, and R&D—in parallel, with at least a loose coordination among the groups involved. As various milestones are reached, there is usually some formal review of the status of projects, as well as a classification system for facilitating further funding requests or additional appropriate action.

Ideally, if a company wished to expand into an attractive new field of business, it would estimate the costs, benefits, and risks associated with such activity in order to determine whether it would be better to invest internally in R&D, plant, inventory, marketing, and so on, or to acquire an existing firm with a position in the new field. The company would have both staff expertise and outside professional expertise available to perform the situation analysis, as well as the other corporate machinery or wherewithal to follow up on the recommended course of action. In practice, few corporations act this efficiently; many are limited by time, resources, and—importantly—by organization structure. This chapter focuses on the types of acquisitions to be considered once a corporation has decided to study the merits of acquisition vis-à-vis an internal-development effort.

Chapter 2 presented an analytical framework within which to study the costs and benefits of acquisitions, and the costs and benefits of de-novo-enterprise corporate R&D strategy. Chapter 7 presents techniques for valuation of an acquisition, chapter 8 covers accounting and financial issues that apply to individual transactions, and chapter 10 discusses the procedures that lead to an effective acquisition program.

Strategic Acquisition Objectives

At least in theory, acquisitions are both capital-budgeting and strategic decisions intended to maximize the value of the firm's common stock. In practice, however, other managerial objectives often come into play and in fact may be dominant. These include the simple desire to show growth, to keep up with competitors, to demonstrate ability to enter new and exciting fields, to fend off potential acquirers of the firm, and so on (see also chapter 10).

Rational acquisition objectives in "creating value for the stockholders" over and above normal management desire for expansion often include the following:

1. A higher level of income from the combination of business entities that can be achieved separately as a result of operating, financial, and/or market economies—that is, *synergy*.

2. Less cyclicality of income: this, for example, might be achieved by means of a highly cyclical company combining with one of low or opposite cyclicality.

3. The achievement of greater market recognition by entrance into a "favored" field: a risky and often costly strategy, but one that sometimes might prove necessary—and successful—for firms in aging industries.

4. The spreading of risk by participating in several rather than a single business or geographic area: the application of portfolio theory to corporate activities. This can also apply to reducing political or geographical risk.

5. The development of a more balanced enterprise in terms of cash flow and stages of maturity. This is in line with product/market-portfolio and maturity-cycle concepts, whereby a firm in a mature or aging product area with a strong positive cash flow might consider acquisition of a growth company with high cash needs. Of course, such an acquisition must be evaluated carefully in terms of its costs and benefits.

These rationales are not mutually exclusive, and usually a combination of objectives is sought. (For completeness here, it is necessary to recognize another alternative (distasteful to management), namely, that when all else fails, liquidation or drastic reorganization of the corporation can sometimes be in the best interest of shareholders.)

Acquisition-Strategy Implementation Options

With the foregoing in mind, let us examine the types of acquisition options available, as a means of organizing the acquisition-evaluation process. (Chapter 5 provides procedures for identifying specific companies and industries that meet certain selection criteria.) The options are as follows:

1. Vertical or horizontal integration.
2. Divestiture.
3. International/foreign business.
4. Business merger (pooling of interests with another corporation of comparable size).
5. True diversification versus related diversification.
6. Special-situation investing.

Vertical integration involves acquiring or merging with sources of supply (backward integration) or users of present output (forward integration); horizontal integration involves acquiring or merging with competing firms. The antitrust laws may preclude certain business combinations of this type, as discussed in chapter 4. They may also be involved in decisions on divestitures. Otherwise, divestiture may be desirable because the business does not fit into the strategic plan. A large number of acquisitions in the last few years have resulted from divestitures by companies of previously acquired businesses that did not work out.

Different philosophies exist with respect to acquiring in such situations. Typically, much more relevant financial-performance data are available than on publicly traded companies' operations, so that one may be able to better estimate the future risk-return characteristics. However, some corporations eschew "turnaround" situations and will seek only companies with an unblemished record of growth in earnings. Among the other options listed, international/foreign-business acquisition is simply one criterion, for example, as part of an expansion strategy. Merger, on the other hand, may be the only way to acquire various strategic assets in a short period of time. The other strategy options are discussed in the sections that follow.

True Diversification versus Related Diversification

The point of diversification is twofold: to spread corporate risk and to enlarge corporate opportunities. Economists and antitrust lawyers still do not agree on many aspects of this subject; and many businessmen and management consultants approach it from an entirely different perspective, as indicated in chapter 2.

We view true diversification as acquisition of a completely different kind of business from that of the acquiring corporation's. What does "completely different" mean here? Generally, it means that the demand for the products or service is driven by different factors. However, in some cases it could mean that an entirely different technology is involved in serving the same general marketplace, or that a different geographic coverage is offered.

An example of the first type would be the acquisition of an oil and gas producer by a cigarette manufacturer. Examples of the latter types would be the acquisition of a laser-hologram entertainment manufacturer by a videotape recorder/player manufacturer, or that of a foreign-based business by a related, entirely U.S.-based business. Only the first type is true diversification; the others represent related diversifications. (Depending on the specific circumstances, the diversification that makes good competitive and strategic sense may or may not be challenged on antitrust grounds.)

Each type of diversifying strategy has certain costs and benefits that should be evaluated. Salter and Weinhold point out the common misconceptions associated with diversification through acquisition, and the fact that one cannot make easy generalizations about unrelated or related diversification.[1] We attempt to shed additional light on this subject by examining actual recent corporate behavior with respect to acquisitions. The next section presents selected examples for discussion.

Special-Situation Investing: Ownership of Minority-Share Positions in Other Corporations

Some corporations purchase and sell shares in other corporations, much as a portfolio manager or individual investor manages an investment portfolio of stocks and bonds. The corporation may be acting either as a risk-taking speculator or as an intermediate-term investor. This activity is incidental to the conduct of the main operations of the corporation, but its persistence and its success deserve notice. It suggests an interesting and somewhat controversial strategy for a publicly owned company.

We use the term *special-situation investing* to denote such activity. It appears to be part of the modus operandi of several corporations, including City Investing, Gulf & Western Industries, and Teledyne. The intriguing aspect of a corporation's taking positions in the stock of other corporations—but not necessarily completing acquisition of them—will be examined through the examples given in the following section.

Examples and Implications

Table 3-1 illustrates actual acquisitions attempted and in most cases consummated by selected groupings of acquirers. Also shown are several divestitures. (For more on divestitures, see chapter 4.) We have chosen these groupings because each seems, on balance, to be associated with a particular corporate strategic problem. Listed at the right side of table 3-1 is a comment on the corporate strategy characteristic of the acquisition. These are meant to be superficial descriptions and are both nontechnical and nonlegal in nature.

The use of the term *vertical integration*, for example, is consistent with antitrust-economics usage only in a broad sense. We imply nothing about likely market definition, market share, number of competitors, and so forth, which might be used in an antitrust context; neither do we imply any grounds whatsoever for antitrust concerns. The term *diversification* is used to refer to true rather than related diversification.

Table 3-1
Illustrative Acquisition Strategies, by Selected Acquirer Groupings

Original Business of Acquirer	Acquired or Merged	Corporate-Strategy Characterization
Cigarettes and tobacco		
R.J. Reynolds Industries, Inc.	Burmah Oil & Gas Co. (1976)	Diversification
Philip Morris	Seven-Up Co. (1978)	Market extension
	Miller Brewing (1975)	Market extension
American Brands	(bal.) Franklin Life Insurance (1979)	Diversification
Food and drug		
Beatrice Foods Co.	Harman Int'l. Industries	Single-industry portfolio extension
	Tropicana Products, Inc. (1978)	Complementary
Foremost-McKesson, Inc.	C.F. Mueller Co. (1976)	Market extension
	American Optical (1967)	Market extension
Warner-Lambert Co.	Deseret Pharmaceutical, Inc. (1976)	Diversification
	Entenmann's, Inc. (1978)	Market related
Pepsico, Inc.	Pizza Hut, Inc. (1977)	Market related
	Taco Bell (1978)	Diversification
Nestlé S.A.	Alcon Laboratories (1977)	Diversification
Pillsbury	Burger King (1967)	Vertical integration
	Green Giant Co. (1978)	Vertical integration
Oil and gas		
Standard Oil of California	(20%) AMAX, Inc. (1975)	Diversification
	(80%) AMAX, Inc. (1981 tender offer)	
Standard Oil of Indiana	Pasco Oil & Gas (Wyoming Properties) (1975)	Vertical integration
	Cyprus Mines (1979)	Diversification
Mobil Oil	(46%) Marcor, Inc. (1976)	Diversification
Union Oil of California	Molycorp, Inc. (1977)	Diversification
Signal Companies, Inc.	Garrett Aerospace (1964)	Diversification
	(49.5%) UOP, Inc. (1978)	Diversification
	(40%) Unitrode, Inc. (1980)	Diversification
Standard Oil of Ohio	Kennecott Corp. (1981 tender offer)	Diversification

Company	Acquisition	Strategy
Oil-field service/engineering		
McDermott (J. Ray) Co., Inc.	Babcock B. Wilcox Co. (1977)	Market extension
	Pullman, Inc. (1980) (unsuccessful tender offer)—lost to Wheelabrator-Frye)	Complementary
Halliburton Co.	Brown & Root (1962)	Market extension
Baker Oil Tools, Inc.	Reed Tool Co. (1975)	Complementary-horizontal
Aerospace		
United Technologies	Essex Wire (1975)	Market extension
	Otis Elevator (1975)	Diversification
	AMBAC Industries (1978)	Market extension
	Carrier Corp. (1978)	Market extension
	Takeover attempt unsuccessful: Babcock & Wilcox (1977) (lost to McDermott)	
Raytheon Company	Beech Aircraft (1979)	Complementary diversification
McDonnell Douglas	Microdata	Complementary diversification
Conglomerate		
Esmark, Inc., International	Playtex Co. (subs. of Rapid American Corp.) (1975)	Diversification
	STP Corp. (1978)	Diversification
Textron	(–%) Scott Paper (1981)	Diversification
Gulf + Western Industries	(9.6%) Allied Chemical (1977)	Diversification
	(25%) Esquire, Inc.	Diversification
	(27%) Xcor International, Inc.	Diversification
	(21%) Amfac, Inc.	Diversification
	(bal.) Simmons Co. (1978)	Diversification
	(–36%) Flying Diamond Oil (sold interest to Bow Valley Industries, Ltd.)	Divestiture
International Telephone & Telegraph Corp.	Carbon Industries (1977)	Diversification
	Eason Oil Co. (1977)	Diversification
	Qume Corp. (1978)	Market extension
	–Avis, Inc. (1977)	Divestiture
Financial		
Prudential Insurance Co. of America	Bache Group, announced 1981	Complementary diversification
American Express Co.	Shearson Loeb Rhoades, proposed 1981	Complementary diversification

Table 3-1 *(continued)*

Original Business of Acquirer	Acquired or Merged	Corporate-Strategy Characterization
Banking		
New England Merchants Corp.	Chatham Trust (1979)	Horizontal, market extension
	TNB Financial Corp.	
	(Third Nat'l. Bank Springfield), announced (1981)	
Financial Security Corp.	International Bank of Wilmington (1979)	Complementary
Key Banks	Citizens National Bank and Trust (1979)	Market extension
Allied Bancshares	Travis Bank & Trust (1979)	Market extension
	Beltway Bancshares, announced (1981)	
Southwest Bancshares	Vidor State Bank (1979)	n.a.
Texas American Bancshares	Fredericksburg Financial Corp. (1979);	Market extension
	Collin County NB of McKinney, announced (1981)	
Mitsui Bank, Ltd. (Japan) subs.,	Manufacturers Bank of Los Angeles, announced (1981)	Market extension
Mitsui Bank of California	First S & L Shares, Inc. (Colo.) (expected 1981)	Diversification
D. Ludwig (as individual)	Fred Meyer Savings & Loan, announced (1981)	Diversification
Foreign Groups		
Flick Group (W. Germany)	(35%) W.R. Grace & Co. (1976-1978)	Diversified/geographic extension
	(34.5%) U.S. Filter Corp. (1978)	Diversified/geographic extension
Sandoz (Switzerland)	Northrup King (1976)	Complementary
Mannesman (W. Germany)	Harnischfeger (1979) (opposed by FTC)	Complementary
	Tally Corp. (1979)	Diversification
Bayer A.G. (W. Germany)	Miles Laboratories (1977)	Geographic extension
Thorn Electrical Industries, Ltd. (U.K.)	Systron-Donner (1977)	Related/geographic
Imperial Group Limited (U.K.)	Howard Johnson (1979)	Geographic extension
Unilever	National Starch & Chemical (1978)	Diversification

The term *market extension* connotes that the acquisition brings an additional product market to the group or groups presently served by the acquiring company. Thus Warner Lambert's acquisition of Deseret Pharmaceutical brought it an extended capability in the medical- and surgical-supply field, which it had been cultivating since its earlier acquisition of Parke-Davis. We may risk an analogous comment with respect to United Technologies' (UTC's) acquisition of AMBAC, after that of Essex Wire, which may be viewed as extending UTC's market from aircraft-engine technology to automotive/truck-engine technology. The broad rationale for selected groupings in table 3-1 is given in the following sections.

Cigarettes and Tobacco

The pattern here is market extending, that is, from cigarettes to food and beverages. The acquisitions capitalize on existing channels of distribution, or on skills in national-media advertising, both serving the mass consumer market. We surmise that the driving force has been concern that the long-range trend in consumption of cigarettes was downward, whereas the consumption of food and drink was likely to keep increasing.

Oil and Gas

Prudence would suggest that oil-company managements diversify away from too heavy a dependence on the politically unstable and unpredictable oil and gas business, especially when they have the cash flow on hand and can make major acquisitions at relatively attractive prices. The preference of oil companies for nonferrous-metals companies and coal has been striking. Another rationale may be that these other industries still receive favorable tax treatment via the depletion allowance, something that major domestic oil companies have lost. Although we refer to such acquisitions as diversification, it may be observed that all these businesses are extractive processes, and that the future of the oil and gas business is tending—through synthetic-fuels and shale-oil development—to become much more closely associated with mining operations and with the lands that are held by these mining companies.

Aerospace

The technology that the major aerospace and defense contractors possess has, even before the completion of the first manned space program, been considered for application to advanced (more efficient) energy-conversion systems for stationary-source power production—particularly electric-utility applications—and also for automotive vehicles (for example, using fuel cells). In recent years, United Technologies (formerly United Aircraft) in particular has exemplified an acquisition program along this and related lines (including some sensitivity to the trend toward energy-conservation systems). McDonnell-Douglas, on the other hand, has built up a substantial interest in data processing and data communications.

The point is that these markets are generally growth markets not subject to the vagaries of defense contracting or to the cyclicality of commercial-aircraft orders.

Conglomerate—Special-Situation Investing

Table 3-1 presents a few examples of acquisition activity by conglomerate firms. Some of this activity apparently is not intended to take the form of complete acquisition of another business, but rather to benefit from an expected return (dividends plus capital gain) on investment in securities, as opposed to profit from operating assets.

The philosophy and organization of several conglomerate firms are conducive to their utilization of special insights (or a belief that they have such insights) to pick up perceived bargains in anticipation of the acquisition by third parties of the companies in which they invest. This activity in and of itself can affect the climate for acquisitions. Moreover, it raises a policy question similar to that raised by corporate diversification itself—namely, should corporate management perform this "mutual-fund" function on behalf of shareholders—even if they do it exceedingly well?

Regulated-Industry Diversification

The diversification of banks is generally subject to regulatory approvals at both state and federal levels. The actual provisions will depend on whether the bank is state chartered (controlled by the state banking commission) or a national bank (controlled by the Comptroller of the Currency and the Federal Deposit Insurance Corporation); and whether the acquisition, merger, or other diversified business proposal is in the name of the bank per se, or that of a bank holding company (Bank Holding Company Act administered by the Federal Reserve Board).

Table 3-1 illustrates considerable recent activity in bank acquisitions and mergers. The motivations of banks are similar to those of industrial corporations (managements)—growth, expanded markets, access to more capital on better terms. The last of these has a special significance in the case of banks.[2]

In the next several years, we anticipate an increase in merger and acquisition activity involving savings-and-loan associations (S&Ls) as a result of conversions to stock corporations and of new banking powers granted them under the Depository Institutions and Monetary Control Act of 1980.

Utility Diversification

Although not shown in table 3-1, an area that has also shown some recent activity is that of utility diversification. Utilities include gas (transmission and distribution companies), electric, and telephone companies. These vital, capital-intensive businesses are regulated by both federal and state regulatory authorities with respect to rates, rate of return, securities issuance, and other matters. Operating companies generally have less freedom than industrial corporations to acquire other firms, merge, or diversify their businesses. Among the utilities, the gas-transmission companies have been most active and effective in reorganizing into holding companies and in acquiring and diversifying under the aegis of a holding company, albeit subject to the former Federal Power Commission (FPC) and now Federal Energy Regulatory Commission (FERC) approvals. Tenneco (formerly Tennessee Eastern Transmission Company) and InterNorth (formerly Northern Natural Gas) are good examples. Investor-owned electric utilities are generally constrained from acquiring other utilities or diversifying into substantially unrelated fields, as a matter of public policy, covered in general by the Public Utility Holding Company Act of 1935, administered by the SEC; and also by requirements set by independent state public-utilities commissions. Some special cases and exemptions have been "grandfathered," such as Citizens and Southern Company. More recently, there have been cases in which an electric utility formed a holding company and then diversified the holding company. Houston Industries (formerly Houston Lighting and Power of Texas), Texas Utilities, and Iowa Resources (formerly Iowa Lighting and Power) are some examples. The recent pattern is one of diversification into fuel resources—either to secure supplies (vertical integration), or as a long-term investment in an area about which the utility is very knowledgeable, and/or to sell on the open market fuel supplies in excess of the utility's needs. The problem faced by an electric utility seeking diversification is that its stockholders, unlike those of most other businesses, would have a difficult time retaining any windfall profits from a subsidiary that "strikes it rich," because of the legal tradition and regulatory philosophy under which utilities are franchised. Nevertheless, recent hard times and slower electricity-demand growth have caused electric utilities to search for ways to diversify to improve their shareholder's lot. Another problem is that they are still in a net-cash-requirements phase, in contrast to many gas utilities, which are throwing off cash.

In the past, there have been proposals with respect to both the banking industry and the electric-utility industry that would foster consolidations among the many companies in these respective industries. There are, for example, some 14,000 commercial banks in the United States. There are several hundred electric-utility companies (albeit fewer generating companies). The dramatic changes underway in each industry may also bring about a change in the regulatory atmosphere conducive to such consolidations.

Some Thoughts about the Future Role of Pension Funds in Acquisition Strategy

Corporate pension-fund assets are expected to aggregate nearly $500 billion in the near future. Accounting for pension-fund assets and liabilities is an area of increasing concern. The types of assets in which pension funds invest, and the performance of such investments, have been of interest for many years. The Employee Retirement Income Security Act of 1974 (ERISA), pending amendments, and related legislation have heightened such interest. Finally, as a consequence of ERISA—and exacerbated by inflation effects on pension plans—the funding of pension obligations has become more of a burden for many corporations.

The pension-fund situation can affect acquisition strategy in several ways.

1. Efforts by the SEC, the FASB, and the Pension Benefit Guaranty Corporation (the U.S.-government agency established by ERISA to insure defined-benefit pension plans) to change the financial accounting and reporting of pension-plan assets and liabilities may result in a changed perception of the value of an acquisition, as well as its impact on the acquiring firm, or on whether an acquisition for cash or an exchange of stock is more advantageous. In short, corporations may have to present, in effect, a new balance sheet. In the long run this change should not cause valuation problems, since investors will have had a chance to evaluate changed regulatory requirements and the economic reality. However, in the short run, confusion may create considerable valuation disparities.

2. Even under the present framework, acquisitions involving the combination of a corporation with a large unfunded past-service liability, with a corporation whose pension plan is fully funded, require careful normalization and adjustment in order to arrive at a correct valuation basis for the exchange of cash or shares in consummating the acquisition transaction. The large accounting firms and actuarial consultants are vital at this stage; the potential differences in valuations can be very large, depending on the assumptions used and the consistency with which they are applied.

3. The debt-rating services have begun to recognize the impact of pension liabilities on corporate creditworthiness. Moody's has begun to compute adjusted fixed-charge coverage ratios.[3] Large institutional lenders have also started to introduce this approach in writing the loan covenants for corporate indentures. The point is that the true assets and liabilities of a target company are never completely and accurately measured by the conventional balance sheet, and that pension assets and liabilities are an additional complicating factor in strategy and valuation today.

4. Another, perhaps more significant, factor for the future is the possibility that pension funds (state, local-government, and corporate) could conceivably own 50 percent or more of the outstanding common stock of corporate America before the year 2000. The management expert, Peter Drucker, among others, has written provocatively about this possibility and its likely consequences. The combination of such ownership structure with a consolidated corporate balance sheet (including pension assets and liabilities) will force a profound rethinking of the issues of stockholder versus management versus employee-beneficiary prerogatives and control. Who will then really vote on an acquisition or merger? Whom will antitrust policy hold responsible for corporate behavior?

Notes

1. See Malcolm A. Salter and Wolf A. Weinhold, *Diversification Through Acquisition* (New York: Free Press, 1979).

2. See also "Bank Capital Issues," by D.H. Korn in *The Bank Directors Handbook*, edited by E.B. Cox (Boston: Auburn House, 1981).

3. See Patrick J. Reagan, "Moody's Gathers Pension Data," *Financial Analysts Journal*, July-August 1980. See also William C. Norby, "Accounting for Pensions," and Fischer Black, "The Tax Consequences of Long-Run Pension Policy," *Financial Analysts Journal*, July-August 1980.

4

Antitrust and Other Legal Impediments to Acquisitions and Mergers

Overview

Corporate management should be aware of current trends in antitrust policy and should request legal counsel to review the likely antitrust implications of a contemplated acquisition, divestiture, or merger. Obviously, such counsel should be sought at the earliest practicable point in the deliberations, in order to avoid commitments that are likely to be unproductive—costly in time and effort that ultimately come to naught.

Antitrust policy views acquisitions and mergers as alternatives to internal development for achieving growth. However, in response to the public interest, antitrust legislation proscribes any acquisition or merger that tends substantially to lessen competition or encourage monopoly behavior.

Indeed, the principal concern of antitrust policy is to maintain competitive industry and market structures. The major authority under which the federal government or competing firms may challenge a merger is Section 7 of the Clayton Act, enforced by the Department of Justice (DOJ) and the Federal Trade Commission (FTC). Section 5 of the FTC act gives the FTC additional jurisdiction over alleged unfair business practices. The FTC and DOJ rules relating to premerger notifications and business-review clearances, and the SEC disclosure requirements governing tender offers and proxy statements, also influence merger trends. State laws are becoming more influential as well. Table 4-1 presents a simplified framework for placing antitrust and antimerger considerations in perspective.

The law distinguishes mergers by their effect on the nature of the acquiring firm and by their competitive impact on the industry or relevant market. *Vertical* mergers involve acquisition of existing or potential suppliers or customers. *Horizontal* mergers involve acquisition of existing or potential competitors. *Conglomerate* mergers typically involve diversification into one or more substantially unrelated businesses. Typically, in such cases the size or *market power* of the business combination is relevant in determining antitrust actions (as is the extent of intercompany sales). The DOJ and FTC have issued guidelines for assessing the legality of various mergers, and court decisions complement these in articulating existing policy. Market share and number of firms in a market are key elements in these guidelines.

Table 4-1
Antitrust and Antimerger Considerations

Antitrust statutes
  Section 7, Clayton Act
  Section 5, Federal Trade Commission Act
  State laws regarding takeovers

Enforcement policy
  Primarily Department of Justice and
    Federal Trade Commission
  Competitive structure emphasis
    Vertical mergers: Market shares
    Horizontal mergers: Concentration guidelines
    Conglomerate mergers: Market power, reciprocity
    Failing-company doctrine
  Premerger notification requirements to Federal
    Trade Commission

Other considerations
  Special regulatory jurisdictions
    (Civil Aeronautics Board, Federal Reserve Board)
  Securities and Exchange Commission rules, disclosures
  State hearing requirements

Enforcement Implications

Often the very condition that makes certain companies attractive takeover targets, such as strong market position, is seen as a powerful anticompetitive weapon in the hands of the acquiring firm. Horizontal mergers between companies with high market shares are virtually impossible. At the other extreme, the *failing-company doctrine* condones mergers that preserve the number of competitors in a field: "weak, dying" firms are sometimes "rescued" in the name of this doctrine. An example was the combination of Lykes Corporation and LTV Corporation, both of whom owned steel-manufacturing operations (Youngstown and Jones & Laughlin, respectively).

The same enforcement policy that denies certain mergers and acquisitions—that is, the policy of antitrust divestitures—is a source of potential acquisition candidates for other firms. We have reviewed the American Bar Association (ABA) study of several hundred merger cases prosecuted by the DOJ and FTC through 1970; some major examples of the corporate activity in divestitures resulting therefrom, and of more recent transactions, appear in table 4-2.[1]

Although many well-publicized acquisitions are classified as conglomerate mergers under strict antitrust definitions, conceptually they are most often "related-diversification" moves from a corporate-strategy viewpoint. Antitrust-enforcement policy has allowed Continental Oil-

Table 4-2
Antitrust Divestitures

Divested Company	Potential New Owner or Offeror	Divested by Action Against
Avis	Norton Simon	International Telephone and Telegraph (ITT)
Peabody Coal	Newmont Mining et al.	Kennecott Copper
Grinnell Corp.	ITT	Grinnell Corp. et al.
Grinnell (Fire Protection business)	Tyco	ITT
Autolite	Bendix Corp.	Ford Motor
Service Bureau Corp.	Control Data Corp.[a]	International Business Machines
Nuclear Chicago	G.D. Searle	Abbott Laboratories
Rome Cable	Cyprus Mines (now part of Std. Oil Co. Indiana)	Alcoa
Okonite	LTV; public; ESOP	Kennecott Copper; LTV

[a]In out-of-court settlement of litigation between the companies.

Consolidation Coal, Mobil-Marcor, Atlantic Richfield-Anaconda, and General Electric-Utah International, among others. It has prohibited Kennecott Copper from retaining ownership of Peabody Coal, Combustion Engineering from owning a minority position in United Nuclear, Ford Motor from retaining Autolite, BIC Pen from acquiring American Safety Razor from Philip Morris, and AMAX from acquiring Copper Range (this last company acquired by Louisiana Land & Exploration).

One of the difficulties in interpreting policy is that there is often a very long lead time between enforcement action and settlement of an antitrust case. Kennecott-Peabody action commenced in 1968, and final approvals of a divestiture were received almost a decade later. Obviously, dynamic industries and the firms within them can change dramatically in this period of time, as can the political and ideological setting for enforcement policy. As this was written, the U.S. government's massive suit against International Business Machines (IBM) was in its tenth year; unless it is dropped, this suit is likely to bring several more years of uncertainty for investors and competitors, regardless of the district-court decision.

Of the merger examples just cited, those that were of a conglomerate type—but that largely involved related diversification in the context of corporate development developed herein—were permitted. Those that were of a substantial vertical or horizontal nature were challenged. In the case of Kennecott, the FTC staff believed that Kennecott could have entered the coal industry itself, thus adding a competitor—which antitrust policy almost always favors, especially vis-à-vis the loss of a competitor (which would have been the case with BIC Pen-American Safety Razor and AMAX-Copper Range). With respect to Combustion Engineering-United Nuclear (now UNC Resources) the management of the latter—not the DOJ—brought the initial action against Combustion Engineering in 1968 (the management also rebuffed a subsequent acquisition offer from Ashland Oil).[2] Judge Fullam's instructive opinion in the United Nuclear suit stated:

> Having determined that this acquisition violates Section 7 because of its horizontal effects, I need not, strictly speaking, consider its vertical implications. However, in the interest of completeness, and because of the importance of the issues involved, I believe the vertical aspects should also be dealt with in this opinion. . . .
>
> The basic guidelines for determining the validity of vertical mergers were established in *Brown Shoe*. Market foreclosure is the initial point of reference. The present case is typical of vertical cases in that the foreclosure is neither of monopoly nor *de minimis* proportions. . . .[3]

Corporations should track closely trends in antitrust enforcement. Investigation of concentrated industries by the DOJ, and attempts to introduce economic models and theory in antitrust proceedings, also merit attention from the business community.[4]

In some respects, however, antitrust policy toward conglomerate mergers could eventually become more liberal. Richard Posner of the University of Chicago has pointed out a way. Posner has written a scathing but scholarly criticism of U.S. antitrust law, particularly the policy interpretation and enforcement that have come about through judicial decisions.[5] He argues that fewer prohibitions on conglomerate mergers, rather than restrictive legislation, would be in the public interest and consistent with U.S. free-enterprise concepts. He points out that the social premise of antitrust doctrine is really economic: that competition is good when and because it promotes efficient (that is, lower-cost and more) production of goods and services. He believes that there is already adequate statutory machinery to deal with any abuses—monopoly, price fixing, conspiracy, restraint of trade. He has seen no persuasive evidence yet against conglomerate mergers.

Various states have laws that delay mergers by requiring the filing of information before an offer can be completed, or by requiring the number of (percentage of) outstanding shares that must approve an offer, or—when a takeover is threatened—by offering other defensive actions to an unwilling management.

The relatively recent Williams Act is the federal statute governing takeovers for cash. As pointed out in chapter 2, once a tender offer is made, purchases of securities can be made only in accordance with the terms of an offering filed with the SEC.[6]

Congress subsequently enacted antitrust legislation (known as the Hart-Scott-Rodino Antitrust Improvement Act of 1976) requiring the filing of a premerger notification with the FTC and the DOJ for all mergers and acquisitions in which one of the companies has sales or assets in excess of $100 million and the other company has sales or assets in excess of $10 million. Completion of an acquisition cannot occur until thirty days after the required filings. The law also applies if the acquirer will hold either 15 percent or more of the outstanding common stock or assets of the company, or $15 million or more in value of stock or assets.

Other Considerations

Antitrust policy is very different in other countries, such as the United Kingdom, the countries of the European Economic Community, and Japan. The Organization for Economic Cooperation and Development (OECD) has developed a system of antitrust review and enforcement policies. And most Western economies, separately, have monopolies commissions. However, there is much closer government-business coordination, and especially government-initiated merger activity, outside the United States. In effect, there is much less litigation and challenge to acquisitions made by European firms in Europe, and relatively little activity yet with respect to Japanese firms. We thus see more the case of government-administered merger, rationalization-of-industry, or joint-ventures policy. This is the result of the different industrial-political structures, and of more nationalistic bases for competition.

As table 4-1 indicates, the economic impact of business combinations in the United States comes under the purview not only of the antitrust laws, but also of various federal and state agencies charged with specific approval responsibilities, such as the Federal Reserve Board (FRB) for bank holding companies, and the Civil Aeronautics Board (CAB) for airlines. At present, it is also conceivable that the sweeping provisions and broad interpretations that the courts have given to the National Environmental Policy Act, and the mandate of the Environmental Protection Agency, could also bring environmental-protection economic-impact doctrine into the field of corporate business combinations. In certain cases, in fact, this apparently has happened.

Notes

1. "Merger Case Digest—1971," Section on Antitrust Law (Chicago, Ill.: American Bar Association).
2. Because the issues in this case touched on projections regarding contracts for uranium—a matter of considerable concern in the more recent and massive Westinghouse-utilities-uranium producers litigation in the con-

text, not only of antitrust, but also of the Uniform Commercial Code—the reader may find some of the details in this older case also of interest.

3. From the court decision in *United Nuclear* v. *Combustion Engineering, Inc.* (E.D.Pa., Civil no. 68-1395, 1968). See also *United States* v. *Combustion* (Civil no. 68-4082, S.D.N.Y., terminated May 13, 1970).

4. See, for example, Gerald G. VanCise, "For Whom the Antitrust Bell Tolls," *Harvard Business Review*, January-February, 1978, pp. 125-130.

5. Richard W. Posner, *Antitrust and Economic Policy* (Chicago: University of Chicago Press, 1976).

6. See comments by Bruce Wasserstein, "A Useful New Guide to Tender Offers," *The New York Times*, 5 February 1978, p. 16.

Part II
Implementation: Systematic Procedures and Innovative Approaches

5

Identification and Selection of Industries and Companies of Interest

Gail V. Ferreira

Scope

This chapter is directed at the acquisition planner or analyst and describes in some detail systematic approaches that can be used to identify and make preliminary analyses and selection of candidate industries and companies. Specific examples are included of the application of these approaches to acquisition searches of several types.

Only limited attention is given here to industry as opposed to company selection and analysis. The pros and cons of various forms of diversification and the question of industry selection, as well as issues of criteria development, are treated in chapter 3. Company valuation is the topic of chapter 7. Chapter 10 summarizes the overall acquisition process, of which analysis and selection of industries and candidate companies are part.

Systematic approaches such as those outlined in this chapter can be useful, particularly in the early stages of planning for an acquisition program. However, in our view they should nearly always be coupled with more opportunistic, intense, pragmatic, and active techniques, at least at the point at which interest in specific industry subsegments has been identified and acquisition objectives quantified.

Industry Identification and Selection: Criteria Development

In most cases, criteria designed to select both industries and potential candidates within an industry include elements of at least some of those shown in table 5-1.

Publicly available data can be helpful in conducting initial screening based on historical performance. This can be done by making use of data from government sources, such as the *Census of Manufactures* of the U.S. Department of Commerce and the same source's annual *U.S. Industrial Outlook*; Standard and Poor's industry data; that of *The Value Line Investment Survey*; and a host of others, as described later on in the section on candidate selection. If one is starting from scratch and wants to look at a

Table 5-1
Sample Criteria Headings

1. Preference, if any, for service versus manufacturing industries.
   Additional preferences as to type of industry.
   Geographic preferences or restrictions.
2. Degree of fit (or lack of it) with the acquirer.
   Includes issues of management comprehension.
   Likely image and market effects if a company in the industry is acquired.
3. Size range of transaction contemplated.
4. Statement as to whether acquisition of a leading company is required or not, and other desired characteristics.
5. Industry makeup of sector(s) considered.
   Number and size distribution of participants.
6. Overall historical profitability.
   Return on assets, total invested capital, sales and other measures.
   Average price-to-earnings ratio and the rough range of price-to-earnings ratios for the industry.
   Cyclicality of sales and earnings.
   Variability among companies and reasons for same.
7. Overall past and expected growth trends in terms of sales (dollars and physical output).
   Short term.
   Long term.
   Expected future financial performance (free standing and if acquired).
8. Capital intensity (useful to screen heavy-capital-requirement industries as opposed to "cash generators").
   Dollars of invested capital per dollar of sales.
   Cash-utilization ratio (cash flow in relation to invested capital).
9. Technological, market, regulatory, and political risks.
10. Perceived risk relative to the capital market in general, as measured by the "betas" of major companies in the industry.
11. Projections of selected-company financial performance.
    Cash Flow.
    Internal rate of return (IRR).
    Return on total invested capital for selected years.
    Earnings-per-share (EPS) effects including dilution, if applicable.

Note: Additional factors must be considered when selecting individual companies within an industry, including issues of management, "culture," and value creation.

very wide range of industries, computer screening techniques can be useful, particularly where quantitative data is concerned. However, a screening based on more detailed qualitative insights than can be "machine searched" is usually desirable. Although the past must be considered, the true test, obviously, is expected future performance.

Company Identification, Selection, and Analysis

This section addresses the practical task of both identifying possible appropriate acquisition candidates and developing sufficient information about them so that they can be screened, analyzed, and placed in perspective in relation to the corporation's interests and criteria. The focus here is toward a planned methodical approach to an acquisition program such as is often carried out by corporate development, corporate planning, or financial departments. This approach is often done concurrently with an opportunistic approach in which potentially available candidates are brought to the attention of the company by outsiders.

Here we are dealing primarily with the issue of identifying and making a preliminary characterization of possible target companies; the question of approaching companies and entering into discussions with them, and of other facets of the overall acquisition process are reviewed in chapter 10.

The primary issues dealt with in this chapter are

1. The need for and development of criteria and selection parameters.
   a. Type of industry.
   b. Financial criteria.
2. Methodologies and sources to identify and develop information on companies (or divisions and subsidiaries of companies that meet screening criteria).
   a. Publicly held companies.
   b. Non-U.S. companies.
   c. Privately held companies.
3. Specific scenarios illustrating the various methods and approaches of identifying and analyzing target companies.

Need for Criteria

The two most important factors in identifying and later analyzing potential acquisition candidates are: (1) knowing what you are looking for in terms of specifics—financial parameters and industry position, growth potential, and so on; and (2) knowing how and where to locate them.

The development of criteria in order to initiate a systematic search is often arduous and time consuming. Hence, criteria development needs to be approached from a pragmatic viewpoint. For example, if a firm wants to strengthen and broaden its own base, then its search will be confined to an industry with which it is familiar. The opposite would be true if the firm desires to expand well beyond its present industry scope. Financial criteria in terms of size, profitability, debt-to-equity ratios, and the effect of the potential acquiree on the income statement and balance sheet of the acquirer also need to be specified.

Establishing realistic, acceptable criteria is a difficult task; staff groups engaged in identifying and analyzing potential candidates, along with top management, must constantly test and revise both criteria and possible candidates as the process proceeds.

Candidate Identification and Information

Assuming that tentative criteria covering appropriate financial and industry attributes have been developed, where does one go to identify prospects or candidates?

Basic directories and data banks usually are a first step. These include Dun & Bradstreet's *Million Dollar Directories* and Standard and Poor's *Register of Corporations Directories*. Internal sources such as marketing and sales departments should also be included as a first step because of their possible knowledge and field contacts. One's own key officers, directors, and other employees also are often good sources of candidates. Since there are several different approaches to locating companies, the most efficient way is to describe the process for different categories of companies. Appendixes 5B and 5C describe in detail many of the more useful sources of data.

Publicly Held Companies as Candidates. Basic information concerning public companies is normally readily available. The identification of publicly held companies is facilitated by the number of different sources from which to choose. When one is beginning from scratch, often the most efficient way to extract a list of companies is to use the Compustat or similar computerized data base. This procedure will enable the user to define its parameters and select a listing of publicly held companies. There are other initial avenues of pursuit, but most are generally more time consuming. If no other alternative is available, then the investigation can proceed manually by using the Dun & Bradstreet *Million Dollar Directories* (product-code listing) and checking these lists against the Securities and Exchange Commission's list of firms that must file reports with the SEC. Although this takes time, in some cases it may be the only feasible approach. A good indication of historical financial position as well as of product lines and equity ownership usually can be easily accessed. In some instances, data on competitive conditions are available.

The most important sources for public companies are the SEC Form 10-K and the Annual Report to shareholders. Also significant are the other SEC documents, such as the 10-Q, Proxy, Registration Statement Prospectus, 13-D, and 14-D1. The 10-Q gives a firm's quarterly financial condition. The proxy statement is the announcement of the annual meeting and lists the management, directors of the company up for election, and owners holding 5 percent or more of the company's outstanding shares. The prospectus is a document containing financial data and other information filed in connection with the registration of the securities offered by a publicly owned corporation under the requirements of the Securities Act. Similar information and documentation is filed in connection with events pertaining to companies where securities are listed on a stock exchange under the Exchange Act. The prospectus gives a description of the securities, market prices, and information regarding the corporation's business, employee stock-option plans, significant recent developments, opinions of outside auditors, legal counsel, and so on. In addition, supplements to the registration statement prospectus will cover offers of acquisition through the exchange of shares of the corporation making the offer and the other party. Form 13-D lists the purchasers of 5 percent or more of the issued and outstanding common equity. Form 14-D1 is filed when a tender offer is being made concerning a company. Sources such as Standard & Poor's *Stock Reports*, Moody's *Investors Service*, and *The Value Line Investment Survey* should not be overlooked. In addition to the bound sources, these organizations and others offer several computerized data bases. These sources have software that allows one to select, organize, and analyze the raw data. One example of a useful service for analyzing candidates is the *X-Forma* S-M program offered through Interactive Data Corporation. Automatic Data Processing offers a similar service called *MERGE*. With this program the merger of two or more public firms can be financially analyzed based on the parameters specified by the user (see chapter 9). More relevant from the standpoint of candidate selection and analysis is the *X-Scan* S-M system of Interactive Data Corporation, which allows one to screen and identify large numbers of potential merger candidates that meet specified financial criteria. The Automatic Data Processing counterpart is called *SCREEN*. Similar programs are also available from other vendors. Chase Econometrics Associates' forecast data bases can be accessed via the *X-Scan* program to generate preliminary sales forecasts for target companies. Not only are *X-Scan* and *SCREEN* useful on a company level, but they are also capable of providing aggregate figures for all companies in a given industry based on Standard & Poor's data. This provides the user with comparative information useful in judging a firm's position within an industry and is one of many sources available for making financial projections.

Another source of information on public companies is the *Computer Credit Analysis* offered by Standard & Poor's. These are twenty-page reports summarizing key numbers and ratios.

In addition to financial data, data on product lines and on marketing and distribution systems are necessary to the selection process. Some of this information is available in the Annual Report or Form 10-K, but other material can also be located in special industry issues of a number of leading periodicals. Most of these special issues appear annually. A few of the periodicals include *Chemical & Engineering News* (June), *Professional Builder & Apartment Business* (July), *Electronics* (January) and *Pulp and Paper* (second issue, June), to name a few.

Interest in the basic industry group to which these companies belong is also important. The industry's strengths and weaknesses can tell one a great deal about whether or not it is cyclical, stable, aging, or growing; subject to unusual federal regulation; and so forth. Industry information is easily accessible. Standard & Poor's prepares *Industry Surveys*, which are updated periodically throughout the year. These reports contain facts about the different segments of an industry (for instance, the electronics industry is analyzed in terms of a consumer segment, a components segment, and others); the key participants in those segments and in the basic industry; and pertinent economic and financial data. The Department of Commerce publishes the *U.S. Industrial Outlook* annually, which gives a composite view of selected industries. Various statistics are available from *Predicasts* (an annual) and from *Predicasts Basebook*, which is historical in nature; and every industry has trade journals that talk about subjects such as new-product development, changes in management, regulation, and price trends.

Non-U.S. Candidates. Comparable information on non-U.S. companies has been relatively difficult to develop until fairly recently; it still is not easy to find. SEC-type disclosure is not strictly required, except to some extent in the United Kingdom and, increasingly, in Canada. A further exception is where shares of a foreign corporation are listed on a U.S. stock exchange. Moreover, each country has a different way of presenting information on companies incorporated there. In more recent times, information has become somewhat more accessible, probably as a result of increased U.S. corporate and banking activity abroad and foreign ownership of U.S. public companies. Surprisingly, however, the largest European-based publicly owned corporations routinely disclose more of certain kinds of information than do their U.S. counterparts—for example, with respect to ownership in various other companies and ventures. This may be due in part to their reduced exposure to antitrust concerns abroad.

If a firm has offices in Europe, Asia, or the Middle East, then these locations are good places from which to base the development of an acquisition study. Additionally, reliance on personal contacts, bankers, and a "big eight" accounting firm can provide reliable information on foreign businesses. The series of publications of the U.S. Domestic and International Business Administration include *Market Profiles, Total Market Surveys*, and *Market Share Reports*. There are several company directories that will give financial data and product-line information, including *Information Internationale, Jane's Major Companies of Europe, Principal International Businesses*, and others that are listed in appendix 5B.

Computerized data bases that provide information on international firms include *The New York Times Information Bank* and the Funk & Scott *International Edition*. These are indexed by product and company. In addition, Standard & Poor's has developed *EXSTAT* which currently lists 2000 foreign companies. Also, Dun & Bradstreet offers *Dun's Worldfile*, which lists almost 300,000 companies in 135 countries. *World Traders Data Reports* are available from the U.S. Department of Commerce. These reports give the size of the company, sales area, products, financial references, and general reputation. Equifax and the Foreign Credit Interchange Bureau of the National Association of Credit Management Corporations both have reports on many companies in the free world, which may be accessible. Various banking and other sources can provide credit checks on foreign companies, including, in some cases, individual-company business profiles. As a final point, a possible source of information is SEC Form 6-K, which is applicable to foreign firms selling securities in the United States.

Privately Held Candidates. Industry information is accessed in the same way for private firms as for public firms. The problem lies in identifying and getting information on individual privately held firms within an industry. One might begin the search with a brief examination of such directories as Dun & Bradstreet's *Million Dollar* and *Middle Market Directories*, Standard & Poor's *Register of Corporations*, and *Thomas Register*. Computerized references include the *EIS Industrial Plants* (which lists both public and private manufacturing establishments with annual sales exceeding $900,000) and *EIS Non-Manufacturing Establishments* (which covers over 200,000 establishments).

The next step is to consult one or more of the following sources in order to find out about a privately held company:

1. State filings: If a company is incorporated and doing business in Massachusetts, for instance, records will be kept about the company's business operation, its board members, and some financials. It is now required by every state that companies doing business must file articles of incorporation. Most states require annual reports; several states require financial information be included in these reports. In addition, companies must file Uniform Commercial Code (UCC) documents that show whether a corporation has borrowed against its assets.
2. Dun & Bradstreet Credit Reports: These reports give various data on companies, including lines of business, history, management, and ownership. They also provide credit information.
3. TRWs National Credit Information Service: This is similar to the Dun & Bradstreet service, with more emphasis on payment practices.
4. The Robert Morris Associates *Annual Statement Studies*: Comparing a publicly held firm of approximately the same size and in the same business as a privately held firm can provide invaluable insight into factors such as relative price-to-earnings (*P/E*) ratios, net worth, and other

financial indicators relative to the publicly held firms. In its reports, Robert Morris Associates summarizes average financial data for companies in a wide range of industries.

5. Field interviews.
6. Product literature.
7. Trade exhibitions shows.
8. Editors of certain periodicals.
9. Special trade directories.
10. Industry associations.
11. Probate court estate and divorce records: These can sometimes provide information about control or ownership of small firms.
12. Special industry studies, such as Frost & Sullivan Studies, Adapso report on data-processing, and so on.
13. Congressional Information Service Index, which gives information on hearings and transcripts.
14. Senate and House committees.
15. Government reports.

To demonstrate how these procedures and sources can be used in typical search work, examples are provided in the following section.

Application Examples

*General Techniques for Candidate Screening
and Evaluation*

As a preface to the examples, it is appropriate to explain and describe briefly two techniques used in screening and initial evaluation. The first one is a "check-off" system, used for checking the appropriateness of a company with respect to the criteria established by the potential acquirer. This chart can be set up as follows:

*Check-Off System
Name of Company*

Examples Criteria or Characteristics	*Fit*	*No Fit*	*Maybe*
1. Sales $10+ million	√12 million		
2. Sales growth > 10 percent			√9.5 percent
3. Earnings growth > 12 percent		√10 percent	

4. Price-to-earnings
   ratio
5. Debt-to-equity
   ratio
6. Net worth
7. Employees
8. Market value
9. Earnings per share
10. Position in the
    market
11. Stage of maturity
12. Number of plants

Any number of criteria can be used in establishing a check-off system. In the example, the candidate company had sales of $12 million (which is greater than $10 million), had a sales growth of 9.5 percent (which is slightly under the established level of 10 percent) and had an earnings growth below the required 12 percent. The purpose of the check-off system is to simplify the process of taking a brief look at a company. This brief look should tell the acquirer immediately whether or not this candidate is appropriate for its program.

The second system, the ranking system, is to be used in conjunction with the check-off system. The purpose of using a ranking system is to create a composite view of all of the prospective acquisition candidates. A great deal of judgment and individual discretion is involved in this system; on the whole, the outcome is usually very helpful.

The ranking system (table 5-2) can help to define succinctly where the target candidates fit and to designate those that seem best to meet the criteria. Such a system is not designed to have all the answers, but it does aid the decision-making process. No ranking system is a substitute for a detailed evaluation analysis.

Example A: Identifying Privately Held Companies

We are about to embark on a project involving consumer electronics. Our client, Musical Noise, Inc., has requested our assistance in locating a firm in its field of consumer electronics. Although Musical Noise makes programmable musical toys, our endeavors are not to be limited to this particular segment. A list of appropriate criteria has been prepared.

Locating companies in the consumer-electronics area is a challenge. Although there are a number of dominant players in certain subfields, there is a very large number of small firms in this highly fragmented field. The criteria set forth include:

Table 5-2
Ranking System
(Ranking Scale: Scores from 1 to 10)

	Company Name	Company Name	Company Name	Company Name	Company Name					
1. Sales $10 million	10	6	9	7	5	8	4	2	3	1
2. Sales growth > 10%	8	10	10	6	4	5	7	1	3	2
3. Earnings growth > 12%	9	7	5	10	3	1	8	6	2	4
4. P/E	etc.									
5. D/E										
6. Net worth										
7. Employees										
8. Market value										
9. EPS										
10. Position in market										
11. Stage of maturity										
12. Number of plants										
Total Score	110[a]	104[b]	101[c]	98	70	73	95	80	82	100

[a]These three companies are best suited according to criteria because they ranked highest in the scoring.

1. Privately held business.
2. No greater than $15 million per year in sales.
3. Early growth stage of maturity.
4. Product line:
    a. Toys—programmable and nonprogrammable.
    b. Games—programmable and nonprogrammable, and video.
    c. Appliances.
    d. Security products.
    e. Unusual gadgetry.

To begin, one approach is to conduct a scan of available literature, either by computer terminal or manually. The results for toys and games, for example, could be as follows:

Computer Scan

```
167275  ELEC NEWS  77/01/24  P58,68
    US  PROGRAMMABLE  VIDEO  GAME SALES IN 1977 WILL TOTAL 1.5 MIL UNITS
ACCORDING TO INDUSTRY OFFICIALS.  LONE  SUPPLIER  FAIRCHILD  CAMERA  &
INSTRUMENT  SOLD  50,000-60,000  UNITS  IN  1976.   FAIRCHILD CAMERA &
INSTRUMENT WON'T REMAIN ALONE IN THE PROGRAMMABLE GAME MARKET, RCA HAS
PLANS TO TEST-MARKET ITS 1802 MPU-BASED GAMES IN  EARLY  1977  AND  10
DISTRIBUTE  THE GAME NATIONWIDE BY MID-1977.  APF ELECTRONICS,  ALLIED
LEISURE,  BALLY MANUFACTURING, COMMODORE BUSINESS MACHINES AND NATIONAL
SEMICONDUCTOR FURTHER WILL HAVE PROGRAMMABLE GAMES IN LATE 1977. ALSO,
IT IS EXPECTED THAT MAGNAVOX AND ATARI WILL BE  INTRODUCING  UNITS  BY
MID-1977.  SOME  65%  OF  THE MARKET,  OR 6.5 MIL UNITS,  WILL BE IN
DEDICATED VIDEO GAMES SAID DR  EA  SACK,   CORPORATE  VP  FOR  GENERAL
INSTRUMENT'S MICROELECTRONICS GROUP.  THE REMAINING 20% OF THE MARKET
WILL BE IN NON-VIDEO GAMES,  SUCH AS ELECTRONIC  HAND-HELD  AND  BOARD
GAMES. TOTAL ELECTRONIC GAMES SALES SHOULD REACH 10 MIL UNITS, UP FROM
4 MIL IN THE BEFORE-CHRISTMAS PERIOD OF 1976.

        398199  OFFICE EQP  77/NO/05  P36
        WORLD   TV GAMES & CARTRIDGES DEMAND (MIL UNITS)
        TYPE                      1977     1978      1980
        LOW-END GAMES             8.5       9.2       9.3
        PROGRAMMABLE GAMES        0.5       2.3       6.2
        PROGRAM CARTRIDGES        1         6         30
```

Manual Search

Advertising Age, 10 April 1978, p. 61.

Newsweek, 11 December 1978, p. 76.

Electronic World, 15 May 1979, p. 71.

Discount Merchandiser, March 1979, p. 96.

By conducting a review of the literature, three tasks are accomplished:

1. A "feel" for the industry is obtained.
2. Names of companies, both prominent and unknown are discovered.

3. Awareness of what journals should be screened for information about these candidate companies.

The next phase is to compose a list of journals that can be used for reference. In this case, appropriate periodicals include: *Consumer Electronics, Electronic News, Merchandising Week, Mart, Home Furnishings Daily, Security World, Discount Merchandiser, IEEE Transactions on Consumer Electronics, Appliance Manufacturer*, and *Journal of Electronics Industry*. In addition to trade journals, some special industry studies can provide invaluable data. Most of these studies are prepared by professional groups and trade associations. For instance, the Electronics Industry Association has a booklet entitled "Consumer Electronics Annual Review." The federal-government studies on consumer electronics are less detailed but do give an overview of the industry. And Standard & Poor's *Industry Survey on Electronics* will give information about the different segments, including the composition of the segment (whether there are a few manufacturers or many) and the financial attributes of the public companies. In the field of consumer electronics, there are a great many "gadgets" manufactured that are advertised in wholesale-house catalogues. Hammacher Schlemmer is an example of such a company, one that would deserve attention in the pursuit of candidate companies.

After this step, a "hands-on," more detailed investigation begins. If a list of prospects has not already been created, then one must begin by compiling this list. The first step is obviously to list the names of the companies that appeared as a result of the literature research. The next step is to look through either the Dun & Bradstreet *Million Dollar Directories* or the Standard & Poor's *Register of Corporations*. Each of these has lists of companies categorized by product or standard industrial classification (SIC). If it is too time consuming to do this manually, a similar approach can be accomplished electronically. At a computer terminal using the *EIS Industrial Plants*, one can retrieve information on plants with twenty or more employees and $900,000 or more in sales. Now the criteria check can begin. Bear in mind that the search is to result in a list of privately held firms, with sales of no more than $15 million. The product criteria have already been fulfilled because of the list that was created. An early growth stage cannot be determined on the preliminary search; that will come later. Any name that was retrieved from the *EIS Industrial Plants* or *EIS Nonmanufacturing Establishments* will list sales, employees, and market share. Therefore, those firms should be easy to distinguish. The other firms have to be checked in Dun & Bradstreet and Standard & Poor's. If a listing for a company cannot be found, a quick look in the Dun & Bradstreet *Reference Book of Manufacturers* should verify its existence. If the firm still does not appear, a last resort is to check the *Dun's Code*, which is a microfiche compilation of all companies. If one does locate the listing, then a Dun & Bradstreet Credit

Report can be ordered. This ought to give one some indication of the viability of the company to date. Organizing the analysis stage of investigation includes using the check-off system and the ranking system. A summary sheet for each of the candidate companies would have the name and address of the target company, a telephone number, its products or services, its ownership, and pertinent financials (if available).

It is evident that identifying smaller, privately owned firms is a multiphased task. Possibly the advent of changes in SEC regulations regarding acquisitions may make information about some smaller firms easier to obtain in the future.

Example B: Non-U.S. Acquisition Candidates

We would like to acquire a plastics manufacturer in Belgium.

The first thing to do is to locate all the non-U.S.-company directories that cover Belgium. These include *Information Internationales, Jane's Major Companies of Europe, Principle International Businesses, Kompass Belgium, Business International Corporation Master Key Index, Fortune World Business Directory, and Europe's 5,000 Largest Companies*, all of which are bound. Computerized material is available on *The New York Times* Information Bank, the Funk & Scott *International Index*, and *Exstat*, and *Chemical Market Abstracts*. Using these sources should give the acquirer some flexibility by providing a number of plastic firms among which to choose. The difficulty arises where the parameters are limited to smaller firms. Dun & Bradstreet has a Dun's World File, which is probably the best place to go for information on smaller-sized firms.

After retrieving the information and compiling a list of prospects, the checking and ranking systems can be implemented. If more or better data is necessary, then a review of major European or other journals is helpful. Companies with foreign offices have the added advantage of having people close to the information. Obviously, in any case, one may have to take the additional step of getting information translated if the user is not fluent in the language provided.

Example C: Publicly Held Acquisition Candidates

A large food manufacturer interested in the food-machinery industry first seeks a list of probable acquisition candidates. The major parameters are: (1) publicly owned, (2) sales between $25 million and $100 million, and (3) principal business in food machinery and equipment.

The conduct of the kind of acquisition program depicted in example C is relatively straightforward. A choice of first phases is available. One procedure is to check manually the reference sources and personal contacts for publicly owned food machinery manufacturers. A much faster technique may be to use the Compustat Data Base which lists over 6,000 publicly held companies traded on the New York Stock Exchange (NYSE), on the American Stock Exchange (AMEX), and over the counter (OTC). The data base will accept commands stating sales ranges and product codes, among other factors. The resultant list will contain the names of most public firms whose sales are between $25 million and $100 million and whose principal business lines are food machinery and equipment.

The process of finding current information on these prospects is facilitated by the use of 10-Ks, Annual Reports, reports by security analysts and brokerage firms, and other documents and published literature. Such documents provide detailed business-line information, current and historic financial data, and more—usually enough to permit a complete evaluation:

Appendix 5A:
General Industry
Information

Census of Manufactures, Census of Wholesale, Census of Retail Trade, Census of Construction Industries, Census of Service Industries, Census of Transportation (Bureau of the Census, U.S. Department of Commerce).

Concentration Ratios (Department of Commerce).

Census of Business (Department of Commerce).

U.S. Industrial Outlook (Department of Commerce).

Robert Morris Associates *Annual Statement Studies.*

Conference Board, Inc.

Chase Econometrics Associates.

Standard & Poor's *Industry Surveys.*

Worldcasts.

Predicasts.

Frost & Sullivan and other studies.

This appendix and those that follow are meant to give an indication of some of the sources available and are not intended to be a complete listing.

99

Appendix 5B:
General Company
Information

Domestic

Computerized

EIS industrial plants
EIS nonmanufacturing
establishments
ABI/Inform
Magazine Index
Management Contents
New York Times Information
Bank
Funk & Scott Index
(Domestic)

PROMT
Value Line
Compustat
Cybernet Technotec
Dun & Bradstreet
Chase Econometrics
Dow Jones *News Retrieval*

Manual

Standard & Poor's
Moody's Investor Services
Value Line
Dun & Bradstreet
30,000 Leading U.S. Corporations
Fortune 1,000
Forbes 1,000
Funk & Scott Index (Domestic*)*
Directory of Corporate
Affiliation
Who Owns Whom
Directory of New England
Manufacturers
Missouri Directory of
Manufacturing and Mining

Thomas' Register
Macrae's
Polk's
Who's Who
Wall Street Journal Index
New York Times Index
Business Periodicals Index
Pennsylvania State Industry
Directory
California Manufacturers
Register
Classified Directory
Wisconsin Manufacturers
Directory of American Firms
Operating in Foreign
Countries
American Register of Exporters
and Importers

Canadian

Canadian Business Periodicals Index (CBPI)
Canadian News Index (CNI)
New York Times Information Bank
Funk & Scott Index (International)
Canadian Key Business Directory

Kompass
Canadian Trade Index
Dun & Bradstreet of Canada
Fraser's Canadian Trade Directory
Who Owns Who

International

The New York Times Information Bank
Funk & Scott Index (International)
Information Internationales
Jane's Major Companies of Europe
Kelly's Manufacturers & Merchants Directory
Principal International Businesses
Europe's 5,000 Largest Companies
Major Companies of the Arab World & Iran

Kompass
Business International Corporation—Master Key Index
Polk's
Japan Directory
Who Owns Whom
International Who's Who
Times 1,000
Fortune World Business
Business Week International Scoreboard

**Appendix 5C:
Examples of Industries
and Their Related
Information Sources**

Industry Category	Bound Sources		Data-Base Sources
	Industry Facts	*Company Facts*	
Agriculture/food	*Census of Agriculture* (U.S. Department of Commerce) *Agriculture Statistics* (U.S. Department of Agriculture) *Frozen Food Pack Statistics* (American Frozen Food Institute) *Frozen Food Almanac* (Quick Frozen Food)	*Almanac of Canning, Freezing, Preserving Industries* (E.E. Judge & Sons) *Candy Marketer Almanac & Buyers' Guide Directory* *Thomas Grocery Register*	*Agricola* *CAB Abstracts* (Commonwealth agricultural bureaus) *Foods Ad libra* *Food Science & Technology Abstract*
Motor vehicles	*Automobile Facts & Figures* (Motor Vehicle Manufacturers' Association of the U.S.) *Ward's Automotive Yearbook* *World Automotive Market* *Auto News: Market Data Book Issue*	*Almanac Issue (Automotive News*—last April issue) *International Automotive Industries Annual Suppliers Financial Analysis* (June)	SAE (Society of Automotive Engineers)
Chemicals	*Facts and Figures for the Chemical Industry (Chemical & Engineering News*—first June issue)	*Chemical Week 300 (Chemical Week*—April issue) *Kline Guide to the Chemical Industry* *Kline Guide to the Paint Industry* (Patricia Noble, editor) *Chemical Week Buyers' Guide*	*Chemical Market Abstracts* *Chemical Abstracts* *CIN (Chemical Industry Notes)*
Petroleum/gas	*Oil & Gas Journal Forecast/ Review* (January)	*LP Gas Buyers' Guide* (March issue) *National Petroleum News Fact Book* (Mid-June issue) *Keystone Coal Industry Manual*	*APILIT* *P/E News* *Tulsa*

Plastics	Plastics World Reference File	Directory of Custom Plastics Processors (Organization of Plastics Processors)	RAPRA Abstracts
Paper/packaging	Marketing Guide to the Paper and Pulp Industry C.H. Kline & Co.	Pulp & Paper Buyers Guide Modern Packaging Encyclopedia and Buyers Guide Lockwood's Directory of Paper & Allied Trades	PIRA Paperchem Abstracts
Pharmaceuticals/ drugs	Prescription Drug Industry Factbook. Pharmaceutical Manufacturers Association	Chain Store Age Drug Edition (April) Drug Topics Red Book Cumulative Supplement)	Pharmaceutical News Index International Pharmaceutical Abstracts
Electronics/ appliances	Home Furnishings Daily Electronics (January) Electrical World (June) Merchandising	Consumer Electronics Monthly (January) Appliance Manufacturer Annual Directory (June issue)	PROMT INSPEC
Banking	U.S. League of Savings Associations Savings and Loan Fact Book National Association of Mutual Savings Banks (Annual Report of the President) (National Fact Book of Mutual Savings Banking) Bankers' Desk Reference	Forbes Annual Banking Issue (April) Finance Annual Commercial Banking Edition (July-August) Business Week Annual Banking Survey	ABI/INFORM EIS nonmanufacturing establishments S & L Data Base Bancall II Bancompare FDIC Tapes FSLIC Tapes

Industry Category	Bound Sources		Data-Base Sources
	Industry Facts	Company Facts	
Other industries	Railway Age (January) DataPro (DataPro Research Corporation—hardware/software reference service)	Datamation (June) Building Supply News (Retail/ Wholesale Giants Report) January (Buyers' Guide) November Guide to Scientific Instruments (American Association for the Advancement of Science) Journal of the American Water Works Association Buyers Guide (November) Aviation Week & Space Technology Marketing Directory Issue (December) Greetings Magazine Buyers' Guide Directory Modern Office Procedures Buyers Planbook Security World Annual Security Product Directory	
Canadian industry	Canadian Packaging (July) Canadian Pulp & Paper (May)	Canadian Plastics (Fall)	CNI CBPI
Miscellaneous useful sources	Sales & Marketing Management: Survey of Buying Power; Survey of Industrial Purchasing Power Guide to American Directories (Klein) Business Information Sources (Lorna Daniells) Statistical Information Sources: A Guide for Financial Industries (Bank Administration Institute)	Institutional Investor Annual Financing Directory Ad Age: 100 Leading National Advertisers; U.S. Agency Profiles Money Market Directory	

Appendix 5D: Computerized Data Bases Useful for Acquisitions

EIS Industrial Plant
Economic Information Systems Inc.
9 East 41st Street
New York, N.Y. 10017

(212) 697-6080

The establishments in this file account for 90 percent of the value of U.S. shipments. Over 120,000 manufacturing establishments are classified. The data given include company headquarters, Standard Industrial Classification, sales, employee range, and market share as a percentage of industry activity.

EIS Nonmanufacturing Establishments
Economic Information Systems Inc.
9 East 41st Street
New York, N.Y. 10017

(212) 697-6090

These data are set up in the same way as those for industrial plants. They cover over 200,000 establishments with twenty employees or more, and include classification of banks and nonprofit institutions.

ABI/Inform
Data Courier, Inc.
620 South Fifth Street
Louisville, Kentucky 40202

(502) 582-4111

Over 400 journals are cited in this business-management data base. Information available includes product information, company facts and trends, and other data.

The New York Times Information Bank
Subsidiary of *The New York Times* Company
One World Trade Center
New York, N.Y. 10048

(212) 775-0552 or (800) 631-8056

The Infobank covers data appearing in all major city newspapers including some in Canada and abroad and major business periodicals. Company and industry information is usually abundant.

Predicasts Funk & Scott Indices
Predicasts, Inc.
200 University Circle Research Center
Cleveland, Ohio 44106

(216) 795-3000

The Funk & Scott indexes, which are also in bound form, reference major business and trade journals, both domestic and international. The subjects covered include management procedures, company resources, market information, government regulations, products and processes, and unit costs and prices.

Predicasts PROMT
Predicasts, Inc.
200 University Circle Research Center
Cleveland, Ohio 44106

(216) 795-3000

This file abstracts major journals and newspapers and provides information on acquisitions, market data, foreign trade, new products, and so on; it covers several major industries.

Compustat and *Exstat*
Investors Management Services, Inc.
Subsidiary of Standard & Poor's Corporation
1221 Avenue of the Americas
New York, N.Y. 10020

(800) 525-8640

The *Compustat Industrial File* contains the New York Stock Exchange companies, the American Stock Exchange companies, and a large portion of the over-the-counter companies. *Compustat* also allows access to business lines of each of the 6,000 companies listed. The financials and product descriptions are given for each. *Exstat* is the foreign counterpart to *Compustat*, listing over 2,000 foreign companies.

Value Line Data Base
Value Line Investment Survey
Arnold Bernhard & Company, Inc.
711 Third Avenue
New York, N.Y. 10017

(212) 687-3965

This is the computerized counterpart of the Value Line Investment Service and contains 1,600 public companies.

Dow Jones News Retrieval
Dow Jones & Company, Inc.
22 Cortland Street
New York, N.Y. 10007

(212) 285-5223

This is a news service of the last ninety days worth of business news. The data base is categorized by company, industry, and government-agency activity.

X-Scan and *X-Forma*
Interactive Data Corporation
486 Totten Pond Road
Waltham, Mass. 02154

(617) 492-7500

This is a software system that will manipulate data from either the *Compustat* Data Base or the *Value Line* Data Base. *X-Scan* and *X-Forma* will compute and calculate any financial variables for use in financial-planning and merger analysis.

ADP Strategic Planning Services
ADP Network Services Inc.
Strategic Planning Services
425 Park Avenue
New York, N.Y. 10022

(212) 980-4880

This is another software package that also uses *Compustat* and *Value Line* data bases. Its package includes SCREEN, ANALYSIS, MERGE, and DEALS. ADP (Automatic Data Processing) also offer a number of other data bases including *S&L Data Base, Bancall, Bancompare.*

Appendix 5E:
References

This is a list of some frequently used services. Most of these are in selected public universities and special libraries.

Dun & Bradstreet, Inc.
99 Church Street
New York, N.Y. 10007

(212) 962-6300

*Million Dollar Directory,
    Volumes 1, 2, and 3*
Metalworking Directory
*Reference Book of Corporation
    Management*
Reference Book of Manufacturers

Principal International Businesses
Dun & Bradstreet of Canada

Company/Credit Reports
Worldfile
Dun's Code

Moody's Investors Services, Inc.
99 Church Street
New York, N.Y. 10007

(212) 553-0300

Industrial Manual
OTC
Transportation

Utilities
Bank and Finance

Securities and Exchange Commission
500 North Capital Street
Washington, D.C. 20549

(202) 755-4846

Disclosure, Inc.
5161 River Road
Washington, D.C. 20016

(301) 951-1300

Form 10-K   Financial condition
                                and
Annual Report   company's business
Form 10-Q (Quarterly Report)
Form 8-K (Current Changes)
Form 13-D (Ownership over 5 percent)
Form 14-D1 (Tender offers)
Form 6-K (Foreign companies selling stock)

Standard & Poor's Corporation
345 Hudson Street
New York, N.Y. 10014

(212) 924-6400

Corporations, directors and executives   *Current statistics*
Stock reports   *Outlook*
Corporation records   *Computer credit analysis*
Industry Surveys

U.S. Department of Commerce
14th Street & Constitution Avenue, N.W.
Washington, D.C. 20230

(202) 377-2000

U.S. Industrial Outlook
U.S. Domestic & International
  Business Administration Reports
World Traders Data Reports (DIB-431)

Value Line Investment Survey
Arnold Bernhard & Company, Inc.
711 Third Avenue
New York, N.Y. 10017

(212) 687-3965

Appendix 5F:
Company-Survey
Checklist

Financial

1. Financial statements for last five years.
   a. Balance sheets.
   b. Profit-and-loss and surplus statements.
2. Projected operating and financial statements.
3. Breakdown of inventory as to raw material, work in process, finished goods.
   a. Any change in this mix through the years?
   b. How is inventory carried—average cost, Lifo, Fifo, and so on?
4. Details of prepaid expenses.
5. Detail of property, plant and equipment.
   a. Any buildings partially completed or under construction?
   b. Any machinery or equipment under construction?
   c. Any leased machinery or equipment? (If so, details concerning quantity, terms of lease, contingent liability, and so forth.)
6. Details of intangible assets including cost of patents and method of amortization.
7. Short-term loans—interest rate, due date, security if any, and so on.
8. Is short-term financing used that does not show on annual statements? Explain.
9. Long-term loans—interest rate, payment dates, prepayment penalty, security, restrictions on working capital and dividends, and so on.
10. Details of reserves and capital surplus.
11. Federal income-tax statute—credits, loss, carryovers, and so on.
12. Details of unrecorded or contingent liabilities.
13. Sales and cost of sales by product classification.
14. Details of nonmanufacturing costs such as selling, advertising, research, and so on.
15. Sources of "other income"—royalties, rent, and so on.
16. Details of "other deductions"—interest, royalties and fees, and so on.
17. Details of any "strange" items on financial statements.
18. Extent of management-control techniques used—budget, standard costs, and so on.
19. Details of data processing, and so on.
20. Information on pension plan and unfunded liabilities, if any.

General

1. History of business.
2. Description of corporate structure.
3. List of officers and directors, their affiliations and background.
4. Stock distribution—number, principal holders, and so on.
5. Organization chart.
6. Policy manual.
7. Extent of integration of company—can it expand vertically?
8. Philosophy of management on matters such as growth, industrial relations, organizational planning, industrial engineering, merchandising, educational selling, advertising, accounting and budgeting, research, development engineering, product design, and so on.
9. Can we evaluate company ourselves or must we hire outside consultants for personnel analysis, market research, or any other factors?
10. Are there any legal problems peculiar to the company, its products, or the industry?
11. What is company's philosophy or policy on dividends, financing expansion, finances in general?
12. What consulting firms have been or are being retained by the firm?
13. How are relations with the community?
14. What is policy concerning patent protection?
15. Are any major capital expenditures authorized at present?
16. Are any major capital expenditures contemplated in the near term? In the long term?
17. Are company's name and trademark well known? Are they confusingly similar to any other firm's name and trademark?
18. How did the company do during the depressed times of the early 1970s?

Sales

General

1. List and evaluate sales personnel—management, inside and outside sales people, advertising, and so on.
2. Describe methods (channels) of distribution.
3. Are any changes in method of distribution contemplated?
4. Complete list of branch offices, warehouses, service facilities.
5. Who are consumers? (List and give locations.)
6. What is the company's geographic distribution of sales, sales people?
7. Breakdown by size (in dollars) of orders received annually.
8. Does company formalize market surveys? Use consultants?

Advertising and Promotion

1. What are the extent, type, quality, and media of the company's past and present advertising program? How does this compare to advertising done by competitors of the company?
2. What is the present status of catalogs, price sheets, sales tools, sales engineering data, service manuals, and parts lists? How does this compare to like material put out by competitors of the company?
3. Does the company participate in trade shows? Do the company's competitors participate in trade shows?
4. How are publicity and public relations handled by the company? How does this compare to the programs handled by the company's competitors?

The Product

1. List product lines with description and history.
2. Volume of each item or line:
   a. Each of past five years.
   b. Budgeted for this year.
   c. Present backlog.
   d. Future outlook (present and new fields).
3. What is the life of the product?
4. How much of annual sales are supply and repair orders?
5. Are any items or supplies purchased for resale? If so, what is the volume and characteristic markup of each?
6. List patents and licenses giving life and degree of exclusivity.
7. What emphasis does the company place on industrial design and packaging?
8. For the past five years, how were the sales broken down by industry (chemical, foods, and so forth)?
9. Do products and facilities have possibilities in the consumer field as well as the industrial field?
10. Do products and facilities lend themselves naturally to other products and new fields?
11. Are there possibilities of using the company's products in "new-growth" industries?
12. Will any foreseeable events bring technological obsolescence to the company's industry or any of its products? Review past, current, and prospective technological trends with relation to company's products, its customers, and its competitors.
13. What is the ability of the company to supply present demands? Anticipated demands?

Personnel

1. Number, sex, age of labor force.
2. Breakdown of personnel by direct, indirect, labor; by department.
3. Breakdown of labor force as to length of service.
4. Are employees paid on hourly or piece rates?
5. What is minimum, maximum, and average wage?
6. Description and cost of fringe benefits (insurances, vacation and holiday policy, pensions, and so on).
7. Are incentive, profit-sharing, or stock-purchasing plans in force? Explain.
8. How do wages and salaries compare with competition and other industries in the community?
9. What degree of skill is required?
10. Has there been any difficulty in obtaining labor?
11. Has there been any unusual turnover of personnel in any division of company?
12. What is union affiliation?
13. Is a written labor contract available?
14. What is history of labor relations?
15. To what schools, courses, conferences, or clinics are personnel sent?
16. Give salary structure of key personnel (officers, salesmen, engineers, factory management, and so on).
17. Are aptitude or psychological tests used in hiring personnel?

Competition

1. What is the competitive position of the company?
2. Who are the company's competitors?
3. By line, what share of the market does the company hold?
4. To what extent do unrelated products indirectly compete with company's product?
5. Do competitors have any natural advantages over this company (location, shipping facilities, priority to raw materials)?
6. What recognizable advantages do company and products have over each competitor and their products?
7. What recognizable advantages do competitors and their products have over this company?
8. To what extent is there competition from the so-called "back-alley" or "garage" shops?
9. Do competitors' merchandising methods differ from company's? Explain.

Appendix 5G: Acquisition Announcements

As an example of the type of information that can be readily accessed by computer, a printout follows of merger/acquisition-related announcements of 2 October 1979. The source of this material, selected at random for one date, was Dow Jones News Retrieval.

```
  TI 10/02 LEE ENTERPRISES INC COMPLETES
     (D-W)   ACQUISITION OF 4 NEWSPAPERS
  TH 10/02 SEABOARD WORLD SAYS JUSTICE
     (D-W)   STANCE WAS RELEASED IN PROXY
  TG 10/02 ATLANTA NATIONAL TRUST HOLDERS
     (D-W)   APPROVE MERGER INTO ANRET UNIT
  TF 10/02 TRANSAMERICA CORP. BOARD CLEARS
     (D-W)   TENDER OFFER FOR NN CORP.
  TE 10/02 NY TIMES CO COMPLETES PURCHASE
     (DJ )   OF ARKANSAS TV STATION
  TD 10/02 BARBER OIL DIRECTORS SEEK
     (D-W)   CLARIFICATION ON HANSON OFFER
  TC 10/02 AGENCY OPPOSES MERGER OF TIGER
     (D-W)   INTERNATIONAL AND SEABOARD
  TB 10/02 CASTLE & COOKE TO BUY CANNERY,
     (D-W)   OTHER WESTGATE-CALIF. ASSETS



  N  I/TNM    05/49
  TA 10/02 KATY INDUSTRIES ACQUIRES
     (D-W)   W.H.E. WATCH CO.
  SZ 10/02 NEW ENGLAND MERCHANTS COMPLETES
     (DJ )   PURCHASE OF CHATHAM TRUST
  SY 10/02 FAY'S DRUG AGREES TO ACQUIRE
     (D-W)   SOME ASSETS OF N.C. DRUG CHAIN
  SX 10/02 ZENITH RADIO COMPLETES PURCHASE
     (D-W)   OF SCHLUMBERGER UNIT
  SW 10/02 POSNER-CONTROLLED FIRMS BOOST
     (D-W)   STAKE IN HOWELL INDUSTRIES
  SV 10/02 TAPPAN IN MERGER TALKS; CALLS
     (D-W)   THEM 'VERY, VERY TENTATIVE'
  SU 10/02 HUNT INTL COMPLETES MERGER
     (D-W)   WITH PLANET INVESTMENT UNIT



  ST 10/02 FTC WON'T NOW BLOCK HUGHES TOOL
     (D-W)   TENDER OFFER FOR OIL BASE INC.
  SS 10/02 REMINGTON ARMS CLEARS SWEETENED
     (D-W)   MERGER OFFER -2-
  SR 10/02 NATIONAL LIBERTY SAYS RUMORS
     (DJ )   OF SALE ARE UNFOUNDED
  SQ 10/02 PACIFIC LUMBER, BROOKS SCANLON
     (D-W)   CALL OFF FURTHER MERGER TALKS
```

```
 N   I/TNM     06/49
SP  10/02 REMINGTON ARMS CLEARS SWEETENED
    (D-W)   MERGER OFFER FROM DU PONT CO.
SO  10/02 RAYTHEON - BEECH AIR MERGER
    (D-W)   PACT -2-
SN  10/02 RAYTHON, BEECH AIRCRAFT
    (D-W)   ANNOUNCE MERGER PACT
SM  10/02 NAPCO INDUSTRIES COMPLETES
    (DJ )   ACQUISITION OF J.D. WILLIAMS
SL  10/02 HEARD ON STREET: MERGER AND
    (WSJ)   BUYBACKS SAID A SPUR TO PRICES
```

6 Alternative-Futures Procedures and Their Application to Acquisition and Corporate Development

Martin L. Ernst

Introduction and Background

This chapter introduces the topic of alternative-futures procedures. Increasingly, this powerful tool is being used in acquisition and corporate-development planning as a supplement to, or an extension of, existing, more conventional approaches.

In recent years, there has been growing recognition of the need to improve procedures for helping businesses develop longer-range planning systems and deal with acquisition and investment-decision issues. Traditionally, most of these have been based on forecasting what the expected future will be and then developing plans for this "most likely future." Unfortunately, the pace of change has accelerated throughout the world; more and more businessmen are recognizing that no one can forecast the future accurately enough so that this forecast, *by itself*, can be used as an adequate base for long-range planning or acquisition analysis. This arises because even the most carefully constructed "most-likely future" (or, more broadly, the set of closely related or similar futures that the most-likely future can be considered as representing) has a low probability of occurrence—and is only slightly more likely than many other, and quite different, representative futures.

There are many reasons for this. The most important, probably, are two related factors: the speed with which our current social, economic, and technological environments can alter direction and the tremendous extent to which our world has become so interconnected that important events in any one area cannot be isolated from those in most other areas. This means that an industry or organization can suffer major impacts from what previously would have been considered relatively remote trends or events.

Basically, an organization can undertake only two sets of activities to deal with future uncertainty. It can attempt to reduce uncertainty through forecasting, and/or it can seek means to live better with the residual uncertainty. The preceding discussion suggests that in this somewhat unstable and highly interactive world, the best of forecasting has very severe limits in providing a sound base for long-range planning. The companion approach—learning how best to cope with residual uncertainty—has had application in some specialized industries (such as the use of portfolio techniques in the management of securities investments) but has had limited explicit application elsewhere.

To deal with this situation, at least three elements must be incorporated in planning tools:

1. The use of not just a *single* most-likely future, but, rather, a *set* of alternative plausible futures for analyzing business threats and opportunities.
2. The use of techniques for incorporating a wide range of trends and possible events, in order to become more sensitive to the possible impacts of our current world interconnectedness.
3. The use of analysis methods that can handle a variety of strategy-related questions, and can help to sort out the kinds of steps that are desirable under almost all circumstances—since they appear robust in the face of a variety of potential futures—from other activities that are highly dependent on the particular type of future that evolves.

The result is an analysis that both establishes perspectives for long-range planning and provides a set of guidelines for the development of explicit strategies, including that of acquisition.

The alternative-futures techniques described in the following section have been developed in an effort to find an efficient and disciplined way to meet the preceding requirements.

Procedures

Our alternative-futures procedures involve the following steps:

1. Development of a data base and "base case."
2. Selection of alternative futures to study.
3. Construction of futures scenarios.
4. Construction of a "questions/futures matrix."
5. Cross-futures analysis.
6. Application

Data Base and Base Case

To provide breadth of coverage, we start with existing data bases that describe expected trends in technological, technoeconomic, sociocultural, national economic, regulatory, and international areas. These data bases are updated as necessary and are tailored to meet the needs of a particular situation. Even more important, the driving forces that are responsible for many of the changes under way in the world are related to the data-base trends. Over time, we have developed a number of explanatory models that are useful in relating broad social thrusts to events of importance to business. One example would be a conceptual model relating "egalitarianism" to (1) the external conditions that have led to its great growth in recent years and (2) the manner in which this thrust influences environmental protection, corporate governance, individual attitudes, drives for greater personal security, problems of individual and group "identity," and other factors of social importance. Other explanatory models used frequently deal with: (1) factors influencing the adoption of different types of regulatory postures by governments and (2) factors influencing the spread of technological innovations and the nature of the byproducts created by that spreading process.

As part of this first step, it is also necessary to study the particular industry or industries of which the candidate company is a part. This part of the analysis establishes: the nature of the industry; the primary factors that influence costs, markets and profitability; the technological, economic, and social factors most likely to influence its growth in the future; and similar factors.

The material from the data bases is used to establish a base case, which represents the most-likely future; this serves as a point of departure for studying alternatives.

Selection of Alternative Futures

The most efficient way we have found for studying alternative futures is deliberately to select future *end states* (brief "pictures" of a particular future state of affairs) that are of importance to the subject under study. These end states are carefully selected to provide combinations of the variables most critically influencing the future operations of the company or industry under study. Therefore, they cover characteristics such as:

1. More or less international interactivity (trade, investment flows, and so forth).
2. The style of government intervention in the private sector (more bureaucracy, or more like "Japan, Inc.").
3. The success or failure of specific institutions of major importance (such as the European Economic Community).
4. The level of availability and costs of key resources (energy and particular raw materials).
5. Higher or lower economic-activity levels.

The selections of variables and variable combinations (combinations of factors such as the foregoing) are based on the sensitivities of a company or industry as determined during the studies involved in developing the base case in step 1.

Construction of Futures Scenarios

The function of the futures scenarios is to describe how we might get from the current state of affairs to each of the previously defined future end states. The scenarios, therefore, deal with subjects such as sources of all types of changes; means of overcoming, or reasons for being defeated by, barriers to change; building facilitating mechanisms or being unable to do so; and so forth. Again, in the interests of efficiency, we have found that it is not necessary to build traditional scenarios in the form of detailed stories, although we have employed these and found them useful in some circumstances. For most types of investigations, however, the primary process involves developing lists of events and measures that will permit movement toward the future end states. The process involved is an iterative one; some of the consequences of the preconditions are used to describe the future in more detail, and the more detailed description is used to determine additional preconditions or features. More explicitly, we iterate through four sets of questions:

1. What will this future be like? How will I be able to recognize that I have "arrived" there?
2. What kinds of things must happen in order for us to move to this future? What side effects or other future characteristics will arise from these preconditions?
3. Do the combinations of preconditions make sense in terms of the driving forces and models developed in step 1? Do we deliberately wish to (or have to) ignore or counter some of these forces—and for what reasons?
4. Do we have enough material yet to deal with the questions of interest?

Construction of Questions/Futures Matrix

Once a future has been fairly well characterized, it becomes possible to "ask questions" of it and to answer these questions. The questions can cover a wide range of subjects, but generally they are established to help search for commonalities and differences among the processes and events necessary to reach different end states and the organizational and business practices most desirable for each. At this point, particular interests and requirements relating to a client company, an industry, or a specific acquisition candidate become dominant factors. The questions typically deal with subjects such as:

The types of products and product lines most apt to be successful in a given future.

The management and professional-staff skills of greatest importance.

The role of governmental relationships and the types most influencing business success.

Particular financing requirements and problems likely to be encountered in obtaining them.

Key technologies to be exploited or avoided.

The question-development process is entirely open ended—new questions may be added at any time. The various questions and their answers are presented in the form of a matrix.

Cross-Futures Analysis

The matrix now is employed in a cross-futures analysis during which comparisons are made to deal with subjects such as:

What questions appear to be relatively future-invariant in terms of having pretty much the same answer no matter what future evolves?

What questions have answers that vary radically across the different futures?

What types of events appear critical to the evolution of a particular future? What types of events influence several or even all of them?

Application

Each application is likely to have its own unique requirements. In some cases, an assignment can end with very limited interpretation of the output of the cross-futures analysis; this would be appropriate, for example, if the only objective has been to provide environmental-background information. In other cases, extensive interpretation of the material may be required, or the results may become one of the inputs employed in a strategy-development process.

In still other situations, the material may enter directly into an investment or acquisition decision-making activity, or lead to the development of new market-segmentation concepts or organization structures.

Generally, in management-strategy planning, the role of alternative futures is best seen as one of establishing the environmental guidelines within which strategy will be developed. Thus this technique is a predecessor of and a complement to more traditional strategic-planning techniques, rather than being competitive with them. In fact, many elements and much of the knowledge gained in more traditional strategy planning are employed in the alternative-futures process—first, in the development of explanatory models and, later, in developing answers to the questions asked in the futures matrixes (both procedures described previously).

For corporate-development planning and specific industry and acquisition-candidate evaluation, step 4 (questions/futures matrix) and step 5 (cross-futures analysis) provide a basis for evaluating the prospects for and viability of specific courses of action and investment decisions under a variety of carefully selected plausible futures—not just the one that is considered most likely to occur.

Finally, the key events described in step 3 (the futures scenarios) provide a starting point for the development of a monitoring or evaluation system. This system can be used to track the extent to which the future actually evolves toward a particular end state (or toward something new that requires addition of a new end state to those that have been analyzed), and to provide warning as to when activation of contingency plans might become desirable in response to future events which, for example, would unfavorably affect a specific business.

Application Example

Since alternative futures techniques provide a framework and a discipline rather than a monolithic methodology, elements of them have been used in a variety of strategy-development and acquisition-analysis tasks.

The following example illustrates one of the roles that can be played by these procedures. The situation, based on an actual acquisition that took place recently, involved consideration of a presently successful and rapidly growing company in the mass merchandising/direct marketing of a financial-service product. Conventional analysis put the proposed transaction in a favorable light. The major unresolved issue was the longer-term-growth and future potential of the particular mass-merchandising/direct-marketing approaches pioneered and emphasized by the firm.

For the most part, established companies employ other marketing techniques, some of which are much more labor and energy intensive and of a much more "personalized" and traditional nature. Although there are very few differences in the product lines offered by the candidate company and its competitors, the particular marketing techniques employed can lead to different purchaser-selection patterns within the product lines.

Alternative-futures procedures were used to address the question of the future viability of the company's unique marketing methods, in which it had a proprietary position. After developing a data base and a "base case" (step 1), the many factors that could influence the relative viability of the unique marketing approach were examined. It was determined that the influences of these factors could be displayed effectively in terms of three key variables: the inflation rate; the future economic-growth rate; and the level and nature of government regulation of the industry. On this basis, four specific futures were selected for study, characterized as:

Future 1
A high inflation rate; no significant economic growth; strong government intervention in a bureaucratic mode (for example, relatively detailed regulation of industry operations).

Future 2
High inflation rate; moderate economic growth; high government-bureaucratic involvement.

Future 3
Low inflation rate; no economic growth; low level of bureaucratic measures in government interventions.

Future 4
Low inflation rate; moderate economic growth; low government-bureaucratic intervention.

The four futures are illustrated in the form of a "map" in figure 6-1.

For step 3, four brief "scenarios" were developed dealing with the viability of the unique marketing approach, given that the conditions of each specific future came into existence. Elements incorporated in the scenarios included: new types of savings and investment vehicles appropriate for the different future conditions; competition among financial institutions; appropriate roles of sales agents or brokers; trends in household composition and age distribution; trends in affluence and consumer spending patterns; energy costs; alternative means for purchasing financial services; and so on. Each of these elements was viewed as varying in form, size, or importance according to the nature of the future.

These elements were then examined in the context of the different futures to determine the relative importance of specific attributes that contribute to the effectiveness of the five marketing approaches under study.

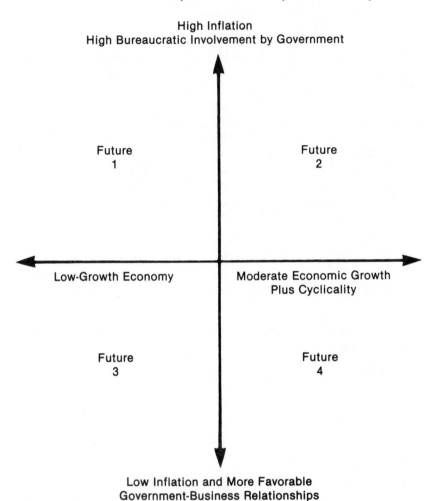

High Inflation
High Bureaucratic Involvement by Government

Future
1

Future
2

Low-Growth Economy

Moderate Economic Growth
Plus Cyclicality

Future
3

Future
4

Low Inflation and More Favorable
Government-Business Relationships

Figure 6-1. Four-Futures Map

Among the attributes were: brand identification, "personalization," and potential for future diversification/innovation. These last items, plus a number of others, were given "scores" for each of the specific future/ marketing-method combinations. These scores made up what amounts to step 4—the answers developed for the questions/futures matrix. The cross-futures analysis was developed by totaling the scores of the five possible marketing techniques against the separate futures. This represented step 5 of the procedure.

The proposed acquisition was a major decision for the buying company and represented a substantial commitment of capital. Thus it was particularly important to minimize risks of failure, even at the expense of some profit potential. The results of the cross-futures analysis showed that the marketing approach of the acquisition candidate, which was the distinguishing characteristic of the company within the industry, was viable under all of the four futures considered. Although it represented the best approach for only one of the futures, and was not the best overall if the different approaches are averaged across all the futures studied, in every instance it was acceptable in the judgment of the acquiring organization. Thus the acquisition decision could be supported on the basis that the acquirer could live with the future uncertainties associated with a set of futures that covered the variables considered to be of most importance for its industry.

This conclusion is illustrated in table 6-1, which also points out that other approaches may be more promising under some particular futures, but would be unsatisfactory under others.

Table 6-1
Simplified Cross-Futures Matrix: Ranking of Marketing Techniques, by Future for Specific Financial-Services Product

Future	Marketing/Merchandising as Represented by Candidate Company	Marketing Technique			
		Traditional Sales Office with Commission Salesmen	"Add on" to Other Financial Services or to Other Retail Sales	Door to Door	Newer Wholesale Methods
Future 1	5.6	5.0	6.6	2.0	7.0
Future 2	7.0	7.0	9.0	3.0	9.0
Future 3	5.6	5.4	4.0	2.4	5.0
Future 4	6.4	7.0	5.6	3.4	7.0
Average for 4 futures	6.2	6.1	6.3	2.7	7.0
Range over 4 futures	5.6-7.0	5.0-7.0	4.0-9.0	2.0-3.4	5.0-9.0

Notes: (1) A score of less than 5.0 in any future was considered unsatisfactory and too risky. (2) Scores in each future represent summary totals from assessment of a large number of factors against each future and marketing technique.

7

Valuation of Companies

Introduction

This chapter describes in some detail and includes several examples of the various approaches often employed in valuing acquisitions. Toward the end of the chapter, a specific example is presented illustrating the interrelationship of these methods in arriving at a fair market value.

A corporation's decision to acquire or merge with another corporation is a capital-budgeting as well as a strategic decision. That is, it is a long-range investment decision, made within the framework of the firm's process of planning expenditures whose returns are expected to extend beyond one accounting period. In theory, the principal duty of management is to make decisions that will likely maximize the value of the firm's common stock; and, in oversimplified terms, the firm should attempt to operate at the point where its marginal rate of return on investment equals its marginal cost of capital.[1] However, as Brealey and Myers point out, "Strategic planning is really capital budgeting on a grand scale . . . [and] deals in intangibles."[2]

Here, the capital-budgeting process thus involves ranking the spectrum of investment opportunities and proposals according to various quantitative *and* qualitative criteria; it necessitates forecasts, as well as assessments of the firm's flow of funds, competitive position, and risks. Capital is allocated among the various alternatives selected—in a manner analogous to the process an investment manager uses to construct a portfolio. However, the commitment of corporate capital to plant and equipment or to acquisition of another operating business results in asset ownership that lacks the liquidity and reversibility of a portfolio of investment securities.

In the United States most of the output of goods and services in the private sector is produced by publicly owned corporations under professional operating management. The shares of the larger corporations are typically widely held and freely traded on the organized stock exchanges, and the shares of many other publicly owned corporations trade in the over-the-counter market. The U.S. securities markets are well developed. In this setting, corporate management, which is accountable to shareholders through an elected board of directors, generally (although not always) pursues policies and strategies designed to increase the value of the firm to shareholders. Because individual or institutional investors normally do not own enough stock in any one large corporation to control management substantially, shareholders who are dissatisfied with the management normally would sell their holdings in the company and seek opportunities for gain elsewhere.

By its very nature, the corporate investor must make a longer-term commitment, implying a longer forecast horizon and greater risk than the portfolio manager typically assumes. Moreover, the corporate investor normally has operating control over the corporate asset(s) acquired. In the context of acquisition, this makes possible large disparities in the subjective valuation of the shares of candidate companies as seen by the corporation vis-à-vis valuation as seen by the passive investor or portfolio manager. (See the discussion at the end of chapter 2.)

We believe that large disparities in asset valuation—between active corporate investors on the one hand, and the typically passive institutional or individual investor on the other hand—account for much of the current acquisition and merger activity. Of course, some transactions reflect opportunities arising from divestitures, as well as normal "background" activity associated with growth and change in various industries.

Scope

The new direction in valuation combines the techniques of economic forecasting, strategic profiling, capital budgeting, and capital-market theory, as illustrated in figure 7-1. The result provides an improved insight and framework for valuation, in which the concepts of risk and return are properly related.

Subjective considerations are still very important in theory, and even more so in practice. These include perceptions of synergistic effects, furtherance of corporate "citizenship," and merger concepts thought to appeal to the investor. However, the achievement of higher total cash flow and/or more predictable cash flow, with higher resultant market value of the firm, is usually the only financial basis for an acquisition.

The negotiating strategy, which reflects the time horizons, risk/return preferences, and experiences of the parties to the transaction, is also colored by emotional factors such as optimism, pessimism, and ego. Thus there is normally no one value; rather, there is a floor, a ceiling price, and a range of reasonableness for negotiation of a deal between the buyer(s) and seller(s).

This chapter first presents a broad view of the subject and the variety of techniques used in valuing a business. It emphasizes the approaches used to determine what a business or a company is worth, that is, to put a price tag on the stock or assets.

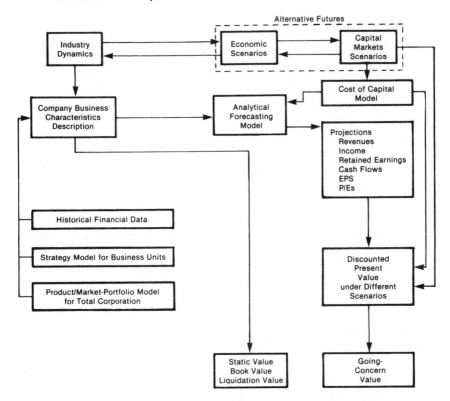

Figure 7-1. The Valuation Process for Acquisitions

Jack L. Treynor, editor of *Financial Analysts Journal*, points out that the main problem in the valuation of businesses is forecasting cash flows. He observes that most investment value derives from the economic rents on productive assets. "An asset has to be scarce before it generates rents." The problem of discounting future rents is one of predicting scarcities, which is also a problem then of predicting capacity entry into an industry. In this framework, value deals entirely with the future, with what is known or can be known. Treynor refers to a "Druckeresque" notion, the "futurity of competitive conditions." In this sense, physical assets and accounting "have nothing to do with value."[3]

Moreover, Treynor asserts that it is now becoming clear that there is enough pattern and shared structure in such important areas as financial strategy[4] and competitive strategy[5] that comparative advantage in such areas belongs to the analyst rather than the corporate executive. "At the present, the principal obstacle to an emancipated conception of the analysts' role is the thinking habits traditionally associated with accounting-centered security analysis."

Valuation Contexts

The following list presents the situations likely to be of interest:

1. Placing a "fair market value" on a going concern (the test used by the Internal Revenue Service and the Courts is that this represents a negotiated price between a willing buyer and a willing seller, both being informed of the facts):
   a. For an acquirer to develop a negotiation strategy.
   b. For potential acquirer seeking to convince candidate that acquisition is attractive.
   c. For seller to provide an offering memorandum for sale or divestiture.
   d. For a parent company to satisfy minority shareholders in merger of two subsidiaries.
   e. For management to satisfy the Board that a fair price was obtained.
2. Other purposes:
   a. Postacquisition or merger allocations of purchase price to specific tangible and intangible assets.
   b. Partnership settlements or partial liquidations.
   c. Evaluation of public offerings, refinancings, or capitalizations.
   d. Administration of incentive compensation and stock-option programs.
   e. Settlement of minority-shareholder claims.
   f. Estate settlement.

In the acquisition and corporate-development context, the value of an operating business is solely a function of its prospects. Uncertainties regarding the firm's future financial performance involve market forces, technological developments, raw-material supplies, labor costs, capital availability, competitive strategies, and the investment climate. All these factors must be reliably assessed; conclusions must not be based only on historical performance, balance-sheet appraisals, or apparent equivalent market-price relationships.

Financial factors to be addressed in valuation begin with accounting and reporting practices and include sales growth, operating margins, earnings, cash flow, return on investment, and competitive environment. In most cases, valuations are based at least in part on projections of future cash flow discounted to present value. Book values and appropriate adjustments are considered. Liquidation value and hidden assets may be taken into account. Where feasible, comparable-company stock-market prices and earnings multiples are assessed. Thinly traded issues and other market factors, if applicable, are evaluated. We thus have several valuation contexts and approaches.

Approach

Consider several methods of valuation:

1. Liquidation value (the floor).
2. Book value (a reference).
3. Public-market value.
4. Public-market value of related firms.
5. Acquisition values of related firms.
6. Normalized price-to-earnings ratio times current normalized earnings.
7. Present value of expected cash flow.

We shall emphasize the last of these methods. The rest rely on historical information. But since in most acquisitions, one is "buying the future," one needs to estimate how it will differ from the past. Thus, depending on the views of the parties, more or less attention is paid to historically based values. Negotiated price tends to fall between a future-based (uncertain) valuation and historically (certain) based results.

We may group the factors to consider in valuation as follows:

1. General:
   a. Status and trends of the national economy.
   b. Status and trends of the relevant industry(ies).
   c. Status and trends of the securities markets.
   d. Fiscal policy of the government.
   e. Regulatory policy of the government.
   f. Tax and accounting regulations and procedures.
2. Specific considerations:
   a. Purpose of the valuation (for example, acquisition, divestiture, stock-option plan).
   b. Nature of the business or asset (manufacturing, service, real estate).
   c. Known strengths and weaknesses:
      (1) Historical performance (sales, profits, investments, dividends, cash flow).
      (2) Competitive position (dominant, follower).
      (3) Technological position (knowhow, patents).

(4) Quality of earnings (operations, speculation, cyclicality).
(5) Management continuity.
(6) Asset condition and adequacy:
    (a) Tangibles
    (b) Intangibles.
3. Quantitative versus qualitative treatment required.

Techniques

Normalizing Financial Data

When one is analyzing company financial data, it is usually necessary to normalize figures both for purposes of intertemporal comparisons of the same business and for intercompany and interindustry comparisons in a given time period.

The balance sheet is examined to estimate normal amounts and ratios for the ongoing business (at a particular level of sales). Current ratio, inventory, plant and equipment carrying values, status of pension funding, use of leverage, are some of the areas of important differences. The income statement requires analysis for the distortions that are produced by "nonrecurring" items such as plant closings, by foreign-currency fluctuations, or by changes in tax accruals. Thus adjustments may be made that add to normalized value or deduct from normalized value. Security analysts and financial analysts following the companies in question can provide valuable insights in this process, which is aimed at estimating, as accurately as possible, the worth of a company in terms of assets and their sustainable earning power.

Present Value of Cash Flows

This refers to a "standard" capital-budgeting technique with which we presume most readers are familiar. However, this is a difficult and controversial area, in which what is evolving is itself a merger between capital budgeting and modern capital-market theory. In short, there is a net present value (NPV) associated with investing in a business, which is determined by its expected net cash flow (CF) to the investor, discounted at the opportunity cost of capital, r (for a business of like risk), over the future time horizon N:

$$\text{NPV} = \sum_{t=0}^{N} \left[\frac{(CF)_t}{(1 + r)^t} \right]$$

For convenience in the calculations, r is usually treated as a constant. One can handle variable rs by estimating an $\bar{r}$ as the effective weighted average; or by expressing the cash flows as *certainty equivalents* and using the average risk-free rate of interest as the discount rate (see also chapters 2 and 9). The above expression is often written inclusive of the Net Present Value of the Investment, which is the algebraic sum of the present value of all cash flows expected, including the initial investment outlay, I_0, to acquire the business or investment position.

$$NPV = (NPV)_{business} - I_0$$

Many well-known problems arise at this point, such as where to get the data to use in long-term projections (for very large N), or how to estimate the residual value, if one projects out only a relatively small number of years.

We find it most effective to work with five- to ten-year financial forecasts, using three economic scenarios. This generates an optimistic, pessimistic, and most-likely environment; and a high (H), low (L), and moderate (M) outcome, to which one can assign subjective probabilities, P. The expected value is then the probability-weighted average of these three outcomes:

$$PV = P_H(PV)_H + P_L(PV)_L + P_M(PV)_M$$

Another problem lies in attempting to agree on what discount rate is appropriate (r in the present-value summation of the previous expression).

Care should be taken in setting up the financial projections on an internally consistent basis. If constant dollars rather than current dollars are used, the discount rate should be, similarly, a constant-dollar cost of capital.

Most businessmen will have difficulty in reconciling historic perceptions of cost of capital with the new realities in an inflationary, multinational corporate setting. That is, estimates by financial economists such as Burton Malkiel at Princeton University indicate the real pretax rate of return on total capital to be on the order of 11 percent in the United States, with real after-tax return on equity around 7 percent or so. With inflation and perceptions of prospective above-average risk for a new venture, the discount rate will be on the order of 20 percent in current-dollar terms, or 10 percent in constant dollars. It will be even higher if one uses earnings before taxes and interest (EBIT) as the measure of return. Such high discount rates, of course, may tend to penalize projects in which returns are deferred to future periods; that is, they discourage the really long-term investment—the type that may be crucial for the future health of the business.

Alfred Rappaport, writing in the July-August 1979 issue of *Harvard*

Business Review, has presented a very complete illustration of the use of the discounted-cash-flow (DCF) technique in acquisition valuations. In his approach, the annual net cash flow from a business being evaluated is formulated straightforwardly—from sales, profit, and investment ratios—as: cash flow = net income plus interest plus depreciation, less capital-expenditure requirements and less working-capital requirements. This stream is projected out the number of years that mangement feels it can confidently expect growth and/or financial parameters to meet a minimum acceptable rate-of-return criterion. He advocates estimating the present value of business beyond that point in terms of an annuity (perpetuity) equivalent. Most precisely, the forecast duration for cash flows should continue only as long as the expected rate of return on incremental investment required to support forecasted sales growth exceeds the cost-of-capital rate.

If for subsequent periods one assumes that the company's return on incremental investment equals the cost-of-capital rate, then presumably the market would be indifferent to whether management invests earnings in expansion projects or pays cash dividends that shareholders can in turn invest in identically risky opportunities yielding an identical rate-of-return. In other words, the value of the company is (theoretically) unaffected by growth when the company is investing in projects earning at the cost of capital or at the minimum acceptable risk-adjusted rate of return required by the market.

Thus, for purposes of simplification, Rappaport would assume a 100-percent payout of earnings after the horizon date or, equivalently, a zero growth rate, without affecting the valuation of the company. (An implied assumption of this model is that the depreciation tax shield can be invested to maintain the company's productive capacity.) The residual value is then the present value of the resulting cash-flow perpetuity beginning one year after the horizon date. If, after the horizon date, the return on investment is expected to decline below the cost-of-capital rate, then this factor can be incorporated in the calculation.

The minimum pretax return on sales (P_{min}) needed to earn the minimum acceptable rate of return (K) on the acquisition, given the investment requirements for working capital (w) and fixed assets (f) for each additional dollar of sales, and given a projected tax rate (T) is:

$$P_{min} = \frac{(f + w)K}{(1 - T)(1 - K)}$$

The duration of a financial forecast for the acquisition would be limited to that period for which management has enough confidence to forecast pretax sales returns above P_{min}.[6]

Other elements of the acquisition valuation approach illustrated by Rappaport are:

1. Use of alternative scenarios to indicate sensitivity to different assumptions.
2. Use of weighted-average cost of debt and equity capital appropriate to the business at hand, as the discount rate for the present value of cash flows (where cash flow *includes* interest). Interest cost on debt is net of tax effect, for cost-of-capital purposes. Cost of equity capital is keyed to market rate-of-return and risk factors.
3. Calculation of the pro forma earnings-per-share impact of the acquisition under various assumptions as to terms and conditions.
4. Calculation of the effect on consolidated debt position and debt capacity, under various terms and conditions.
5. Comparison of acquisition for cash versus an exchange of stock.

Table 7-1 illustrates a typical worksheet to examine the pro forma impact of an acquisition deal. Note that the last three items of the foregoing list do not affect the going-concern valuation of the target business.

In theory, if no better alternative is available and the present value of the cash flow is greater than the cost to acquire, then the acquisition investment should be undertaken—regardless of the immediate impact on reported earnings—because the capital market is not fooled by short-term accounting effects and will figure out the incremental wealth of the firm resulting from such an acquisition.[7] However, as has been pointed out earlier, it is often difficult for management and directors to give enough weight to the long-run as opposed to the short-term financial impact of an acquisition. In any case, an acquisition involves a dynamic interaction of several business and market factors, none of which usually reflects long-run equilibrium values and other assumptions usually made in studying the theory of the firm. Thus, for example, it is important to examine the pro forma consolidated capital structure, since one cannot assume it is necessarily optimal; and this examination has a feedback effect on the valuation process.

The Cost of Equity Capital

The discount rate obviously has a major effect on the present value that is calculated for the acquisition in question. Hence, the cost of capital is always a major issue. There is a vast literature on this subject, and we comment here on the contemporary use of, and controversy over the use of, the

Table 7-1
Acquirer and Target: Pro Forma Analysis of Proposed Deal

	100%-Cash Offer	50% Common, 50% Cash	100% Common Stock
Per-share	$ 53.4	$ 53.4	$ 53.4
total value ($ millions)	525.7	525.7	525.7
Cash ($ millions)	525.7	262.85	—
Common Stock ($ millions)	—	262.85	525.7
P/E current	10.0×	10.0×	10.0×
Outstanding shares			
(million-fully diluted)			
Acquirer[a]	12.00	12.00	12.00
Target[b]	—	2.63	5.26
Pro forma	12.00	14.63	17.26
Full year—1981			
Earnings ($ millions)			
Acquirer	167.7	167.7	167.7
Target[c]	51.0	51.0	51.0
	218.7	218.7	218.7
Less: Interest foregone[d]	(3.2)	(3.2)	—
Interest to finance[e]	(28.3)	(12.6)	—
New goodwill	—	—	—
Pro forma	187.2	202.9	218.7
Earnings per share-fully diluted			
Acquirer	13.98	13.98	13.98
Pro forma	15.60	13.87	12.67
Acquisition effect (dilution)	1.62	(0.11)	(1.31)
Percentage increase in EPS	11.6%	(0.8%)	(9.3%)

[a] Based on a price of $100 per share.

[b] Based on 9.58 million common shares outstanding, plus 270,000 outstanding common-stock options.

[c] Assumes target earns $5.32 per share in current year.

[d] Assumes acquirer would earn 6.0 percent effective after tax-rate on surplus cash held of $53 million (10 percent of acquisition amount).

[e] Assumes 6.0 percent effective after tax on short-term borrowings; 6.0 percent effective after-tax rate on long-term borrowings contemplated to finance transaction.

so-called beta coefficient β of a stock in determination of the cost of equity capital. The usual model is the capital-asset pricing model (CAPM), as follows. (All values are expected (ex ante) values.)

Cost of equity capital = risk-free rate of interest
+ $\beta \times$ (stock market rate of return
− risk-free rate of interest)

The second term is the equity risk premium.

Usually, current-dollar financial projections are used. Then:

risk-free rate = rate of interest in constant dollars + inflation rate.

The values of β are usually derived by regressing individual security rate-of-return data against the return on a stock-market index (usually the S&P 500 stock index) as a proxy for the market.

Controversy exists as a result of low regression coefficients and instabilities in the measured values of βs over time. In addition, the capital-asset pricing model from which β is derived is only a one-period rate-of-return model, whereas corporate acquisitions are capital-budgeting decisions requiring a multiperiod analysis. Usually the appropriate risk/return parameters for this multiperiod analysis cannot easily be derived from historic one-period data using the CAPM unless one makes a host of assumptions.[8]

A related complicating factor is that the true return on the total market portfolio is itself not observable, as pointed out in the important recent work of Richard Roll.[9] Despite these limitations, there seems to be increasing use of stock "betas" in the above form to approximate the cost of equity capital.

Another model is derived from the Gordon-Shapiro long-run growth model of the firm.[10] This is expressed as follows:

Expected average cost of equity capital =
current dividend yield + sustainable growth rate

For a zero-growth situation, with all earnings paid out as dividends, this model reduces to the familiar and important perpetuity relation:

$$\text{Cost of equity} = \frac{1}{P/E}$$

Such analytical expressions suffer from the lack of information about investor expectations and future financial-performance capabilities of the firm.

Since most of the rate of return from holding stocks per se is usually expected in the form of price appreciation, we should keep in mind the fundamental tautology:

$$\text{Stock price} = \frac{\text{Price}}{\text{Earnings}} \times \text{Earnings}$$

Call stock price P, earnings E, and price-to-earnings ratio P/E. Then,

$$P = (P/E) \cdot (E)$$

The derivative of this is:

$$dP = (E) \cdot d(P/E) + (P/E) \cdot dE$$

Dividing by P,

$$\frac{dP}{P} = \frac{d(P/E)}{P/E} + \frac{dE}{E}$$

This may be expressed as:

$$\text{Percentage change in stock price} = \text{Percentage change in } P/E$$
$$+ \text{ Percentage change in } E$$

Because of the tautology, this must hold both ex ante and ex post. The ex ante value changes (expectations) are captured implicitly in the capital-asset pricing model (CAPM) and the dividend-discount model (see later on). The ex post values are simple arithmetic.

Weighting Systems

Weighting of the various factors, both subjective and objective, allows one to qualify the overall valuation of a company. Thus one could assign numerical "scores" or weights to various selection criteria, as illustrated in chapter 5, in order to compare companies.

Investment bankers and consultants often weight reported earnings performance over the last five years by assigning weights of 5, 4, 3, 2, and 1, respectively, to the most-recent year, the next-most-recent year, and so on. Assigning subjective probabilities to financial outcomes and determining an overall, expected value is also a weighting procedure.

The weighted average score or ranking, rather than the raw data, is then used as the input for further analyses and comparisons. Thus, for example, the valuation may be determined through normalization and weighting procedures as follows:

Price/Share $=$ Normalized P/E $\times$ Weighted average earnings per share

The foregoing is the historical approach. The following is a future-oriented valuation approach.

$$\text{Expected value} = p_1\, (PV)_{\text{Scenario}_1} + p_2\, (PV)_{\text{Scenario}_2} + \cdots$$
$$p_j\, (PV)_{\text{Scenario}_j} + \cdots$$

where $p_j =$ Subjective probability of occurrence.

                       $PV =$ Present value of future business cash flows.

and

$$\sum_j p_j = 1$$

Valuation Models

There are a number of valuation models in use by security analysts, investment institutions, investment banking firms, and management consultants which apply to the valuation of publicly owned common stocks. (The techniques are applicable to valuation of any stock, but the parameters are derived from the financial and market performance data for stocks of publicly owned corporations.) Before we discuss them, it is helpful to review some fundamental financial and growth relationships for a business as illustrated by tables 7-2 and 7-3. Although these suggest an over-simplified picture, they do provide a perspective on the importance of return on equity and the use of leverage, behind the apparent growth in corporate earnings. That is, it is important to distinguish between growth due to inherent profitability (with no debt) and that due to leveraging. At the same time, in modern corporate-finance theory it is important to take advantage of prudent leveraging, due to the worth of the tax shield associated with interest charges on debt.

Many stock-valuation models have appeared in the literature (see, for example, the *Financial Analysts Journal*). Since most of the corporate acquisition activity of interest focuses on acquiring the stock of other publicly held corporations, we shall comment on them here.

The Dividend Discount Model. This widely used model is the mathematical equivalent of calculating the true yield on a bond using discounted cash flow over the period to maturity (or redemption). It is attributed to John Burr Williams, in his classic *Theory of Investment Value*.[11] The calculation is the same as the foregoing present-value calculation, except that dividends over a projected time horizon are used as the measure of return to the in-

Table 7-2
Sustainable Growth of a Business: Case A—No Debt

Basis: Assume sales per dollar of assets and profit margin are constant.
Assume there is no external financing.

$$G = (\text{ROE}) (1 - d)$$

where

G = Annual percentage growth sustainable.

ROE = Return on equity.

d = Fraction of earnings paid out in dividends or equivalent.

Example: If $d = 0$, then G = the rate of return on equity. Thus, if ROE = 30 percent and there is no dividend payout, the business can grow at 30 percent per year; if, however, sales grow 60 percent, we would have $0.6 = 0.3 (1 - d)$, and $d = -1$. This means that outside equity capital would have to be supplied, in an amount equal to earnings.

vestor, instead of interest payments or net cash flow generated by the corporation. A residual value is estimated as the price-to-earnings ratio at the end of a forecast period, times the projected earnings at that time.

For a corporate investor, this model can serve as well, assuming the business that is acquired continues its operations as it would have independently. That is, cash flow is reinvested commensurately with the

Table 7-3
Sustainable Growth of a Business: Case B—with Debt (Leveraged)

$$G = (1 - d) \left[(D/E \, (\text{ROA} - I) + (\text{ROA}) \right] , \text{ at constant } D/E.$$

where

D/E = Debt/equity.

ROA = Return on total assets, after taxes.

ROE = $(D/E) (\text{ROA} - I) + \text{ROA}$.

I = Interest rate (net after tax).

d = Fraction of earnings paid out in dividends or equivalent.

Example

$$\text{ROA} = 10$$
$$I = 5$$

If $D/E = 1$, $G = 7.5\%/\text{yr}$, for $d = 50\%$

$$= 15\%/\text{yr}, \text{ for } d = 0\%$$

Note that for G to be constant, debt must be added commensurately with the growth rate so that D/E, the debt-to-equity ratio, also remains constant.

perceived growth prospects of the business, over the same time horizon. This may be a tricky assumption because of the interaction between a business's earning power, growth, and earnings-retention rate. If we have an average return on equity (ROE) (after tax), and if ROE and all other financial ratios remain constant, then the rate of sustainable growth may be calculated as shown in tables 7-2 and 7-3.

The following section illustrates the application of this model to an acquisition situation. For this example, which is fairly typical with respect to time horizon, we chose a ten-year forecasting period and estimated the worth of the acquisition target company (or business under consideration) at the end of that period, that is, the "residual value," using an assumed market capitalization rate and discounting to present value. The assumption is that the investment generates cash during the interim through dividend payments. Reinvested earnings and depreciation are used to fund required capital investments consistent with growth. Debt is assumed to be added to maintain the debt-to-equity ratio.

The approach is analogous to that of the equity investor considering purchase of stock in the target company. The appropriate discount rate here is the risk-adjusted cost of equity capital.

In mathematical terms:

$$I = \text{Investment} = \sum_{n=1}^{10} \frac{(E_A^0)\, d_A\, (1 + g_A)^n}{(1 + r)^n} + \frac{R_V}{(1 + r)^{10}}$$

where: E_A^0 = Initial earnings of acquired company.

I = Initial investment.

d_A = Fraction of earnings paid out by acquired company (effective annualized payment).

g_A = Growth rate in earnings = $\text{ROE}_A\, (1 - d_A)$, assumed for simplicity to be constant over the forecast.

R_V = Residual value at end of ten-year period.

r = Return on investment (ROI) of venture (to be solved for).

$$I = (P/E \text{ paid for target company}) \cdot (E_A^0)$$

Thus:

$$E_A^0 = \frac{I}{(P/E)_{\text{Acquisition}}}$$

$$(P/E)_{\text{Acquisition}} = \frac{I}{E_A^0}$$

If d_A = constant, then

$$P/E_{\text{Acquisition}} = d_A \sum_{n=1}^{10} \left[\frac{(1 + g_A)^n}{(1 + r)^n} \right] + \frac{(1 + g_A)^{10}}{(1 + r)^{10}} (C)$$

Where C = Capitalization rate on "residual" earnings, employed here
for simplicity in the tenth year $[1 \div (P/E)_{10}]$.

The foregoing equation may be solved for r as a function of P/E and g, d_A.
One can thus construct a tradeoff figure, as in figure 7-2.

Figure 7-2 is an example of an analytically simple but operationally useful
illustration in which all earnings are reinvested ($d_A = 0$). It also assumes the
earnings in year 10 are capitalized at a P/E multiple of 10. The figure indicates that under these constraints the ROI of the acquisition varies as a
linear function of the growth rate. Recall, however, that this treatment
assumes return is realized by sale in year 10, or is computed in terms of
market value in year 10 as a proxy for the DCF rate of return realized over a
very long period of future operations.

The candidate business may be examined with the aid of a matrix of
parameter combinations and tradeoffs. The following would indicate conditions associated with a given P/E:

I	E_A^o	P/E	$g_A = \dfrac{(ROE)_A \cdot (1 - d_A)}{ROE \quad\quad d_A}$	ROI
		4		
		8		
		12		
		16		
		20		

Valuation for Estate Purposes. In this section we illustrate the approach to
valuation of a business that was owned by an individual, such ownership
consisting of all the outstanding common and preferred stock. After the individual's death, it was necessary to have an independent, objective value

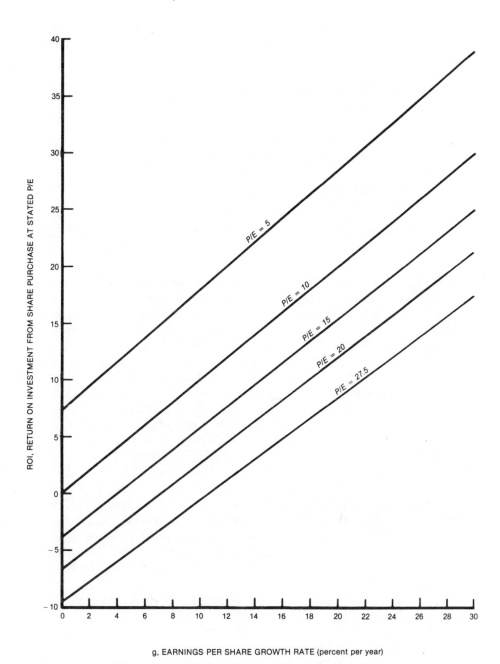

g, EARNINGS PER SHARE GROWTH RATE (percent per year)

Basis: All earnings of acquired business reinvested. Earnings capitalized at 10 percent in year 10 as estimate of market (terminal) value.

Figure 7-2. Hypothetical ROI as Function of Growth of Acquisition and Acquisition Price per Dollar of Earnings (P/E)

placed on the corporation for estate and tax purposes. Litigation was involved, and an appraiser was appointed. The appraiser prepared the valuation, taking into account:

1. History and nature of the corporation.
2. Dividend history.
3. Prior sales of stock (purchase prices).
4. Operations and earnings record, balance sheet.
5. Price-to-earnings ratio of publicly owned companies similar to the corporation.
6. Market- versus book-value considerations.
7. Marketability factors (regarding the absence of a public market for the stock).
8. For the preferred stock, yields on industrial issues, liquidating value of the preferred, marketability.

The preceding factors are substantially the valuation factors listed in the Internal Revenue Code and Regulations. *Revenue Ruling 59-60* (59-60) is intended as a guide in valuing closely held stock or stock of corporations where market quotations are either lacking or not indicative of fair values for the purpose intended. In determining for income-tax purposes the fair market value of stock in closely held companies, 59-60 includes factors recognized by the courts and the appraisal profession. However, the ruling notes that there is no single formula that can be applied to all cases. Indeed, variations are found between IRS recommendations and the factors considered in tax-court cases. Historical earnings and prior sales of stock are two of the recommended IRS factors most frequently used, however.

The notion of a premium for control is firmly established in the appraisal profession, and borne out in actual transactions. The IRS and the courts also have recognized the difference between share prices established in normal trading in the stock market, which are devoid of control, and the total value of an enterprise including a premium for control.[12] (In fact, in 1974 Chris Craft was awarded damages in a court decision, based on the decline in value of a large block of previously acquired stock it held in Piper Aircraft, after Bangor Punta subsequently obtained a 51-percent—and controlling—position.

The following information from the appraiser's report illustrate the various judgmental bases of valuation:

History and Nature of the Business. The corporation was incorporated in the 1950s to engage in the general-contracting business. The corporation was formed from the general-contracting business of a partnership that had been in business for many years.

The corporation, since its incorporation, has been engaged in general contracting and engineering in the heavy-construction industry, including primarily the construction of highways, airports, dams, and so on.

This was characterized as a very high-risk, competitive, and volatile business. As the corporation's financial statements indicate, many of the undertakings, most importantly some joint ventures, have resulted in substantial losses to the corporation.

Dividend History. [The dividend history of the corporation was examined, for both the preferred and common shares.]

Prior Sales of Stock in the Corporation. A few years back, 20 percent of the shares of the corporation's common stock were purchased at [price noted] from another estate. Another 20 percent was purchased from an individual subsequently [terms noted]. Recently, 20 percent of the corporation's preferred stock was purchased at par from other individuals.

Valuation. The corporation was an operating company, and there was no indication that it was considering liquidation. Therefore, the appraiser placed primary significance on the corporation's earning capacity in valuing its stock. As evidenced by financial statements, revenues and earnings have fluctuated over the past five-year period. Past losses from nonrecurring factors were eliminated from the computation of annual net income, and the appraiser then valued the business on the basis of capitalization of earnings. The real estate owned was valued separately. These two separate valuations were combined to arrive at the fair market value of the corporation at the death of the owner.

Although gains realized from the sale of real property were eliminated from the computation of annual net income, the adjusted earnings still showed a fluctuating trend; therefore, an average net income for the five-year period was used as the proper measure of the *future* earning power. The average adjusted net income available for the common stock was about $1 million pretax.

In order to determine a price-to-earnings ratio that could be applied to the average adjusted net income of the corporation to produce the fair market value of the stock, the price-to-earnings ratios of a group of publicly held companies that were engaged in activities similar to those of the corporation were computed. The comparable companies were selected from *Moody's Industrial Manual* and *Moody's OTC Industrial Manual.* The average annual net earnings of each of the comparable companies for the five years prior to the decedent's death were determined. The market price of each of the comparable companies on the date of decedent's death was then applied to the average annual net income of each such company to produce price-to-earnings ratio or multiple for each company. The average price-to-earnings ratio was 8.9 to 1.

The market price of each of the comparable companies was below the respective net book value (stockholder's equity) per share. The discount of market price per share from stockholder's equity per share ranged between 20 and 70 percent, with an average discount of 50 percent.

Although the comparable companies studied were all larger than the subject corporation, with greater resources, the trends of revenues and earnings are basically the same. The appraiser noted that book value is a factor to be considered in the selection of a price-to-earnings ratio, but that the corporation's present ability to generate earnings is most important to investors.

All the foregoing factors entered into the selection of an appropriate price-to-earnings ratio. In addition, consideration was given to the depressed levels of the general market at the valuation date. Because of the lack of market transactions in this stock, the most proper price-to-earnings ratio to apply to the corporation was stated to be the average (8.9) ratio for the comparable publicly traded companies. This produced a market value, exclusive of real estate, of about $5 million.

The appraiser added a discount because there was no listed or quoted market for the corporation's stock, and added a premium factor because the shares of common stock of the corporation represent control of the company. A net discount of 10 percent was considered appropriate.

The value of the real estate was approximated at about $1 million (net of capital-gains taxes). Combining the value of the real estate with the value of the common stock as previously, the value of the corporation's common stock was determined to be $5.5 million at the time of the owner's demise.

Preferred Stock. The terms of the preferred stock provide that the holders are entitled to receive noncumulative dividends at a specified rate. Upon any liquidation of the corporation, the holders of the preferred are entitled to receive $100.00 per share plus unpaid dividends before any distributions are made to holders of common stock. The corporation at its option may redeem in whole or in part any outstanding shares of preferred stock at a price of $100.000 per share plus unpaid dividends. The holders of the preferred stock and the common stock are entitled to one vote for each share of preferred stock or common stock held. The balance sheet showed the liquidating value of the preferred stock to be very small relative to the common stockholders' equity.

The market value of the preferred stock is related to the general level of yields of preferred stocks in the public markets. New issues of preferred stocks were being offered during the month prior to the valuation date at yields of 11 to 12 percent.

The appraiser's opinion was that, based on the preceding factors, the appropriate yield to apply is 11 percent, which gave a price of $36 per share. In addition, a discount of approximately 20 percent should be applied for the lack of marketability, which gave a price equivalent to slightly over a 13-percent yield. Reflecting this discount (for lack of marketability), the opinion was that the fair market value of the corporation's preferred stock (as of the date of the decedent's death) was $30.00 per share.

Selection Models from Securities Analysis.

Computer Screens. In 1977, Essex Investment Management Company, Inc., a Boston-based investment and money-management firm, ran a series of computer screens on Value Line's list of 1,400 stocks. The screening process has been developed further and has proved a useful tool for identifying under- and overvalued issues.

In addition to screening on rate of return on equity (ROE), earning-per-share (EPS) growth, and other benchmarks, Essex displays five items that address the "sociology of the stock": price-to-book, *P/E*, dividend yield, market capitalization, and ten-year price change. Essex points out that the companies that passed the fundamental sort are those with superior characteristics, but that one also needs to know how much recognition they have already been accorded, which is what the latter display items contribute.

Only 187 stocks out of 1,400 (13.4 percent) passed the fundamental screen. When the "sociology" factors were examined, it became apparent that in general this is a better group and that investors know it.

However, the analysis then proceeded to find discrepancies. This was studied by dividing the 187 stocks into quartiles, in descending order of total market capitalization, as shown in table 7-4.

The indications were that the top-capitalization issues have been granted higher investment premium than the smaller ones, but with no fundamentally better performance to account for the difference. Thus superior growth and current value are available across the spectrum of capitalizations, perhaps more so if the investor is not constrained to the largest capitalization issues.

Superior Companies: Investment Characteristics. David L. Babson & Company, Inc., of Boston, has consistently monitored the long-term results of a twenty-eight-company list of firms, ranging from high-technology-equipment manufacturing to commodity nondurable-goods merchandising. Although their businesses differ widely, Babson notes that they share certain investment characteristics:

1. Above-average growth in unit demand for their products and services.
2. Valuable proprietary products, services, or skills.
3. Ability to develop important new products and markets.
4. Relatively low capital requirements and/or labor costs.
5. Consistently high profit margins.

Table 7-4
Illustrative Computer-Screen Results

Superior-Characteristic Stocks	Average P/E	Ten-Year ROE (%)	Ten-Year EPS Growth (%)	Ten-Year Book-Value Growth (%)	Average Price to Book	Average Dividend Yield (%)	Average Market Capitalization ($ Million)
1st quartile	12.9×	17.7	17.3	17.6	2.9×	2.6	2,700
2nd quartile	10.3×	17.3	18.3	18.0	2.1×	2.8	429
3rd quartile	10.1×	18.0	17.0	17.2	1.9×	3.1	183
4th quartile	7.9×	16.8	16.9	20.3	1.2×	3.8	66
Standard & Poor's 400-Stock Average	9.9×	12.3	5.6	4.9	1.4×	5.0	—

Source: Essex Investment Management Company, Boston, Mass. Courtesy of Joseph C. McNay. Reprinted with permission.

Table 7-5
Superior Growth Companies

	Percentage Change in Per-Share Earnings					
	1975	*1976*	*1977*	*1978E*	*1974-1978E*	*1979P*
Air Products	+36	+17	+ 6	+13	+ 90	+ 9
American Home	+11	+11	+11	+13	+ 55	+11
AMP	−40	+87	+47	+26	+108	+ 4
Burroughs	+13	+12	+15	+15	+ 67	+15
Capital Holding	+ 9	+13	+13	+14	+ 59	+11
Citicorp	+10	+15	− 6	+31	+ 57	+15
Coca-Cola	+22	+19	+12	+12	+ 83	+12
Colgate	+14	+13	+ 6	+ 4	+ 41	+ 7
Dow Chemical	+ 5	− 1	− 9	+ 3	− 2	− 7
Eastman Kodak	− 3	+ 6	− 1	+29	+ 32	+12
Exxon	−20	+ 6	− 8	+11	− 15	+20
Georgia-Pacific	−12	+38	+20	+12	+ 62	+ 5
Gillette	− 9	− 3	+ 3	+17	+ 6	+ 8
Halliburton	+52	+36	+16	+11	+166	+14
Hewlett-Packard	− 2	+ 7	+32	+23	+ 71	+19
IBM	+ 7	+19	+15	+13	+ 66	+18
Johnson & Johnson	+14	+11	+20	+21	+ 82	+15
K mart	+89	+31	+13	+ 7	+199	unch.
Marathon Oil	−25	+52	unch.	+ 7	+ 23	+14
Merck	+ 9	+12	+ 9	+12	+ 47	+16
Minnesota Mining	−14	+28	+21	+33	+ 79	+14
Pfizer	+ 9	+ 9	+10	+18	+ 53	+12
Procter & Gamble	+ 5	+20	+15	+11	+ 61	+12
Provident L & A	+16	+23	+19	+16	+109	+ 4
Revlon	+10	+28	+29	+19	+102	+16
Sears, Roebuck	+ 2	+32	+20	+11	+ 79	unch.
Standard Brands	+19	+ 1	+ 1	+11	+ 33	+ 9
Xerox	+ 3	+ 5	+12	+14	+ 38	+10
28 Growth Companies	+ 8	+20	+12	+15	+ 66	+11
28 cyclical companies	−11	+42	+ 6	+22	+ 54	unch.
28 income companies	− 1	+10	+10	+ 6	+ 23	+ 8
Dow 30	−24	+28	− 8	+15	+ 3	− 5
S&P 500	−12	+27	+10	+11	+ 36	− 2

Source: David L. Babson & Company, Inc., Boston, Mass.: Mary J. Wilson. *Weekly Staff Letter*, 18 January 1979. Reprinted with permission.

6. Good product-pricing flexibility.
7. Ability to finance most of their expansion from retained earnings and depreciation.

The firm points out that such characteristics promote strong earnings growth under any economic conditions. Moreover, as inflation has accelerated, they have become even more vital, since all seven help companies to control costs and/or to pass on unavoidable cost increases through price increases. In the twenty-year period 1957-1978, the twenty-eight companies listed in table 7-5 increased their earnings 1,778 percent, compared to 183 percent for the Dow Jones Industrials, 249 percent for the Standard & Poor's 500 stocks, and 132 percent for the consumer-price index.

Although many of these companies might not be acquisition or merger candidates because of antitrust or other policy considerations, their attributes might usefully be studied as a possible model, and employed in constructing various comparisons in the valuation of any particular situation.

Valuation in the Corporate-Planning Framework

Figure 7-1 illustrates the framework we advocate for performing the valuation of any business. This framework includes various building blocks, and provides inputs, as appropriate, either to a going-concern valuation or to a liquidation.

It should be apparent that placing a value on a business is generally not a neat analytical process. Numerous factors must be weighed and considerable professional judgment used. In general, when it is not feasible to make reliable projections of the cash flows, and/or to estimate reliably future market value by capitalizing future earnings, one places greatest weight on historical earning power and on capitalization rates (*P/E*s) for comparable publicly traded companies. If the subject business ceases to operate as presently constituted, then more emphasis will be placed on liquidating value.

The following example illustrates the valuation of a potential acquisition on a going-concern basis, with emphasis on the future prospects of the business.

The XYZ Company is a small, diversified, new-technology-based company, with a lackluster recent record. It is the successor to the merger several years ago of two previously separate companies, and it is in the process of turning itself around. Earnings performance has been volatile. Capital expenditures necessary to improve market position have been deferred. In recognition of this, the stock has been selling at a depressed valuation relative to its peer group.

However, a new management team has recently been brought in by the board, and proprietary rights have been acquired to a new genetic-engineering product successfully introduced and manufactured by a joint-venture partner abroad. This news was disclosed publicly to the trade, and the corporate-development group of another company (the ACQ Company) is evaluating XYZ as a possibly undervalued acquisition candidate. ACQ sees several features, namely:

1. XYZ will need financing in the next five years.
2. XYZ's business is turning around and will show less volatile performance, plus new growth.
3. These factors will have a direct impact on the financial parameters used

by ACQ in the valuation, such as discount rate, time horizon for forecasts, and *P/E* or other capitalization basis for XYZ's value.

The approach involves the following steps.

Understanding the Basic Business and the Industry or Industries in which the Company Competes

Industry and company markets, technology, sales, and financial statistics are the starting points. This step produces information about the company's overall strategic position—that is, its strengths and weaknesses, stage of maturity, basis for competition, by product/market grouping. A diagrammatic representation, as in figure 7-3, is often useful.

Detailed Financial Analysis

Historical data are analyzed to determine the basic earning power of the target company and to estimate the financial requirements to sustain and increase earnings. What are the real sources of profitability? Conversely, where are the trouble spots? Are these factors transient, or are they inherent in the company? How does the company compare with a peer group? Does it use an accounting policy similar to that of its competitors (for example, with respect to depreciation or inventories)? Does it lease or own facilities? Does it accumulate large amounts of tax-deferred or tax-sheltered income (for example, through foreign or export subsidiaries)? Can it repatriate these funds for redeployment as it sees fit?

What has been the pattern of valuation for such companies, in *P/E* terms? In the latter respect, we have found it useful to perform both simple and multiple regression analyses to test for any significant correlations among *P/E*, earnings growth rates, dividend payout, dividend yield on common stocks, ROI. Sometimes relationships among the company financial variables and external valuation parameters can be found that have statistical significance at high confidence levels. The historical relations are compared with current and prospective values of parameters. These correlations can then be employed in estimating both absolute and relative market values.

Forecasts

Figure 7-1 also illustrates the use of forecasts in arriving at going-concern valuation. In reality all economic forecasts are interdependent, and a rigorous approach requires solving a general or partial equilibrium

Company's Competitive
Position in Specific
Industries

Industry Stage of Maturity

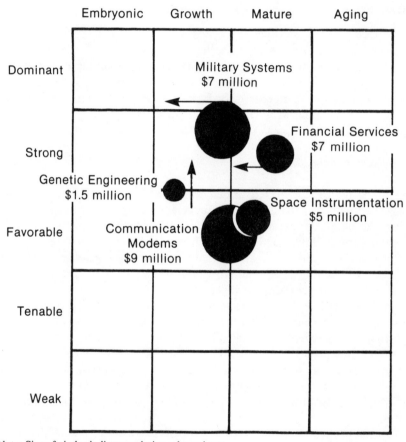

Note: Size of circles indicates relative sales volume.

Figure 7-3. Strategic Position of XYZ Company as of 1981

model—of the world economy—over the period of the forecast horizon. Since no such model is available, one uses simpler, separate models, with exogenously specified variables as required, taking care to make adjustments for internal consistency. In general, one will have a general forecast for the economic environment, including inflation; a forecast of the capital markets consistent with this; a related forecast for the industry(ies) of interest; and a forecast of the company's sales, earnings, cash flow, and other factors of interest to the valuation. High, low, and medium forecast values can be generated, which indicates the sensitivity of results; and one can subjectively estimate the probability of occurrence for each case and hence derive the *expected value* as the probability-weighted average of the scenarios studied (see table 7-6).

Develop Pro Forma Financial Statements
Consistent with Macro- and
Microeconomic Forecasts

One uses generally accepted accounting principles together with the expected income-tax treatment over the period of interest. Then, sets of sales forecasts, expense and capital-investment assumptions, and financial ratios (working-capital ratio, inventory turnover, debt-to-equity, and so on) are used as the inputs to the financial model of the company being evaluated. The outputs are the projected income statement and balance sheet year by year (see tables 7-7 and 7-8). (These can be generated using a standard computer-software package, or can be programmed for the case at hand.)

Calculate Present Value of Cash Flow

A corporate investor purchasing the company in question expects to receive some net cash flow from operations and/or some cash in the future from the sale (or mortgaging) of the corporation at its market value at that future time. The estimation of the latter usually makes a significant difference in the value placed on the business today. Moreover, it will be influenced by the tradeoff between reinvestment (which builds equity) and cash taken out by the parent.

The *P/E* at the end of, say, seven years, other things being equal, will be influenced by the growth rate experienced over that period and by that expected by investors in the following years. The present value in this illustration includes a significant component from the residual value in the last (N) forecast year (based on an estimated *P/E* at the time of 19 $\times$). This residual value, equal to $(P/E)_N \cdot (E)_N$, is used as the proxy for the worth of the company at that future point in time—which in turn represents the discounted cash flow that could be expected by shareholders at that future point. A discount rate ranging from 20 to 25 percent was selected as the appropriate range expected for the risk-adjusted opportunity cost of capital from the point of view of a potential acquisition.

Table 7-6
Worksheet: Selected Expense- and Capital-Investment-Variable Inputs to Financial Model (Illustrative Case Using Discrete Probabilities)

	1981			1982			1983			1984			1985			1986		
	High	Most Likely	Low	High	Most Likely	Low	High	Most Likely	Low	High	Most Likely	Low	High	Most Likely	Low	High	Most Likely	Low
Sales (millions, current $)[a]																		
Cost of sales ($ sales)																		
SG&A (% sales)[b]																		
R&D (% sales)[c]																		
Total operating expenses (% sales)																		
Capital expenditures[d]																		
Working capital (% sales)																		
Estimated probability of scenario occurence																		

Note: High, medium, and low outcomes assigned with a three-point probability distribution.

[a]From macro- to microlevel forecasts.
[b]Based on historical data and competitive factors.
[c]Based on strategic position analysis.
[d]From specific announced plans and/or capital-ratio study.

Table 7-7

XYZ Company: Projected Income and Cash Flow, Most-Likely Case
(Millions of Current Dollars)

	1981	1982	1983	1984	1985	1986	1987
Sales	29.4	37.2	42.4	50.0	59.0	69.6	80.0
Operating expenses	24.7	30.7	35.2	41.6	49.0	57.8	65.8
Depreciation	0.9	0.9	1.0	0.8	1.0	1.2	2.2
Operating profit	3.8	5.6	6.2	7.6	9.0	10.6	12.0
Other income (interest), net	0.0	0.2	(0.6)	(0.6)	(0.8)	(1.4)	(1.6)
Profit before tax	3.8	5.8	5.6	7.0	8.2	9.2	10.2
Taxes (including deferred)	1.8	2.8	2.6	3.2	3.8	3.6	4.6
Net income	2.0	3.0	3.2	3.8	4.4	5.6	5.6
Depreciation and deferred tax (add back)	1.0	1.0	1.1	0.9	1.1	1.3	2.3
Increase in working capital (subtract)	(1.6)	(2.2)	(3.4)	(4.0)	(4.6)	(5.0)	(1.5)
Capital expenditures (subtract)	(2.0)	(0.4)	(0.8)	(0.8)	(5.0)	(9.4)	(1.6)
Net cash flow	−0.6	+1.4	+0.1	−0.2	−4.2	−7.5	+4.8

Develop the Fair Market Value

1. Look at weighted-average historical earnings to develop price on a historical basis.
2. Investigate past and present public-market *P/E* ratios of similar companies (table 7-9).
3. Investigate recent acquisitions to determine actual *P/E*s paid (market plus a premium) (see table 7-10), and judge what future *P/E* would be likely in a "normal" market environment. Estimate future market (table 7-11).
4. Review the present value calculated from expected cash flow (table 7-7).
5. The discounted cash flow from the business is added to the present value of the future market value of the acquired firm to get the NPV of the acquisition.
6. Weigh (weight) these factors to arrive at an *intrinsic value*. This procedure suggested a fair market value of $26 million, as illustrated in table 7-12.

The keys to valuation here are sales forecasts, financial forecasts, appropriate *P/E* determination, appropriate discount-rate determination, understanding valuation disparities.

Table 7-8
XYZ Company: Consolidated Balance Sheet (at 31 December)
(Millions of Dollars)

	1980 Actual	*1987 Projected (Most-Likely Case)*
Assets		
Current assets		
Cash	0.7	2.7
Accounts receivable	7.8	24.5
Inventories	7.1	22.0
Other	0.4	—
Total current	16.0	49.2
Property plant and equipment		
Gross book value	9.1	29.8
Less accumulated depreciation	2.0	10.0
Net plant and equipment	7.1	19.8
Other assets	0.5	—
Total assets	23.6	70.0
Liabilities		
Current liabilities		
Notes payable	2.2	4.6
Accounts payable	1.4	8.3
Accrued taxes	0.6	2.0
Other	1.1	0.2
Current portion long-term debt	—	1.1
Total current	5.3	16.2
Long-term debt	2.0	15.6
Deferred tax	0.1	0.8
Capital stock	5.2	5.7
Retained earnings	11.0	31.7
Net worth	16.2	37.4
Total liabilities	23.6	70.0

The last point relates to the fact that "beauty is in the eye of the beholder"; and that, moreover, there is a premium or discount from values as established in an efficient auction market, due to the elements of share marketability and control that are inherent in an acquisition or divestiture situation.

Financial Simulation and Multielement Decision Analysis

There are often large uncertainties about many differential financial variables, as well as complex interactions among the variables used in

Table 7-9
Public-Market Performance of Comparable Companies Studied

Company	Stock Exchange	P/E	Growth Rate of EPS (% per Annum)	Market Liquidity and Ownership Consideration
A	ASE	30	25-30	Small capitalization, 20 percent closely held.
B	NYSE	18	18.5	Company G and directors control about 23 percent.
C	OTC	10	13	CEO and family own 65.7 percent.
D	NYSE	6	Nil	Family and directors control 22 percent.
E	NYSE	17[a]	20-25	Company H and family interests control about percent.
F	OTC	15	19	Insiders believed to control more than 10 percent; small capitalization.

[a]*Fully diluted* earnings (adjusted for conversions, options, warrants). This adjustment can be especially important in an acquisition valuation, for example, when any premium offered is likely to trigger conversion or exercise of options.

generating the projections and related valuation. It is then usually worthwhile to write equations expressing the various relationships, also as functions of time, and simulating the performance of the investment under consideration, under various scenarios or strategies. This is efficiently done today with the aid of readily available computer hardware and software (plus relatively straightforward programming, as necessary). The technique

Table 7-10
Recent Acquisition Characteristics of Related Companies

Acquired Company	Acquirer	Adjusted P/E Paid[b]	Five-Year Average EPS Growth Rate (%)
I	J	16 (3 × BV)	14
J	E	16	13
K	L	27 (6 × BV)	20
M	N	15	10
O	P	10 (near BV)	7
D	Q[a]	7 (below BV)	0

[a]Not consummated.

[b]Normalized to current market conditions by dividing the *P/E* at time of acquisition by the following ratio:

[S&P average *P/E* in acquisition year] ÷ [current S&P average *P/E*].

Table 7-11
Expected Future Market Value—Illustration

Valuation Factor	Probability of Scenario		
	Pessimistic (P = 0.2)	Most Likely (P = 0.6)	Optimistic (P = 0.2)
1987 net earnings ($ millions)	4.4	5.6	7.4
Corresponding growth rate (%)	14	19	24
Expected P/E	13	19	22
Market value ($ millions)	57.2	106.4	162.8
Expected value 1987 ($ millions)		108	

of Monte Carlo simulation to handle probability distributions of variables is well developed, and standard computer software packages are available.

Another technique that aids in the analysis of an acquisition, and its alternatives, is the use of decision diagrams or decision trees. Many companies also need to optimize multiple objectives simultaneously; that is, *a decision based only on the greatest expected NPV may not be the best decision, given the alternatives and their combined attributes*. The approach that includes a systematic treatment of time, uncertainties, risks, and multiple-objective tradeoffs is called decision analysis and is the subject of chapter 9.

Arthur D. Little, Inc., has developed a business-planning and risk-analysis model that incorporates the elements of decision analysis and Monte Carlo simulation. It is particularly applicable both to single-objective projects (such as determining which of several capital-investment alternatives has the highest risk-adjusted rate of return or NPV) and to multiple-objective decision situations where such objectives as the decision to maximize financial returns may be coupled with other quantifiable objectives such as minimizing dependence on a single facility.

The model is a financial simulator with the ability to incorporate the elements of risk in all the critical variables. Such a model can be used to:

1. Examine the implications of alternate strategies and "what if" scenarios.
2. Explore the probable consequences of any business decision over a wide range of future conditions.
3. Identify those variables that are critical to the success of any strategy.
4. Develop robust strategies to optimize performance in an uncertain future.

The model forces its users to analyze assumptions about the future of key variables and, in turn, provides realistic insights into the tradeoffs involved.

Table 7-12
Salient Items in the Valuation of XYZ Company for Acquisition (as of 31 December 1980)

Book value of common stock	$16.2 million
Current market value of shares	$17.0 million
Valuation based on historical earnings and industry *P/E* comparisons	$17.0 million
Net present value (based on cash-flow/earnings forecast and assumed residual value/sale 1/1/88)[a]	
At 20-percent discount rate	$27.6 million
At 25-percent discount rate	$20.6 million
Range for negotiations on intrinsic value per se	$19-27 million
Memo: Value based on current market plus 50-percent premium (environmental benchmark and/or premium for control)	$25.5 million
Values based on NPV	$20-28 million[b]
Recommended fair market value for acquisition	$26.0 million

[a]If an acquisition were consummated at these price levels, and the company actually sold subsequently, say in 1988, for the residual value as determined, the NPV could be reduced by approximately 15 percent, in this example, because of the effect of capital-gains taxes.

[b]This could be higher if one could establish synergy leading to higher cash flows from the business combination.

It also calculates the odds for alternative decisions or courses of action, thus permitting the selection of the one that has the highest probability of success.

We have used this model in commercial-feasibility studies and venture simulation. (These capabilities result in such models often being termed "venture" models.)

The model requires, as a first step, the identification and forecast of those variables that are critical to the desired outcome of the decision to be made. The outcome is defined by the decision maker, usually as high NPV or high return on investment (ROI). The variables include investment required, production costs, market size, prices, market growth, market share, and project-phase duration. The analysis of these variables and their inter-relationships is what forces explicit consideration of the uncertainties attached to them, since any of the variables may deviate from the value forecast for it.

For each decision alternative, the model generates the results of a realistic range of future values assigned to all critical variables, and provides a risk profile that summarizes the impact of these results on the desired

NPV or ROI. The optimal decision is derived from a comparison of the risk profiles for the decision alternatives.

A risk profile is a frequency distribution that demonstrates the risks involved and estimates the statistically most-probable outcome. For example, if NPV is the main criterion of a desired outcome, then the model will indicate the probability that a given decision will generate an acceptable value. The model can also provide analyses of the sensitivity of the NPV or ROI to extreme values of the critical variables.

For any chosen values of the critical variables, the model provides pro forma: balance sheet, income statement, working-capital table, gross- and net-cash-flow statements, sources- and uses-of-funds statements, profitability table, and NPV and ROI analyses. Chapter 9 illustrates the potential application of decision analysis, for example, to the question of acquisition(s) versus corporate development, with multiple objectives to be satisfied.

Notes

1. Fred Weston and Eugene F. Brigham, *Managerial Finance*, 3d ed., 5th ed. (New York: Holt, Rinehart & Winston, 1969, 1975).

2. Richard A. Brealey and Stewart C. Myers, *Principles of Corporate Finance* (New York: McGraw-Hill, 1981).

3. Jack L. Treynor, "The Emancipation of Security Analysis." Presentation to the Boston Security Analysts Society, 5 February 1981.

4. Fruhan, William E., Jr. *Financial Strategy—Studies in the Creation, Transfer and Destruction of Shareholder Value* (Homewood, Ill.: Richard D. Irwin, Inc., 1979).

5. Porter, Michael E. *Interbrand Choice, Strategy, and Bilateral Market Power* (Cambridge, Mass.: Harvard University Press, 1976); and *Competitive Strategy* (New York: The Free Press, 1980).

6. Reprinted by permission of the *Harvard Business Review*. Excerpt from "Strategic Analysis for More Profitable Acquisitions," by Alfred Rappaport (July-August 1979), pp. 102-104. Copyright © 1979 by the President and Fellows of Harvard College; all rights reserved.

7. See, for example, J.L. Treynor and Fischer Black, "Corporate Investment Decisions," in *Modern Developments in Financial Management*, ed. S.C. Myers (New York: Praeger, 1976). See esp. chapter 16, pp. 310-317.

8. Taken from the authors' letter in *Harvard Business Review* November-December 1978, p. 210.

9. See Richard Roll, "A Critique of the Asset Pricing Theory's Tests, Part I: On Past and Potential Testability of the Theory," *Journal of Financial Economics* 4 (1977):129-176; and Richard Roll, "Ambiguity When Per-

formance is Measured by the Securities Market Line," *Journal of Finance* 33 (1978):1051-1069.

10. M.J. Gordon and E. Shapiro, "Capital Equipment Analysis: The Required Rate of Profit," *Management Science* 3 (October 1956):102-110.

11. John Burr Williams, *Theory of Investment Value* (Cambridge, Mass.: Harvard University Press, 1938).

12. See John Heath, "Appraisal Processes in Mergers and Acquisitions, *Mergers and Acquisitions*, Fall 1974, p. 11.

8

Selected Accounting, Tax, and Financial Issues

Introduction

In this chapter we present an overview of a number of the important "nuts-and-bolts" factors that corporate management must bear in mind when considering the possible alternative accounting and financial methods used to treat business combinations and to structure deals. These issues are complex but can strongly influence the economics and feasibility of a transaction. The focus here is on the financial-reporting, tax, and structuring approaches that one faces when a transaction is being considered. (An introduction to the general legal, accounting, and income tax considerations was presented in chapter 2.) Acquisition-candidate evaluation/valuation and financial-modeling issues, on the other hand, are discussed in chapters 7 and 9.

The details and options involved in the structuring of transactions and the consideration of tax effects are best left to specialized professionals. Early and continuing consultation with accounting, financial, and legal counsel is essential. Nevertheless, executives responsible for planning, implementing, and overseeing acquisitions, as well as all those concerned with the acquisition process, must have at least a preliminary appreciation of these factors. Without this it is impossible to begin to think in terms of a transaction that meets the objectives of all parties. Lack of such basic knowledge can make the negotiation process extremely difficult, put one party at a severe disadvantage, cloud the true economics of transactions, and generally cause considerable agony. Moreover, it can expose one party to unforeseen future problems and liabilities.

Much of the material in the earlier part of this book applies to any level of investment in another corporation. However, the main focus in this chapter is on transactions involving the acquisition of 80 percent or more of the stock or assets of a company. In general, acquisition of 20 percent or less of another company's stock is carried on the investor's (acquirer's) balance sheet as an investment at cost, with dividends only reflected in the income statement. Under the *cost method* of accounting, no balance-sheet adjustment is made for profits or losses of the company in which the investment has been made. For less than 50-percent but at least 20-percent interest, some control or influence is implied. Here, typically, the *equity method* is required, with the stock carried on the balance sheet of the acquiring company at cost and adjusted for the proportional share of subsequent net earnings or losses. Often the investment is made above net asset value. Where this excess on a fair-market-value basis can be attributed to real assets or specific intangible assets, the excess is depreciated or amortized. If the excess is goodwill, it is accounted for as required by APB no. 17, as described later on in this chapter. In addition, the proportional share of net profits or losses of the minority-owned company is reflected in the investing (acquiring) company's income statement. APB no. 18 and the reference cited at the end of this chapter provide further details on the equity and cost methods. Where 50-percent ownership (or more) is involved, consolidation of the balance sheets and income statements occurs (with breakout of any minority interest).

The following material is intended to summarize broadly many of the important financial and accounting issues of acquisitions from the standpoint of both the corporate buyer and the seller, as well as from the point of view of the selling stockholder.

The issues principally addressed include:

1. The general types of transactions to effect an acquisition or merger and the advantages, disadvantages, and implications of each to both buyer and seller including:
   a. Stock versus cash and/or other consideration.
   b. Taxable versus nontaxable transactions.
2. Pooling versus purchase accounting.
3. Other issues, including earnouts, installment purchases, and legal/regulatory questions.

The objectives of this chapter, therefore, are to relate the foregoing points to the requirements of carrying out the transaction, the effects on the acquirer's balance sheet and income statement, the earnings-per-share implications, and the financial and tax impact on stockholders of the acquired corporation. In this discussion, the terms *acquirer, acquiring corporation, buyer,* and *buying corporation* are used interchangeably. The same are true of *acquiree, acquired corporation, seller,* and *selling corporation.*

Types of Transactions and Form of Consideration

The five basic types of transactions employed to effect a business combination, three nontaxable and two taxable, are outlined in this section. In this discussion we are assuming that 80 percent or more of the assets or stock of a company are acquired. Figure 8-1 is a flow diagram illustrating the overall mechanics of the various transaction types. A simplified summary of the types of transactions; the form of consideration possible; and some of the more important characteristics, requirements, and implications of each are summarized in table 8-1.

I. Statutory Merger or Consolidation

"A" type of tax-free reorganization

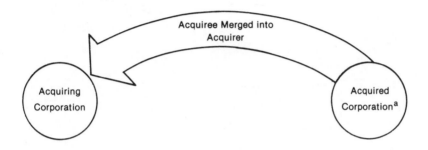

II. Acquiring Corporation's Stock for Stock of Acquired Corporation

"B" type of tax-free reorganization

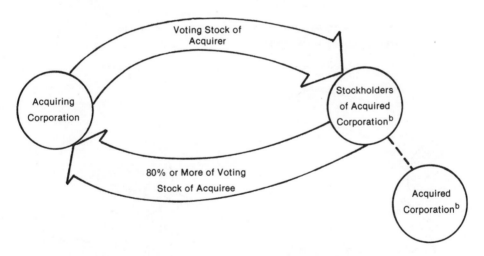

[a]Stockholders of the acquired corporation become stockholders of the acquiring corporation, and acquired corporation ceases to exist. Example given is illustrative of a merger. In a consolidation, stockholders of both corporations become stockholders in a new entity and the two original corporations cease to exist.

[b]Stockholders of acquired corporation become stockholders of acquirer and acquired corporation becomes a subsidiary of acquirer.

III. Acquirer's Stock for Assets of Acquired Corporation

"C" type of tax-free reoganization

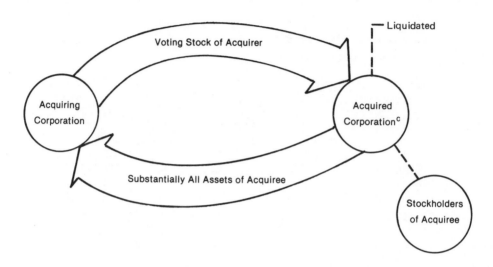

IV. Acquirer's Cash or Nonvoting Securities for Stock of Acquired Corporation

Taxable; similar in mechanism to 11

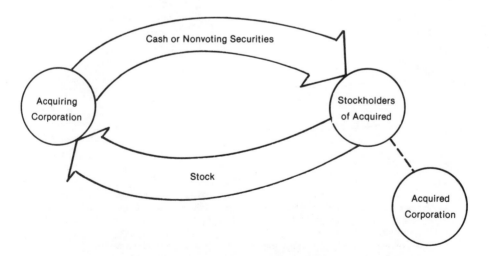

[c]As part of the reorganization, the acquired corporation may subsequently distribute its assets (i.e., voting stock of the acquirer) to its stockholders in accordance with the internal revenue code. Stockholders of acquiree then become stockholders of acquiring corporation.

V. Acquiring Corporation's Cash or Nonvoting Securities for Assets of Acquired Corporation

Taxable; similar in mechanism to III.

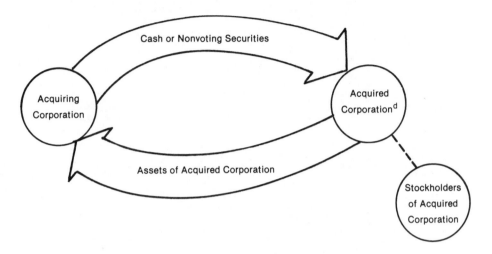

^dTo avoid double taxation, acquired corporation must be subsequently liquidated in accordance with provisions of the internal revenue code.

Note: Although not shown, subsidiaries are often used to effect acquisition transactions.

Figure 8-1. Simplified Flow Diagram, by Type of Transaction

Nontaxable Transactions

These transactions are nontaxable in the sense that neither the acquired corporation nor its stockholders incur a tax liability as a result of the acquisition for stock of the acquirer. (When such stockholders do sell their stock, however, a tax liability is incurred if the stock is sold at a gain.) Consideration other than stock or sometimes other securities is termed *boot* and is taxable.

To be tax free, a reorganization must satisfy the following basic requirements:

It must have a business purpose;

Stockholders in the acquired corporation must retain a continuity of interest in the acquiring corporation through an equity position in that corporation; and

A continuity of the business enterprise of the acquired corporation must be maintained by utilizing a significant portion of the assets, or by continuing a significant business line of the acquired corporation.

Table 8-1
Simplified Guide to Transaction Types and Their General Characteristics, Requirements, and Implications

| Characteristics/ Requirements Implications | Type of Business Combination | | | | |
	I Statutory Merger (A)	II Exchange of Stock for Stock (B)	III Purchase of Assets for Stock (C)	IV Purchase of Stock for Cash or Nonvoting Securities	V Purchase of Assets for Cash or Nonvoting Securities
Nontaxable to shareholders of acquiree if specific requirements met	Yes, except for "boot"	Yes	Yes, except for "boot"	No	No
Transaction Medium and steps	Generally 50% or more of purchase price must be in stock to meet continuity-of-interest rule.	Voting stock only. Voting preferred stock may be possible but not for pooling treatment.	1. Voting stock with possibility of up to 20% nonstock. 2. Corporate shell of acquiree remains and may be liquidated.	No restriction as to purchase medium.	1. No restriction as to purchase medium. 2. Corporate shell of acquiree remains and may be subsequently liquidated to avoid double taxation.
General requirements in addition to disclosure; regulatory approvals; and where securities are involved, registration unless an exemption applies	1. State law and other regulations must be met. 2. Continuity of interest and business enterprise. 3. Business purpose must exist. 4. Approval by selling company's directors and stockholders required.	1. Minimum 80% control for tax-free status. 2. Continuity of interest and business enterprise. 3. Business purpose must exist. 4. No "boot" allowed.	1. Transfer of "substantially all assets." 2. Continuity-of-interest and business enterprise. 3. Business purpose must exist. 4. Approval by directors and share holders of selling company required.	—	Approval by directors and shareholders of selling company required.
Type of accounting treatment	Purchase or pooling of interests.	Purchase or pooling of interests.	Purchase or pooling of interests	Purchase only.	Purchase only.

	I	II	III	IV	V
Financial accounting basis of acquired assets	If pooling accounting, no revaluation; if purchase accounting, assets revalued to fair market values.	Same as I.	Same as I.	Assets revalued to fair market values if acquired corporation liquidates.	Assets revalued to fair market values.
Position of minority stockholders of selling company after acquisition	By definition 100% control achieved. Minority stockholders cease to exist after merger but may have appraisal rights.	Dissenting selling stockholders can remain; if 20% or more interest remains, the acquisition is not tax free.	Stockholders of acquired corporation who dissent may have right to receive cash; can affect tax-free nature of transaction.	—	Minority stockholders may or may not have appraisal rights.
Tax basis of acquired assets and related issues	1. Old tax basis maintained of acquired property	Same as I.	Same as I.	1. Step up (revaluation) of assets for tax purposes if buyer liquidates seller under internal revenue code provisions. 2. *Buyer* liable for ordinary income taxes on depreciation and investment-tax-credit recapture if buyer liquidates seller.	1. Step up of assets (revaluation) for tax purposes 2. *Seller* liable for ordinary income taxes on depreciation and investment-tax-credit recapture.
Advantages to buyer	1. Flexibility of payment medium and still retain tax-free status. 2. Eliminates minority interests. 3. Pooling may be possible.	1. Corporate existence of seller can be continued. 2. A possible mechanism for unfriendly tender offers. 3. Pooling may be possible.	1. Pooling may be possible. 2. Liabilities assumed can be selected. 3. Eliminates minority interests.	1. Simplest form of acquisition. 2. Appropriate for unfriendly tender offers. 3. Corporate existence of seller can be continued. 4. Few approvals required.	1. Liabilities to be assumed can be selected.
Disadvantages to buyer	1. All assets and liabilities assumed (triangular or reverse triangular mergers may alter this). 2. Transaction often complex and time consuming; for example, shareholder	1. 100% voting stock required. 2. Lacks flexibility. 3. No "boot" allowed. Buyer cannot absorb sellers acquisition-related costs and maintain tax-free status.	1. Asset deals tend to be complex. 2. Transaction lacks flexibility. 3. Not suitable for unfriendly tender offers.	1. Pooling not possible.	1. Asset deals tend to be complex. 2. Not suitable for unfriendly tender offers. 3. Pooling not possible.

Table 8-1 *(continued)*

Characteristics/ Requirements Implications	*Type of Business Combination*				
	I Statutory Merger (A)	*II* Exchange of Stock for Stock (B)	*III* Purchase of Assets for Stock (C)	*IV* Purchase of Stock for Cash or Nonvoting Securities	*V* Purchase of Assets for Cash or Nonvoting Securities
	approval of both parties often required. 3. Not suitable for takeover since seller's directors must approve.				
Short-term total reported earnings and earnings-per-share (EPS) implications	1. Under pooling accounting: a. No change in reported total earnings from that of the entities prior to merger. b. EPS can be higher or lower as determined by number of shares issued to effect transaction; EPS impact can be positive or negative. Dilution results where a greater number of buyer's than seller's shares are required for the transaction. c. Combined entities restated for financial-reporting purposes for the entire current period in which	Same as I.	Same as I.	1. Use of cash itself does not reduce EPS from premerger position regardless of amount paid. 2. EPS of buyer increased by earnings of seller less any interest costs on borrowed money or on debt issued to effect transaction. 3. EPS contribution shown from date of acquisition only as required by purchase accounting. 4. Revaluation of assets may create goodwill and an annual charge against earnings as well as different annual depreciation, and may thus affect earnings. Typical effect is to reduce earnings and increase cash flow.	Same as IV.

acquisition took place, and usually for previous periods.

2. Under purchase accounting:

   a. Goodwill created, if any, will result in an after-tax charge and reduced earnings.

   b. Asset revaluation can change annual depreciation and affect earnings. Usual result is lower earnings and higher cash flow.

   c. EPS contribution shown from date of acquisition only, as required by purchase accounting.

   d. Some EPS effects due to number of shares issued as in 1b above.

In determining whether a transaction meets the requirements for a tax-free reorganization, other transactions preceding or following the reorganization (for example, sales of assets or stock, or stock redemptions) may be considered as part of the reorganization transaction. Such other transactions may result in the reorganization failing to qualify for tax-free treatment. For example, the purchase of stock for cash by an acquiring corporation may invalidate an otherwise tax-free stock for stock "B" reorganization if considered part of the plan of acquisition.

A tax-free organization may provide advantages by preserving the acquired corporation's tax attributes such as net-operating-loss carryovers. Also in a tax-free reorganization the assets of the acquired company will retain their tax basis and tax holding period.

Statutory Merger or Consolidation. This type of transaction involves the merger or consolidation of two or more corporations under the laws of the states involved. For purposes of this discussion, a *consolidation* is the combination of two or more corporations into a third, new corporation; a *merger* occurs where one corporation continues as a survivor. A *statutory merger* or consolidation is commonly known as an "A" reorganization, so named for section 368(a)(1)(A) of the Internal Revenue Code.

In concept at least, and often in concept alone, statutory mergers offer the greatest flexibility and simplicity. A statutory merger can apply only when the directors of the companies involved and usually the stockholders of at least the acquired company specifically approve the transaction. Obviously, then, this is not a vehicle for an unfriendly tender offer. On the other hand, under some state laws the only recourse for minority stockholders is to claim appraisal rights and receive cash payment for their shares. In other words, minority stockholders of the selling corporation are removed as such. A major advantage of the statutory-merger route is that acquisition can be for a combination of stock, cash, or other consideration, as long as stock represents 50 percent or more of the total price. Selling stockholders who are not concerned about their tax liabilities can accept cash, and others can have a tax-free exchange. Thus the buyer has considerable flexibility in terms of payment.

As noted previously, the continuity-of-interest test must be met for a tax-free reorganization. Under IRS guidelines for the issuance of favorable rulings on tax-free reorganizations at least 50 percent or more of the value of the stock surrendered by the selling stockholders must be paid for in stock. Here a nonvoting preferred stock possibly may qualify. For "B" and "C" tax-free reorganizations, which are described later on, the statutory rules with respect to the percentages and type of stock are more stringent.

In a statutory merger, the acquiring corporation would normally assume the assets and liabilities of the acquiree. Assumptions of liabilities, however, may be modified in a so-called triangular merger, where the acquired company is merged into a subsidiary of the acquirer that may have been created for this purpose. Thus the liabilities are not directly assumed by the parent corporation. In another variation—the reverse triangular merger—a subsidiary of the acquirer is merged into the acquiree, and the latter becomes the subsidiary of the acquiring corporation. A reverse triangular merger is sometimes used where the acquired corporation has valuable contractual rights, licenses, leases, or similar assets that may be jeopardized if the acquired corporation were not the surviving corporation.

Although on the surface the statutory merger would appear to have important advantages, the complexity of such transactions, the time and costs they involve for the acquirer, and the fact that stockholders of both parties may have to approve the merger are disadvantages. Furthermore, this type of transaction requires the approval of the directors of the seller and is thus unsuitable for an unfriendly takeover.

Exchange of Stock of Stockholders in the Selling Company in Exchange for Voting Stock of the Acquiring Corporation. This is the so-called B reorganization. Although, like the statutory merger, this can be a tax-free exchange, here 100 percent of the consideration must consist of the voting stock of the acquiring company. In addition, the acquirer must achieve ownership of stock possessing 80 percent of total combined voting power of all classes of stock entitled to vote and 80 percent of the total number of shares of all other classes of stock. Minority stockholders who choose not to exchange their stock may remain.

Purchase of Assets of the Selling Company for the Acquiring Corporation's Stock. This, the so-called C reorganization, involves exchange of voting stock in the acquiring company for substantially all of the assets of the acquired company. Under such circumstances it can be a tax-free transaction. The shell of the acquired company may be liquidated after the assets have been exchanged for the acquirer's stock. The transaction may remain tax free with a small percentage of the purchase price—up to 20 percent—in the form of cash. The rule requiring acquisition of substantially all the assets must be carefully observed. For example, if appreciable assets have been sold off by the seller prior to the transaction, then it may not be construed as a tax-free reorganization.

A principal advantage of the acquisition of assets is that the acquirer can select those liabilities that it chooses to assume. Also, this transaction differs from the B reorganization previously described (stock-for-stock transaction) in that a small percentage of the purchase price may be permitted to be nonstock. On the other hand, asset transactions involve transfers of titles, which by nature are more complex than transfers of stock.

Taxable Transactions

These are taxable transactions in the sense that the stockholders of the selling company may incur a long-term capital-gains liability at the time of the transaction. (If the stock has been held for less than the minimum of twelve months required for long-term capital-gains treatment, then the stockholders will be subject to taxes at short-term capital-gains rates.) In taxable transactions, a new tax basis would develop for the selling corporation's assets where the assets are purchased directly or the acquired corporation is liquidated in accordance with provisions of the internal revenue code. Allocation of purchase price among assets and their effects can be a major issue. (See also the discussion on investment credit and depreciation recapture later in this chapter.)

Purchase of the Selling Company's Stock from its Stockholders for Cash or Nonvoting Securities of the Acquirer. Unlike the A, B, and C tax-free transactions previously discussed, this is always a taxable transaction. Beyond the question of taxes, there are other important advantages from the purchaser's standpoint, since board approval by the selling company is not required and the purchase transaction is with existing stockholders. Therefore, this is a route frequently taken with tender offers. Minority stockholders remain and may be a factor.

Purchase of Assets of the Acquired Company for Cash or Nonvoting Securities of the Buyer. Except for its taxable nature, this is quite similar to a C tax-free reorganization. The advantage of purchase of assets rather than of stock is primarily that the liabilities to be assumed can be selected. The shell of the acquired corporation is typically liquidated within twelve months of the plan of liquidation adopted prior to the asset sale to avoid double taxation.

General Comments on Taxable versus
Nontaxable Transactions

A few basic concepts are given in this section. Bear in mind that this is a discussion of tax issues and not of the accounting-treatment question of pooling of interests versus purchase accounting.

Each situation must be considered separately in order to determine whether a taxable or a nontaxable transaction is more desirable and, in the latter case, if such a transaction can be achieved. Where the interests of buyer and seller favor different approaches, an agreement on one form or another and possible adjustment of price may have to take place during the negotiations.

From the buyer's standpoint, it may be a matter of indifference whether the deal is taxable or nontaxable, since the tax liability generally involves the stockholders of the seller. Moreover, taxable transactions may be simpler to effect; and the exchange of stock required for a tax-free deal can be avoided, if that is desired. In some cases a taxable transaction may be desirable from the buyer's standpoint. This is true, for example, where (1) the purchase price is above book value of the seller's assets, (2) the transaction is accounted for as a purchase, or (3) the fair value of the assets approximates the purchase price. Here the buyer in a taxable transaction may be able to write up the tax basis of the assets, incur no goodwill, and increase both depreciation and cash flow. In a tax-free acquisition, such write-up of assets generally is not possible.

Selling stockholders typically prefer a tax-free deal. However, where the purchase price is less than their tax basis, selling stockholders may want a taxable transaction, in order to establish a loss.

Pooling of Interests versus Purchase Accounting

From an accounting standpoint, a merger is treated either as (1) a pooling of interests or (2) a purchase. Important differences in balance-sheet and income-statement effects for the combined company can result from these two approaches. In some instances these differences can be very great: some acquisitions that would be attractive to a buyer on a pooling basis would be difficult or impossible to justify if purchase accounting were required. These are cases where, under purchase accounting only, the purchase price exceeds the fair asset value of the seller and the difference becomes goodwill that must be amortized against after-tax earnings.

Acquisitions must be accounted for by one of these two methods according to specific rules. APB Opinion no. 16, issued in 1970, sets up criteria for the conditions under which pooling is mandatory; if these conditions are not met, then acquisition must be treated as a purchase. The net effect is to restrict the number of deals in which pooling is possible. It is often difficult or impossible to meet the conditions required to effect a pooling. Generally speaking, where companies desire purchase accounting, this can often be effected by seeing that one or more of the conditions required for pooling is not met. Effecting a pooling, if that is desired, is usually far more difficult.

Under current economic conditions and in the current acquisition environment, purchase versus pooling accounting is less of an issue in merger negotiations because of the effects of inflation. Assets can often be acquired for cash at below "fair market value" but well above a company's stock-market value. These assets can be revalued upward without creation of significant goodwill and resulting charges against after-tax income. In pooling, no asset write-up occurs.

Pooling of Interests

In the pooling-of-interests method, the balance sheets of the two firms are simply added together and treated as if they had always been one entity. The only exception that may be required is a reallocation among the equity accounts, but not total equity. No write-up or change in asset values occurs. Regardless of purchase price, no goodwill is created by the transaction. Earnings of the combined entity can be restated from the beginning of the accounting period as if the two firms had been merged for the entire period. For pooling to be allowed, some of the requirements are that 90 percent or more of the stock of the selling company must be acquired for voting stock of the acquirer; the acquisition must be accomplished in one step; contingent payments (earnouts) are not allowed; each of the two companies must have been an independent entity for at least two years; and the new entity cannot dispose of a significant portion of the assets of the combined companies for a two-year period. These, along with other conditions that must be met in order to effect a pooling, are shown in figure 8-2. If any of these conditions is not satisfied, then the combination must be accounted for as a purchase.

A strong argument against pooling is that the assets of the acquired business are not recorded at either purchase or fair market value, but rather at existing book values. This obscures the investment on which management should earn a return and be measured. However, where companies are of approximately the same size and where both managements are to continue, a pooling of interests by means of an exchange of voting stock may be more justifiable.

Purchase

As previously indicated, purchase accounting must take place where one or more of the conditions for pooling does not exist. As a practical matter where purchase accounting is desired, conditions can usually be set up so that this occurs.

In a purchase transaction, the assets and liabilities of the acquired companies are not recorded at book value, but are shown at "fair market value," as described in APB no. 16. Where purchase price exceeds the fair market value of tangible assets—a fairly common occurrence today—the difference must be attributed to identifiable intangible assets such as patents, or to goodwill. Goodwill typically is not a desirable balance-sheet item, and only after revaluation of other assets does goodwill come into play. Sometimes patents, technology, and other intangible assets can be determined to have substantial values and an expected life for amortization purposes; thus the creation of goodwill can be minimized or eliminated.

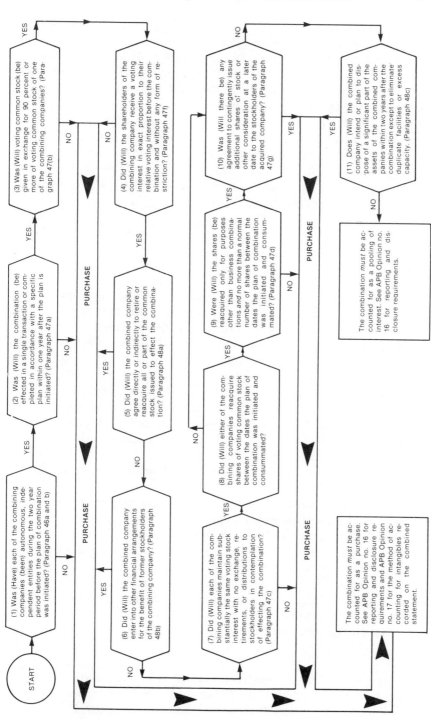

Figure 8-2. Accounting for Business Combinations: A Decision Chart

However, any goodwill created must be written off for financial-reporting purposes against after-tax income on a straight-line basis over forty years or less. This is outlined under APB no. 17 issued in 1970. It should be noted that this goodwill amortization, unlike identifiable intangible assets, is *not a deductible expense for tax purposes*. On the other hand, if the purchase price is less than the fair market value of the assets, the property assets are written down. (In extremely unusual situations where the purchase price is such that a balance exists after property assets are written down to zero, *negative goodwill* is created, which may be credited and taken into income, much as goodwill is written off against income.) A purchase differs from a pooling of interests in that earnings of the combined entity are reported only as of the date of the transaction.

*Effects of Pooling of Interests versus
Purchase Accounting*

Where both the reported book value of the net assets of the selling company and their fair market value approximate the purchase price, the question of pooling versus purchase treatment should be largely a matter of indifference, since no recurring balance-sheet or income-statement effects occur with regard to tax liability or goodwill amortization.

In a more probable situation, however, where the purchase price exceeds reported net book value, the effects can be quite important. A revaluation of assets and liabilities to fair market values may or may not result in creation of goodwill or an attendant non-tax-deductible charge to net income. Even where goodwill can be avoided, reevaluation can create a new depreciable base for assets and higher depreciation charges, which may or may not be desirable. Certainly, under such circumstances, reported earnings will be reduced and cash flow increased.

The basic differences between pooling of interest and purchase accounting are illustrated in the simplified hypothetical merger situation that follows. Salient data on the two firms are shown in table 8-2.

Assume that a merger takes place involving the tax-free exchange of 650,000 shares of company B's stock, which sells on the market for $17 per share (ten times earnings) for all the stock of company A. New stock in the combined companies is issued to the stockholders of A. To simplify the example, assume that company A is privately held, with no public market for its stock. What are the effects of pooling versus those of purchase accounting?

Pooling of Interests. The new combined balance sheet and income statement would reflect the addition of company A's assets, liabilities, and stockholders' equity at historical costs to those of company B. The

Table 8-2
Salient Premerger Reported Financial Data

	Thousands of Dollars	
	Company A (Seller)	Company B (Acquirer or Issuer)
Current assets	$ 1,000	$ 2,000
Fixed plant and equipment net	11,000	17,500
Total assets	$ 12,000	$ 19,500
Current liabilities	500	700
Long-term debt	4,500	2,000
Total liabilities	$ 5,000	$ 2,700
Common stock	4,000	4,000
Additional paid in capital	1,000	3,000
Earned surplus	2,000	9,800
Total stockholders' equity	$ 7,000	$ 16,800
Net income ($)	$1,100,000	$1,700,000
Number of shares outstanding	550,000	1,000,000
Net income/share ($)	2.00	1.70
Book value/share ($)	12.73	16.80

$11,050,000 purchase price for company A is nowhere reflected on the books of the separate or combined companies. Only a modification in the allocation between equity accounts, but not total equity, would take place, as explained in table 8-3. Net income of the combined entity would be $2,800,000 (the total for the two companies) and earnings per share based on 1,650,000 shares now outstanding would be $1.70. The overall effect of pooling accounting is shown in table 8-3.

Under pooling-of-interests accounting, unlike purchasing accounting, the reported financial statements can reflect the combined companies for the full fiscal year even though the merger took place at some point during the year.

Purchase. Under purchase accounting, assets (and liabilities) of the acquired company must be restated at fair value. Assumptions as to fair value are given below in table 8-4.

In this situation the entire $2,000,000, representing the excess of the purchase price of $11,050,000 over adjusted book value of $9,050,000, must be attributed to goodwill if no values can be assigned to other identifiable intangible assets. Although under APB no. 17 goodwill can be amortized over a period of up to forty years, assume that the outside accountants rule that twenty years is appropriate here. The annual figure for goodwill amortization, which is not a tax-deductible expense, will result in a reduction in earnings reported for financial purposes. The resulting reduction in reported net income of $100,000 per year, or 6¢ per share, would not have occurred if

Table 8-3
Effects of Pooling and Purchase Accounting, Combined Companies A and B
(Thousands of Dollars)

	Pooling	Purchase of Assets
Goodwill	—	2,000
Current assets	3,000	3,100
Fixed plant and equipment	28,500	30,450
Total assets	$ 31,500	$ 35,550
Current liabilities	1,200	1,200
Long-term debt	6,500	6,500
Common stock	6,600[a]	6,600[a]
Additional paid in capital	5,400[a]	11,450[a]
Earned surplus	11,800	9,800
Total liabilities and stockholders' equity	31,500	35,550
Number of shares outstanding	1,650,000	1,650,000
Net income	2,800	2,800[b]
Amortization of good will	—	100
Reported net income	2,800	2,700
Reported net income/share ($)	1.70	1.64

[a]Common-stock figure is total of premerger account for company B plus par value of stock issued to acquire company A; 650,000 shares company B common stock issued at $17 per share with a par value of $4 per share. Difference of $13 per share ($2,145,000) assigned to additional paid in capital. Final additional paid in capital figure adjusted to meet required total equity value.

[b]Does not reflect higher depreciation charges following acquisition from step up of asset values.

pooling had taken place. In addition, under purchase accounting, depreciation would be taken on the new values of fixed assets, further reducing future reported earnings but having a positive effect on cash flow.

The overall effect is shown in table 8-3. Note the addition of goodwill to the balance sheet, the revaluation of assets to higher levels, the effect on overall equity, and the reduced reported earnings under purchase accounting in this example.

Other Issues

Installment Purchases

Installment purchases can be desirable and come into play for taxable transactions where selling stockholders want to reduce or defer taxes by spreading the gain on the sale of stock over several taxable years and where the buyer agrees to pay for the purchase over the same period. Only purchase accounting applies. Debt is issued for future payments; interest (stated or imputed) on such debt will be taxed at ordinary rather than capital-gains rates.

Earnouts (Contingent Purchase Price)

Sometimes the seller's price is such that the transaction can only be justified by the buyer at levels of future earnings considerably above what the buyer can expect with any degree of certainty. Here an earnout may allow the deal to be consummated. Basically, earnouts call for part of the purchase price to be paid in later periods based on future earnings according to a formula worked out between buyer and seller.

Earnouts may qualify as nontaxable transactions if the usual conditions for a tax-free reorganization are met and if all stock used in the purchase is issued within five years of closing. Usually an upper limit to the potential number of shares is stated, and 50 percent or more must be issued at the time of closing.

A contingent purchase may allow some deals to go through that would otherwise be impossible. However, a series of difficult management and control problems between buyer and seller during the earnout period may easily develop when the seller's management is attempting to meet its earnings goals. Purchase accounting applies to earnouts.

Related Legal/Regulatory Issues

Antitrust and legal issues have been discussed in chapter 4. Compliance is also necessary with many SEC and other government regulations. For ex-

Table 8-4
Revaluation of Company A Assets under Purchase Accounting
(Thousands of Dollars)

	As Originally Stated	Fair Value	Change
Current assets	1,000	1,100	+ 100
Fixed plant and equipment	11,000	12,950	+ 1,950
Other assets	12,000	14,050	+ 2,050
Current liabilities	500	500	—
Long-term debt	4,500	4,500	—
Total	5,000	5,000	
Book value as originally stated	7,000	—	—
Adjusted book value	—	9,050	—

ample, except where the private-placement or other exemption applies, stock or other securities used to effect an acquisition transaction must be registered. Disclosure must be made of any 5-percent or greater interest in another corporation. As noted in chapter 4, tender offers must comply with the Williams Act, premerger notification under the Hart-Scott-Rodino Act must take place where larger acquisitions are involved, various state laws must be observed, and so forth. Therefore, close coordination with legal counsel is of absolutely critical importance.

References

Acquisitions. New York: Practicing Law Institute, 1975.

Arthur Anderson & Company. *Accounting and Tax Considerations for Business Combinations in the United States.* Chicago: Arthur Anderson & Company, 1980.

———. *Tax Economics of Business Combinations.* Chicago: Arthur Anderson & Company, 1980.

Brigham, Eugene F. *Financial Management.* Hinsdale, Ill.: Dryden Press, 1977. (See chap. 21, pp. 745-785.)

Dearden, John, and Shank, John. *Financial Accounting and Reporting.* Englewood Cliffs, N.J.: Prentice-Hall, 1975. (See chap. 2, pp. 251-285.)

Financial Accounting Standards. Stamford, Conn.: Financial Accounting Standards Board, 1979. [APB Opinion no. 16, 1970 (business combinations); APB Opinion no. 17, 1970 (intangible assets); APB Opinion no. 18, 1971 (the equity method of accounting for investment in common stock).]

Freund, James C. *Anatomy of a Merger.* N.Y.: Law Journal Press, 1975.

Nickerson, Clarence B. *Accounting Handbook for Non-Accountants.* Boston: CBI Publishing Company, 1979. (See chap. 20, pp. 384-396.)

Scharf, Charles A. *Acquisitions, Mergers, Sales and Takeovers.* Englewood Cliffs, N.J.: Prentice-Hall, 1971.

Wasserstein, Bruce. *Corporate Finance Law.* New York: McGraw-Hill, 1978. (see pt. III, pp. 181-252.)

9

The Application of Decision Analysis to Acquisition versus Internal-Capital-Investment Choices

Karl M. Wiig

Introduction

As indicated in chapter 7, a corporation's decision to acquire or merge with another firm may usually be viewed as a capital-budgeting, as well as a strategic, decision. In this sense, it competes with or complements decisions to invest in new plant and equipment for the currently owned enterprise. We term the latter the internal-investment choices in the context of this book.

Capital investments, including acquisitions, are made (required) to secure, renew, and expand the resources of a firm. Such capital investments usually consist of the allocation of large amounts of money with plans for recouping the initial investment plus adequate profits from cash flows generated during the economic life of the investment. The decisions associated with these allocations of funds normally are the responsibility of a firm's top executives, and these decisions constitute the major tools used to implement the strategic actions of an enterprise.

Once the investments are committed, the decisions are very hard to reverse without creating significant economic disturbances to an organization. Thus capital-investment decisions require very careful analysis and are among the most important and difficult decisions that managers must make.

It is important at this point to emphasize certain characteristics always present in capital-investment decisions, because they will play an important role in the methods used to analyze the consequences of these decisions.

Time

The long-lasting effects of capital-investment decisions imply that long planning horizons (in some instances spanning ten or twenty years) should

This chapter includes an adaptation of Arnoldo C. Hax and Karl M. Wiig, "The Use of Decision Analysis in Capital Investment Problems," *Sloan Management Review* 17, no. 2 (Winter 1976). We gratefully acknowledge permission to reproduce portions of that article.

be adopted in their analysis. This forces recognition of the time value of money (that is, a dollar spent or earned today is worth more than a dollar spent or earned in the future).

Uncertainties

The long-lasting consequences of the investment decision also create the problem of uncertainties. With long planning horizons, a wide variety of future conditions is possible. It is important to account for these uncertainties in order to avoid severe oversimplifications that may lead to the selection of an investment alternative that can be expected to perform poorly under many likely futures.

Risk

Uncertainties create an environment in which risk attitudes play an important role. It has long been recognized that investors are normally risk averse. Their degree of risk aversion depends on their personal preferences, their present assets, and the nature of the uncertainties they have to face. A complete analysis of an investment decision has to provide the decision maker with the means to evaluate properly, in view of his risk attitudes, each strategy option under consideration.

Tradeoffs between Multiple Objectives

The selection among competing alternatives cannot be resolved in many practical applications by means of a single objective or attribute. In these cases it is necessary to provide a mechanism that permits evaluation of the tradeoffs existing between multiple objectives.

   This chapter therefore describes an approach to dealing with a capital-investment decision, including treatment of multiple-objective tradeoffs.[1]

The Capital-Investment-Decision Problem

Two basic questions should be raised at the outset of the investment-decision analysis: (1) What is the decision that is about to be made? (2) Who are the decision makers? A decision in this context is an irrevocable allocation of resources. It is irrevocable in Howard's sense of being impossible or too costly to reverse after it has been made.[2] This implies an actual commitment of funds on the part of management. The definition of the investment decision requires much creativity on the part of management, not only to identify the most attractive opportunities for capital investment (which determines the environment in which the decision takes place), but also to construct all the relevant alternative ways of approaching the decision that are open to the decision maker. Our approach provides a systematic way to structure the elements of a given decision so as to facilitate the process of selecting the most promising alternative available to the decision makers. This is what Simon calls the *choice phase*.[3] The approach takes as input the definition of the investment problem; therefore, it does not contribute to the process of identifying investment opportunities—the *intelligence phase*.

The second basic element of the capital-investment problem is the identification of the decision maker(s). This is an essential element since we need to incorporate (1) the scope of the analysis, (2) the decision options that the decision maker wants to consider, (3) his or her attitude toward risks,[4] and (4) the tradeoffs that one is willing to make at various levels of outcomes. This approach calls for a personal interaction with the decision maker; therefore, there are significant differences between dealing with a single individual and dealing with a group of individuals making a collective decision.

The example concerns a major mining company, A, which is in short supply of ore and therefore entertains projects to increase its supply capability. An opportunity for decision making is expected to occur soon, because of the U.S. government having settled an antitrust suit against another company, C, in a consent decree requiring that company to divest itself of a subsidiary, B, which, fortuitously, owns extensive ore deposits. It is expected that other companies will also be interested in B. There are two major decisions to be made in this situation:

1.   The *bidding decision*, which includes, primarily, the amount to bid for B and whether to bid alone or with a partner.
2.   The *production decision*, which includes the options of developing and operating a plant alone and of developing and operating a plant with a partner.

If the bidding were successful, the property owned by B would be developed. If the acquisition were to be won with a development partner, the partnership should be extended to the exploitation phase. If the bidding were unsuccessful, some other partnership would be required since the deposits currently owned by the firm are not enough to allow a large-scale exploitation. Moreover, the company is considering heavy investment in another venture that would soon have to be decided on. If those funds were committed, the company would be forced to develop the project analyzed herein with a partner. In the following analysis this alternative project will be referred to as the *competing internal venture*.

The following characteristics are significant in the analysis of these alternatives:

1. The project has a planning horizon of twenty-eight years, consisting of three years of engineering studies and plant design, five years of construction, and twenty years of plant operation.
2. Great uncertainties are associated with the required mining technology and the future product prices.
3. The total capital commitments may be on the order of $500 million.
4. The president is the single decision maker because of his authority and personal interest in the decision problem.

Modeling and Data Collection Phase. Having defined the decisions and selected the major alternatives, we shall proceed to describe the investment problem in a systematic and rational way. This is accomplished by the development of a mathematical model that provides a simplified representation of the capital-investment problem under consideration. We will list each step in the model formulation. Although this sequence of steps provides an orderly approach to formulating the decision-making model, we will not expect the analysis process to be exhausted by just one pass through the sequence. In practice, several iterations might be needed, with loops interjected between each step.

Selection of a Planning Horizon and Number of Time Periods. Here, we use twenty-eight one-year time periods.

Selection of the Decision Variables. Decision variables are those factors under the control of the decision maker. As explained earlier, the decision variables in this case are (1) bidding alone or with a partner, (2) bidding value for B, and (3) developing and operating deposits alone or with a partner.

Variables 1 and 3 are bivalued. Variable 2 is a continuous variable that can assume an infinite number of values. However, it is common practice in decision analysis to limit such variables to a discrete number of options so as to reduce the computational burden. For these reasons, this analysis is confined to three bidding values: high, medium, and low for B.

Selection of Parameters. Parameters (exogeneous variables) are those elements of the problem that are beyond the control of the decision maker; they are imposed by the external environment. In this project the most important parameters associated with the investment decision are:

1. Schedule and magnitude of capital investment.
2. Product market prices over planning horizon.
3. Plant capacity.
4. Operating costs over planning horizon.
5. Tax rates (corporate-income-tax rate, investment-tax-credit rate, and depletion-allowance rate).
6. Depreciation (periods and methods for book and tax depreciation for each cash-flow category).
7. Inflation rates over planning horizon.
8. Fraction of capital investment subject to investment credit.

In addition, there are parameters associated with the probabilities of winning bids and the success of the competing venture. The project is to be totally financed by internally generated funds, and hence interest rates on financing sources were not required parameters.

There are two important issues associated with the specification of the parameters.

1. The level of aggregation of the information contained in the parameter specification must be determined. In the analysis of capital ventures it is necessary to describe the parameters in enough detail to allow the capture of the essential differences between the alternatives being tested. However, one should avoid using excessive detail, which would burden the data-collection and analysis process.

2. Most of the values of the parameters described previously are subject to much *uncertainty* throughout the planning horizon. Therefore, it is necessary to describe the uncertain parameters by means of probability distributions. However, it is a common and useful practice to begin by assigning a single-valued estimate (single-point forecast) to each parameter, thus initially ignoring the uncertainties that are associated with the data. The deterministic case that is thus established is normally referred to as the *base case*. The base case is used as a standard for comparison and verification for the uncertainty analysis that follows.

Cash-Flow-Projection Model. The cash-flow model is developed and used as discussed in chapter 7.

Transformation of Cash Flows into a Single Profitability Measure. In order to compare the different cash flows generated by the decision alternatives, it is convenient to reduce them to a single measure of profitability. This measure of profitability should provide a consistent indicator of the preferences of the decision maker toward alternative cash flows. Several measures of profitability have been proposed.

We strongly recommend the adoption of net present value (NPV) as a measure of profitability in capital-investment decisions. In order to obtain the NPV of a stream of cash flows, it is necessary, of course, to define a discount rate. The classical approach to this issue is to select as the discount rate the cost of capital. Another approach is to consider the discount rate as a statement of time preference on the part of the decision maker. It is also important to emphasize that the discount rate chosen should be consistent with the methodology used to handle uncertainties or risks.

Selection of Objectives and Measures of Effectiveness. The transformation of the cash-flow stream into a single measure of profitability provides the specification of a criterion and a measure of performance that could be of great assistance to the decision maker in his attempts to distinguish between various alternatives. In fact, many investment opportunities in the private sector can be properly decided on by using profit maximization (or cost minimization) as the single objective. However, in some applications it is extremely difficult to identify a unique objective that represents adequately the preferences of the decision maker with respect to the outcomes of his decisions. It could be that there are several attributes that he considers important (such as profit, share of market, employment stability, and customer satisfaction), some of them offering conflictive objectives.

There are various ways of approaching this problem. One is to select the most important of these attributes as the objective and to incorporate the others in the constraint set so as to generate a minimum level of accomplishment in the secondary attributes. Sensitivity analysis may help in gaining a better understanding of the tradeoffs obtained by changing the minimum required level of accomplishment for the secondary attributes. A second way around this problem is to reconcile the conflicting goals by establishing a global objective function by heuristic means.[5] These two approaches, although relatively straightforward to implement, are arbitrary and pragmatic and do not necessarily resolve the basic issues behind the multiple-objective question. A third approach, which is conceptually extremely attractive but requires much work in its implementation, is to assess directly the multiattribute preference (or utility function) of the decision maker. Extensive research is being conducted in this important field.[6] Regardless of the type of approach used to deal with the multiattribute problem, each approach has the same final consequence—to transform the multiple-objective problem into a single measure of effectiveness.

For our project the decision maker felt it was essential to incorporate two objectives into the analysis: (1) *maximization of profit* as measured by the net present value of the projected cash flows and (2) *maximization of product output* as measured by the company's share of total yearly production.

Identification of Parameters Whose Uncertainties Have to Be Treated Explicitly. Although the values that every parameter of the problem can take during the planning horizon are subject to some degree of uncertainty, the impact that this uncertainty has on the selected objective(s) (for example, the NPV of the investment) could be quite different. In many cases, therefore, it is possible to classify the parameters into two groups: the deterministic parameters and the uncertain parameters.

Deterministic parameters are those whose uncertainties can be ignored without causing undue oversimplifications in the analysis. The expected range of variability of the parameters is small, and/or the change of the objective's value within that range is negligible. Their values will be assigned constant numbers, normally the most-likely values or "best single estimates" available, in each time period of the planning horizon.

Uncertain parameters, also called critical parameters, are those whose uncertainties have to be properly recognized and dealt with. Otherwise, we will be ignoring a critical element of the problem that could cause the wrong alternative to be chosen.

There are basically two ways in which to perform this classification.

1. *Subjective classification*. In some situations it is possible for the decision maker to determine a priori which parameters should be treated deterministically and which should be regarded as uncertain parameters. This decision may be based on intuitive or subjective feelings or may be supported by previous engineering, marketing, and feasibility studies.

2. *Sensitivity analysis*. Whenever the identification of uncertain parameters becomes too complex an issue to be resolved subjectively, it is possible to perform this task by conducting sensitivity analyses with the cash-flow-projection model developed so far.

We are confronted with the following uncertain parameters:

1. Probability distribution of winning bids given a specific bid value.
2. Probability of success of competing venture.

The selection of the remaining uncertain parameters for the project was done subjectively.

The following parameters of the project were considered to be deterministic:

1. Plant capacity.
2. Tax rates.
3. Depreciation rates.
4. Fraction of capital investment subject to investment tax credit.
5. Inflation rates (inflation was taken into consideration by expressing all costs and prices in terms of constant dollars).

Construction of a Decision Tree. After the uncertain parameters have been specified, it is useful to structure the investment problem by using a decision diagram or decision tree. The decision tree provides a graphical representation of the way in which decision variables interact with the uncertain parameters. These interactions are presented sequentially through the time spanned by the planning horizon in the order in which (1) decision variables are chosen by the decision maker and (2) uncertain parameters are known to him.

The construction of the decision tree corresponding to the investment problem is performed to organize clearly the elements of the problem, to recognize and communicate the alternatives that are meaningful to the decision maker, and to program the remaining computations necessary for the analysis.

The decision tree for our project is shown in figure 9-1. The initial decision node (1) has four initial alternatives: (1) bid for company B alone, (2) bid with a partner, (3) stay with own property, and (4) do not pursue or develop project. The bidding process is represented by nodes 2 through 3 (with a like set of nodes for bidding with a partner). The bidding decision is represented by bid levels (high, medium, low) for B (node 2) with a resolution of uncertainty associated with each (node 3).

Node 4 represents the outcome of the competing venture. If that venture were successful, the company would have only sufficient resources to develop the mining project with a partner. If the venture turned out to be a failure, any previously agreed-on partnership arrangement would continue. Nodes 5, 6, and 7 represent uncertainties associated with capital investments, operating costs, and product prices, respectively.

Assessment of Probability Distributions of Uncertain Parameters. Once the parameters whose uncertainties will be treated explicitly have been determined, the next stage of the analysis consists of measuring the likelihood of occurrence of the possible outcomes of the uncertain parameters. This is accomplished by specifying the probability distributions of those parameters. If the parameters are independent of each other, each probability distribution can be determined separately. However, if the outcome of one parameter depends on the level of achievement of another parameter, we might have to assess conditional and marginal probability distributions. In these cases the problem of characterizing the probability distribution of the uncertain parameters could be quite complex.

There are two approaches regarding the concept of probability. The *classical* (or *clinical*) *approach* equates the probability of a given outcome of an uncertain event with the relative frequency of occurrence of that event after a large number of independent trials. Whenever there is access to past history on the uncertain parameter behavior, or whenever one can obtain sample information on a given parameter, this concept could be of help in

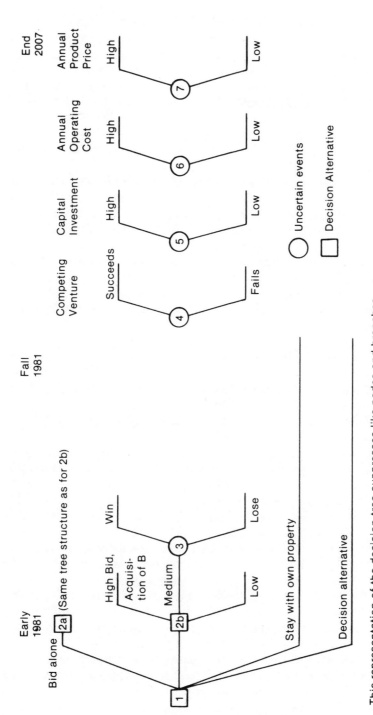

This representation of the decision tree suppresses like nodes and branches.

Figure 9-1. Decision Process for Capital-Investment Project

quantifying the parameter probability distribution, provided the conditions prevailing when the data were collected are similar to those expected in the future.

A second approach associated with the concept of probability is the *Bayesian* (or *subjective*) *approach*. This approach considers probabilities to reflect the state of mind or current knowledge of the decision maker regarding the outcome of an uncertain event. Since many investment decisions are unique and there is little room for experimentation or empirical observation, this concept of probability is considered quite useful and is being widely used.

Normally, these two approaches for describing the probability distribution of an uncertain parameter lead to the definition of a continuous distribution. Often it is useful for computational purposes to transform this continuous distribution into a discrete one. An effective way to accomplish this is to use the *bracket median technique*.

In our project, because of the unique nature of the mining venture and the lack of previous history with regard to the parameters' behavior, we relied completely on subjective assessment to characterize the nature of the probability distributions of the uncertain parameters, for example, figure 9-2.

Definition of Relevant Strategies and Computation of Risk Profiles. After the decision tree has been constructed and the uncertainties have been assessed, we are ready to evaluate the consequences of the decision maker's actions with respect to a single criterion.

There are two ways of conducting the necessary calculations to perform this stage of analysis.

1. The *backward-induction process* begins by calculating the terminal values of the objective at each of the terminal points of the decision tree and proceeds backwards to define the optimal strategy. At every event node, we calculate the expected value of the criterion corresponding to all the possible outcomes of that event. At each decision node, we select the alternative that leads to the highest expected value for the criterion.

2. *Monte Carlo simulation* is useful when the number of terminal points of the decision tree becomes so large that the backward-induction process could be infeasible or impractical to implement. In this case, it might be desirable to sample among the distributions that characterize the uncertain events and to obtain an estimate of the expected value of the criterion for each strategy that the decision maker wants to consider by performing the sample computation a sufficient number of times.

A *strategy* is a rule that prescribes exactly what act shall be chosen in every situation in which a choice may have to be made over the planning horizon. In this simulation approach, it is imperative to define in advance the strategies that the decision maker wants to evaluate. In the backward-induction process, the evaluation of the pertinent strategies can be extracted

Probability
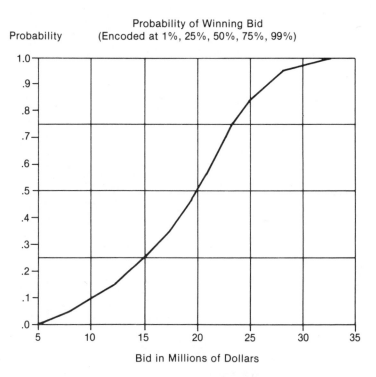

Figure 9-2. Expected Bid Sensitivity as Encoded by Company Decision Makers

from the decision tree after the necessary computations have been completed. In both cases, however, it is important for practical reasons to eliminate all those strategies that are obviously nonoptimal.

In this example, eight strategies were defined to be evaluated. There strategies refer to the conditions—bidding either alone or with a partner; the bidding level (high, medium, and low acquisition prices) if a bid is made; or not bidding at all, but developing previously owned property.

It is not enough to measure the profitability of each strategy by the expected net present value (NPV) or expected return on investment (ROI) for that strategy. Since the uncertainty present in the project will not guarantee the achievement of a specified NPV or ROI, we need to include some measures of the variability of the NPV and ROI resulting from the investment. These measures of variability can be the standard deviation of RPV and ROI or some selected fractiles of the NPV and ROI distributions. However, it has become common practice to represent the performance of the project by providing the complete probability distribution of the selected measures of profitability, NPV and ROI. This distribution is known as the *risk profile* of the investment. Figure 9-3 provides the NPV

Legend and Statistics

Strategies	Means	Standard Deviation of NPV
◯ 1	71	53
☐ 2	81	26
⬡ 6	87	43
△ 7	101	30
Do Nothing 8	0	0

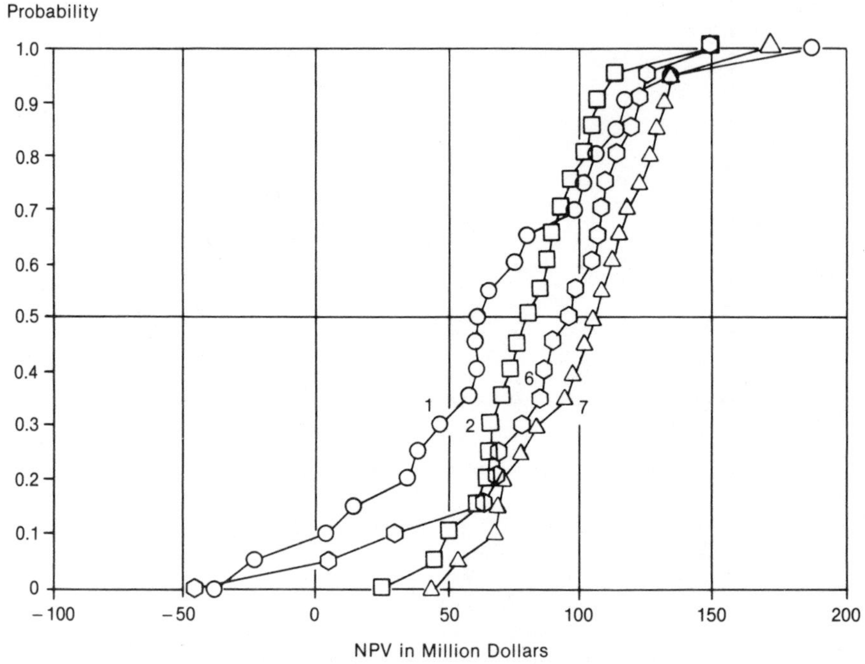

Figure 9-3. Risk Profiles (in NPV) for Four Selected Strategies

risk profiles for four of the strategies (strategies 1, 2, 6, and 7). These strategies stochastically dominated all other strategies; their means and measures of variability are shown on the figure. The NPVs were calculated for a discount rate of 10 percent. Figure 9-3 shows that strategy 7 also dominated all other strategies, except for a minor end effect, where strategy 1 becomes preferable.

The risk profile is useful to evaluate the risk associated with each strategy by examining the probability of occurrence of undesirable outcomes. There are only two strategies that can take on negative net present values: strategy 1 has a 9-percent chance of yielding a negative NPV, and strategy 6 has a 4-percent chance of such an outcome. The lowest possible

NPV for strategy 1 is − $40 million, whereas that amount for strategy 6 is − $48 million. Strategies 2 and 7 will always have positive NPVs. Although strategy 2 has a lower expected NPV than strategy 6 ($81 versus $87 million), a sufficiently risk-averse decision maker might prefer strategy 2 over 6 because of the undesirable outcomes that strategy 6 could produce.

Treatment of Risk Attitudes for Single-Objective Projects. In some instances when dealing with projects with single objectives, the risk implications of each strategy can be resolved by carefully analyzing each strategy's risk profile. If a clear dominance exists, as seems to be the case with strategy 7, the decision maker could feel confident enough to reach a decision at this stage of the investment analysis. In any event, the risk profiles could serve the purpose of eliminating from further consideration a number of the strategies selected initially that seem to be clearly dominated by a subset of superior strategies. Whenever a clear dominant strategy cannot be identified at this stage, it might be necessary to assess explicitly the attitude of the decision maker toward risks by encoding the *utility function* (or *preference function*) of the decision maker. A utility function provides a complete description of the decision maker's attitude toward risk over the range of all the possible consequences related to the project under analysis.

A common procedure used to define the utility function for a given decision is to assess the *certainty equivalents* of specified 50/50 gambles presented to the decision maker. A certainty equivalent is that amount offered to the decision maker that will make him indifferent as to whether to accept the amount or to accept the risks implied in the gamble. The process of assessing a given utility function is well understood and straightforward. The corresponding utility function in terms of NPV for our example was determined from gambles that have been used to assess utilities 0.25, 0.50 and 0.75, as shown in figure 9-4.

An exponential function was fitted to the data points. An exponential function has some very desirable properties that can be used to characterize utility functions. First, if all the outcomes of the gamble are increased in the same amount, then the certainty equivalent of the gamble also increases in that amount. Only linear and exponential functions satisfy this property. Second, exponential utility functions can be expressed in the following form:

$$U(x) = \frac{1 - e^{cx}}{1 - e^{-c}}$$

which allows for easy normalization, that is, $U(0) = 0$, $U(1) = 1$. The quantity c is called the *risk-aversion coefficient* and is the only parameter to be assessed if exponential utility functions are used. When $c = 0$, the deci-

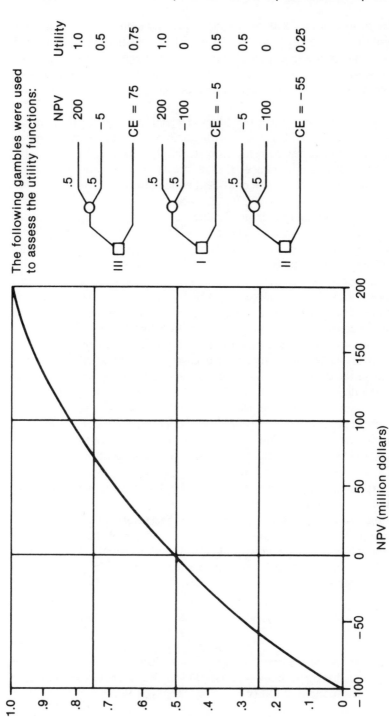

Figure 9-4. Utility Function for NPV with Assessment Gambles

sion maker is risk neutral. Positive values of c indicate risk aversion; negative values of c indicate risk-seeking attitudes. Thus c plays a role similar to that of the discount rate for time preferences.

The utility function developed for this project was:

$$U(\text{NPV}) = 1.3 \, [1 - e^{-.055(\text{NPV} + 100)}].$$

The utility function allows characterization of each individual strategy by a single number, its expected utility. Then the optimal strategy is selected by simply choosing that strategy with the highest expected utility.

Therefore, if a backward-induction process were used, each of the terminal values of the criterion should be converted into utilities. The optimal strategy is determined by working backward through the tree computing expected utility values for the events and by selecting those alternatives that lead to the highest expected utility.

If a Monte Carlo simulation approach is used, at each trial the value of the criterion is converted into corresponding utility. The expected utility value is calculated for each strategy, and the strategy having the highest expected utility will be optimal. It might be desirable to transform the expected utility of the optimal strategy into a certainty equivalent to provide the decision maker with a feeling for the amount of money he would accept instead of undertaking the venture.

For our project, the leading strategies had the following expected utilities and certainty equivalents.

Strategy	Bid High for B Alone (1)	Bid High with Partner (2)	Bid Low with Partner (6)	Develop Own Property with Partner (7)	Do Nothing (8)
Expected Utility	.704	.747	.750	.797	0.512
Certainty Equivalent (million $NPV)	56	71	72	90	0

As was evident from the NPV risk profiles, strategy 7 is still dominant. It is now also clear that strategies 2 and 6 are almost indistinguishable and that strategy 1 is much poorer than the other strategies.

Optimal Strategies with Two Objectives. The steps described so far provide a complete and comprehensive analysis of capital-investment decisions with a single objective. The consequences of our project could not be evaluated properly by considering merely profitability measures. A second objective of great significance was the availability of products.

A highly simplified treatment of multiple-objective decisions can be performed by assigning a weight to each objective that reflects its importance to the decision maker. This approach will transform the multiple-objective analysis into a single-objective problem. This procedure neither recognizes nonlinear tradeoffs that frequently exist among competing objectives nor considers interdependencies among these objectives.

The two competing objectives and their associated attributes that the decision maker considered important in our decision situation were:

1. Maximizing economic return from the venture (NPV).
2. Maximizing product availability.

The ranges of the attributes were -100-200 for NPV and 0-100 for available percentage of production (P). The single-objective utility function for NPV was established earlier (for $P = 100$). In order to evaluate the proper functional form of the two-objective utility functions, it was necessary to determine the utility dependence of the two objectives. By reassessing the certainty equivalents of NPV at several values of P, and then by repeating the procedure for P at several values of NPV, it was concluded that the two objectives were utility independent. A quasi-additive utility-function form was adopted.[7]

The single objective utility functions $U_1(NPV)$ and $U_2(P)$ were fitted to first-order exponential functions. The assessment of the constants was performed and resulted in the function:

$$U(NPV,P) = 0.988(1 - e^{-.005[NPV + 100]}) + 0.197(1 - e^{-.03P})$$
$$+ 0.067 (1 - e^{-.005[NPV + 100]})(1 - e^{-.03P})$$

A corresponding utility *surface* can be constructed and the point of indifference used to determine the constants in the utility functions. This utility function expresses the values of tradeoffs for the decision maker. The results are discussed later on.

Conclusions

In many corporate-development and acquisition projects there are several competing objectives that need to be considered in order to determine the optimal strategy. For the project analyzed in this chapter, the two-objective optimal strategy (strategy 2) was not found to be optimal when only monetary objectives were considered. The ranking of strategies in the three methods of analysis was:

Strategy	Bid High for B Alone (1)	Bid High with Partner (2)	Bid Low with Partner (6)	Develop Property with Partner (7)	Do Nothing (8)
NPV analysis rank	4	3	2	1	5
NPV risk utility rank	4	3	2	1	5
Two-objective utility rank	2	1	4	3	5

It can be seen that the rankings change significantly when the additional objective is introduced. The difference in terms of NPV between strategies 7 and 2 is $20 million, whereas the difference between the two strategies' certainty equivalents (in NPV) with two objectives is − $5 million. If the certainty equivalents from the NPV analysis had been chosen as the basis for the decision on which alternative to pursue, the wrong strategy would have been chosen. In addition, the relative value of the chosen strategy 1 would have been overestimated by $25 million when compared with the multiattribute optimal strategy: 2 value.

In our example, the decision maker chose to pursue strategy 2 as a result of the analysis outlined.

Notes

1. Much of the conceptual basis for the approach relies on the field of decision analysis and on Raiffa, *Decision Analysis*; Schlaifer, *Analysis of Decisions*; Keeney and Raiffa, "Decision Analysis"; Howard "Decision Analysis"; and Spetzler and Zamora, "Decision Analysis."
2. Howard, "Decision Analysis."
3. Simon, *New Science of Management Decision.*
4. de Neufville and Keeney, "Use of Decision Analysis."
5. Briskin, "Method of Unifying Multiple Objective Functions."
6. See Fishburn, *Utility Theory*; Raiffa, *Decision Analysis*; de Neufville and Keeney, "Use of Decision Analysis"; Keeney, "Utility Functions"; and Keeney and Raiffa, "Decision Analysis."
7. Keeney and Raiffa, "Decision Analysis."

References

Bernhard, R.H. "Mathematical Programming Models for Capital Budgeting—A Survey, Generalization, and Critique." *Journal of Financial and Quantitative Analysis*, June 1969, pp. 111-158.

Bierman, H., and Smidt, S. *The Capital Budgeting Decision*. New York: Macmillan, 1966.

Briskin, L.E. "A Method of Unifying Multiple Objective Functions." *Management Science* 12 (1966):B406-B416.

Brown, R.V. "Do Managers Find Decision Theory Useful?" *Harvard Business Review*, May-June 1970, pp. 78-89.

de Neufville, R., and Keeney, R.L. "Use of Decision Analysis in Airport Development for Mexico City." In *Analysis of Public Systems*, ed. A.W. Drake, R.L. Keeney, and P.M. Morse. Cambridge, Mass.: MIT Press, 1972.

Ellis, H.M., and Keeney, R.L. "A Rational Approach for Government Decisions Concerning Air Pollution." In *Analysis of Public Systems*, ed. A.W. Drake, R.L. Keeney, and P.M. Morse. Cambridge, Mass.: MIT Press, 1972.

Fishburn, P.C. *Utility Theory for Decision Making*. New York: John Wiley & Sons, 1970.

Fishburn, P.C.; Murphy, A.H.; and Isaacs, H.H. "Sensitivity of Decisions to Probability Estimate Errors: A Reexamination." *Operations Research* 16 (1968):254-267.

Hammond, J.S., III. "Better Decisions with Preference Theory." *Harvard Business Review*, November-December 1967, pp. 123-141.

Hertz, D.B. "Risk Analysis in Capital Investment." *Harvard Business Review*, January-February 1964, pp. 95-106.

_____ . "Investment Policies That Pay Off." *Harvard Business Review*, January-February 1968, pp. 96-108.

Hespos, R., and Strassmann, P. "Stochastic Decision Trees for the Analysis of Investment Decisions." *Management Science* 11 (1965):B244-B259.

Hillier, F. "The Derivation of Probabilistic Information for the Evaluation of Risky Investments." *Management Science* 9 (1963):B443-B457.

Hirschleifer, J. "On the Theory of Optimal Investment." *Journal of Political Economy*, August 1958, pp. 329-352.

Howard, R.A. "The Foundation of Decision Analysis." *IEEE Transactions on Systems Science and Cybernetics* SSC-7, September 1968.

_____ . "Decision Analysis: Applied Decision Theory." In *Proceedings of the Fourth International Conference on Operational Research*, ed. D.B. Hertz and J. Melere. New York: John Wiley & Sons, 1968.

_____ . "Risk Preference." In *Readings in Decision Analysis*. Stanford Research Institute, 1974.

Keeney, R.L. "Utility Functions for Multiattributed Consequences." *Management Science* 18 (1972):276-287.

——— . "An Illustrated Procedure for Assessing Multiattributed Utility Functions." *Sloan Management Review*, Fall 1972, pp. 37-50.

Keeney, R.L., and Raiffa, H. "A Critique of Formal Analysis in Public Decision Making." In *Analysis of Public Systems*, ed. A.W. Drake, R.L. Keeney, and P.M. Morse. Cambridge, Mass.: MIT Press, 1972.

——— . "Decision Analysis with Multiple Objectives." Forthcoming.

Magee, J.F. "Decision Trees for Decision Making." *Harvard Business Review*, July-August 1964, pp. 126-138.

——— . "How to Use Decision Trees in Capital Investment." *Harvard Business Review*, September-October 1964, pp. 79-96.

Modigliani, F., and Miller, M.H. "The Cost of Capital, Corporation Finance and the Theory of Investment." *American Economic Review* 48, no. 3, 1958.

Naylor, T.H.; Balintfy, J.L.; Burdick, D.S.; and Chu, K. *Computer Simulation Techniques*. New York: John Wiley & Sons, 1966.

Pratt, J.; Raiffa, H.; and Schlaifer, R.O. *Introduction to Decision Under Uncertainty*. Boston: Graduate School of Business Administration, Harvard University, 1964.

——— . *Introduction to Statistical Decision Theory*. New York: McGraw-Hill, 1965.

Raiffa, H. *Decision Analysis: Introductory Lectures*. Reading, Mass.: Addison-Wesley, 1968.

Raiffa, H., and Schlaifer, R.O. *Applied Statistical Decision Theory*. Boston: Division of Research, Graduate School of Business Administration, Harvard University, 1961.

Salazar, R.C., and Sen, S.K. "A Simulation Model of Capital Budgeting Under Uncertainty." *Management Science* 15 (1968):B161-B179.

Schlaifer, R.O. *Analysis of Decisions Under Uncertainty*. New York: McGraw-Hill, 1969.

Simon, H.A. *The New Science of Management Decision*. New York: Harper & Row, 1960.

Solomon, E. *The Theory of Financial Management*. New York: Columbia University Press, 1963.

Spetzler, C.S. "The Development of a Corporate Risk Policy for Capital Investment Decisions." *IEEE Transactions of Systems Science and Cybernetics* SSC-4, September 1968.

Spetzler, C.S., and Zamora, R.M. "Decision Analysis of a Facilities Investment and Expansion Problem." Stanford, Calif.: Stanford Research Institute.

Swalm, R.O. "Utility Theory—Insights Into Risk Taking." *Harvard Business Review*, November-December 1966.

Weingartner, H.M. *Mathematical Programming and the Analysis of the Capital Budgeting Problems.* Englewood Cliffs, N.J.: Prentice-Hall, 1963.

———. "Capital Budgeting of Interrelated Projects: Survey and Synthesis." *Management Science*, March 1966, pp. A485-A516.

Winkler, R.L. "The Consensus of Subjective Probability Distributions." *Management Science* 15 (1968):B61-B75.

Part III
Organization and Policy Issues

Part II

Orientation and Performance

10

Functions and Roles in the Acquisition Process

Introduction and Operating Modes

As a step involving a substantial degree of risk and with a major impact on the future of the enterprise, the acquisition (or divestiture) decision is clearly a matter reserved for top management and the board of directors. Increasingly, however, specialized inside corporate-development staff are being used as part of the acquisition process.

One force in the evolution of corporate development has been the acquisition of U.S. companies by foreign interests. U.S. corporate culture differs markedly from those of, for example, Japan, Germany, or the Middle East. This, together with the interest of these latter acquirers in acquisition here in the United States (see chapter 1), means that all parties require a knowledge and understanding of the cultural differences in order to negotiate effectively and to reach agreements in the 1980s.

There are few general rules pertaining to functions and roles. Each corporation has its own personality, style, culture, and biases. In the last analysis, these factors will determine the types of situations that will be of interest and ultimately approved, as well as the approach and organization of the acquisition effort itself.

Formerly, acquisitions were too often made largely on the basis of a situation brought to the parties by outsiders (reactive mode) and after only brief analysis of short-term earnings potential, plus some consideration of fit and longer-term issues. Although the services of finders and intermediaries remain important, and although short-term earnings effects cannot be overlooked, today's efforts are more likely to involve heavier staff inputs with much more consideration given to an organized search rather than simply to a reactive or opportunistic mode. There is also more attention to the analysis of alternative strategic possibilities, longer-range implications, and postmerger management questions. Portfolio theory, asset management, and related concepts from contemporary corporate finance and managerial economics are increasingly a part of the work of investment bankers, consultants, and staff groups within large corporations. Our experience is that these approaches to diversification and acquisition are not yet fully understood or appreciated generally by the active chief executive officer (CEO) and board. However, these concepts appear to be in the process of being adopted, if not formally then at least implicitly.

Five typical operating modes or styles, three of them active and two passive, to carry out the acquisition/corporate-development process are shown in table 10-1. We include, from our experience, comments on the appropriateness and effectiveness of each. Some of these issues are further discussed in the next section.

Nature of the Corporate-Development/ Acquisition Organization

Formalization of the corporate-development function, including that of acquisition, is a relatively new phenomenon. For most companies, a formal corporate-development/acquisition organization is of relatively recent origin; the majority of such departments have been formally organized only since 1974.[1] Merger and acquisition activities are commonly, although not always, part of or allied with strategic planning and general corporate development.

Unless tied in with operational planning, business analysis, or economics—as opposed to mainly strategic-planning activities—most departments tend to be very small, with one to four professional staff members working with the department head. The manager frequently has a financial or strategic-planning background and may have come from an investment-banking or consulting firm. The composition of the staff varies, but often includes one or two recent business-school graduates who rotate out of the department into other positions in the corporation after two years or so.

Ad hoc groups or task forces are commonly formed by corporate-development departments to address questions of industry outlook, to search for and analyze candidates, and to conduct detailed reviews of promising situations. Finance, legal, economic, and tax staff are often involved, along with managers from operating divisions. Clearly, unusually good working interpersonal relationships and the ability to "sell" or "unsell" ideas to top management are key. The permanent corporate-development staff will also be interacting with outsiders—investment bankers, finders, consultants, and others. In fact, a significant portion of the director's time may be spent developing and analyzing ideas with outsiders. Some departments regularly meet with selected groups of outsiders to explore acquisition ideas. This contact may include not only investment and commercial bankers and "financial consultants," but also former company presidents, "head hunters," and other knowledgeable individuals. However done, informing the financial community and others of the corporation's goals and "needs" is important to generating the leads for a successful acquisition program. Formal steps may include speeches and putting such in-

Table 10-1
Alternate Operating Modes for the Acquisition Process

Mode	Comments
A. Active	
1. CEO, chairman, or president makes commitment to program, but delegates major authority and responsibility to corporate-development department.	Typically an effective mode. Particularly useful in getting an acquisition program off the ground. Makes use of full corporate resources.
2. CEO, chairman, or president carries out and takes full responsibility for the program.	Can be a good approach where strong CEO exists, but can lead to an overly opportunistic emphasis. However, the development of internal-staff expertise is usually required for ongoing programs.
3. Corporate development develops, presents, and supports recommendations and is involved in implementation.	Appropriate for ongoing efforts in organizations that have a record of past success and management support.
B. Passive	
1. Investment bankers, brokers, finders, "friends," and others bring situations to the attention of CEO and/or directors.	Without goals and commitment to acquisitions, this opportunistic approach is a long shot. Where specific corporate interests are articulated, this sometimes can be a satisfactory approach.
2. Internal staff generates and presents ideas, but no commitment to specific acquisition plan or goals has been made by CEO or the corporation.	Least-effective approach. Without top-management commitment and support this approach is unlikely to produce significant results, except possibly over the very long term.

formation in the Annual Report. Communicating the company's financial and management culture can also be crucial.

The effectiveness of the corporate-development function depends to a major degree on its relationship to the chief executive officer or chairman; to the heads of operating units who often must support the proposed acquisition or other course of action; and to staff heads, such as those of finance, legal, and marketing departments, with whom corporate-development staff must work. A wide spectrum of effectiveness can be attributed to the corporate-development function. Some departments importantly influence the growth of the corporation and operate in line with the roles outlined later on. Others, in a lesser position of influence, are basically researchers, list generators, and financial analysts. In many firms a major task of the corporate-development/acquisition manager is to evaluate potential deals that reach the company after its interests and general criteria have become known. Sometimes acquisition groups concentrate largely on generating ideas for top management's reaction, thereby hoping that an outline of the scope and criteria of a "plan" for the corporation and their own efforts will slowly evolve.

In many companies the organization and role of the corporate-development department undergo relatively frequent change due to varying levels of activity, changes in the chief executive officer or others in top management who have the ultimate corporate development responsibilities, or other factors. In a few large companies where divisional acquisitions are common, a substantial part of the function is carried out at divisional levels, with final approval made centrally.

A corporate-development department can work well in a corporation with a successful record of acquisitions, internal development, and joint ventures. However, getting a new function off the ground can be extremely difficult. We have seen this effectively done where the chairman, president, or CEO takes on the formal responsibility himself—a common occurrence—or where a strong corporate-development officer is appointed who is committed to acting as a change agent and is not afraid to step on toes.

In its idealized form, the corporate-development department is a major force behind acquisition and other forms of growth and diversification. However, the head of this function is a delegate of the CEO and the board and, in effect, often acts primarily as an "air-traffic controller" rather than a "pilot" in marshaling the resources of the corporation toward its acquisition and corporate-development goals.

In our experience, corporate-development responsibility generally, and the acquisition/merger effort in particular, are among the most difficult staff-management tasks in a large organization. For many executives this represents a frustrating career period, with results few and far between. For others, fortunately, it can be one of the most creative, exacting, and rewarding functions in corporate life. Much depends on corporate development's relationships with the CEO and key officers; whether the enterprise and corporate development have a strategic plan, mission, and commitment; and the degree to which the function is more than just a supporting internal-staff function that generates data and reports in support of work by others, including other officers, outside advisors, and consultants.

A Protocol for the Acquisition Process

Although a series of steps or a protocol can be useful in conceptualizing the overall role of corporate development and the steps in carrying out an active acquisition effort, such a scheme or methodology represents at best only a guide or checklist. It should not serve to create obstacles to opportunities meeting the company's criteria that present themselves. One useful protocol, summarized and adapted from that developed by Robert K. Mueller, chairman of Arthur D. Little, Inc., is shown in table 10-2.[2]

A matrix applying to a medium-to-large corporation and showing the roles of various functional elements is given in figure 10-1 for those nine steps of the protocol. It should be recognized that every situation will be different, that some corporations will have a more formal approach than

Table 10-2
A Protocol for the Acquisition Process

Determinative stage
   Clarify and state acquisition objectives.
   Determine top management and board commitment to the extent possible.

Scouting stage
   Search for and/or otherwise identify acquisition candidates.
   Make initial candidate assessment.

Consultation stage
   Consult with outside legal, accounting, banking, and other professionals, possibly including
      consultants.

Strategic stage
   Determine impact of the transaction on both parties.
   Develop negotiating strategy and more detailed company analysis, including consideration
      of accounting/financial and legal issues as well as personalities of the "key players."

"Sensor" stage
   Determine likely potential interest via direct or indirect contact.

"Vamp" stage
   Carry out the "act of seduction" coupled with regulatory notice and approvals

Proposal stage

Deal stage (execution)

Management (post-acquisition) stage

	Board of Directors	Top Management	Planning and Corporate Development	Finance/ Accounting	Legal	Technical
			Parties Involved			
Stage						
Determinative	+	+	+ +	+		+
Scouting	+	+	+ +	+	+	+
Consultation		+	+ +	+	+	+
Strategic		+	+ +	+	+	+
Sensor	+	+ +	+			
Vamp	+	+ +	+			
Proposal		+ +	+	+	+	
Deal	+ +	+	+	+	+	
Post Merger Management		+ +		+		

+ + — Primary Responsibility
+   — Participation and/or Approval

Source: Reprinted by permission of the publisher from James W. Bradley and Donald H. Korn, "Acquisition and Mergers: A Shifting Route to Corporate Growth" *Management Review*, March 1979, © 1979 by AMACOM, a division of American Management Associations, p. 50. All rights reserved.

Figure 10-1. Example of Functional Roles in Stages of the Acquisition Process

others, and that in some the roles shown for corporate development will be taken by one or two key officers or by outsiders.

Not shown are the important roles often played by investment bankers and consultants. For example, these organizations or individuals may bring acquisition opportunities to the company or may serve in the key role of evaluating the acquisition from an independent, outside viewpoint.

**Organizational, Cultural, and Financial
Conditions for Success**

From our experience with over a hundred corporate assignments relating to mergers and acquisitions, we find that most successes are characterized by the following:

1. Top-management involvement and commitment.

2. Sound rationale for acquisition, with explicit objectives.
3. Flexible, realistic screening criteria.
4. Persistence in the acquisition process and sound negotiating skills.
5. Willingness to take significant risk.
6. Favorable business climate and timing.
7. Availability of adequate financial and management resources.
8. Appropriate corporate linkage and integration.

The last point, linkage and integration, is central to the "sensor" and "vamp" stages of the acquisition process and to the postmerger management of acquired companies. The degree to which independence is expected to be granted or allowed can be a determining factor in interesting some candidate companies, particularly young, high-technology ventures. One format we have found useful in viewing these issues and discussing them with candidate companies is shown in table 10-3. A face-to-face meeting at which both parties fill out the chart and reach a tentative understanding of the roles of each is a powerful negotiating tool.

Acquisitions and mergers are risky decisions and, as explored in chapter 11, results do not always match expectations. Statistics on corporate acquisitions and mergers indicate that a high percentage of transactions constitute divestitures; aside from antitrust-forced divestitures, the majority are symptomatic of the fact that many corporate marriages fail. The reasons for failure are numerous, but the most common are overoptimism and the lack of adequate contingency planning. Major examples are failure to exercise healthy skepticism with respect to business projections and failure to see a mismatch in personalities between managements. Proper organization of the acquisition effort and assignment of responsibilities can materially improve the chances for success.

**The Role of Personality, Whim, and
Chance Occurrences**

The experience of the authors and of most other practitioners leads to the conclusion that issues of personal chemistry, chance occurrences, and subjective influences—including the actions and opinions of peers—are usually as important as rational quantitative analysis in making a final corporate decision regarding an acquisition or merger.

Some observers feel that a significant amount of acquisition activity is a result of management's protecting itself and its corporate assets from a raid by an outside group. That is, one corporation may seek to combine with another firm or firms as a means of reducing or eliminating the chance that

Table 10-3
Suggested Linkage Models and Mechanisms

	Independent Authority	Independent Authority After Consultation	Shared Authority	Consent—No Authority	No Authority
Resources					
Long-term financing					
Key staff appointments					
Asset management					
Major capital expenditures					
Actors					
Officer appointments					
Major organizational changes					
Management process					
Corporate concepts/purpose/objectives					
Corporate identity					
Long-range planning					
Strategy(ies)					
Measurement/control/acct/MIS					
Research and development					
Legal and patents					
Marketing					
Budgets					
Working capital					
Public relations					
Purchasing					
Other management policies					

it will, itself, be an easy target for takeover. Such action is not always consistent with classic stockholder-wealth-maximization models of the firm, but it is perfectly consistent with contemporary managerial-welfare-maximization models.

Notes

1. O'Connor, *Managing Corporate Development*.
2. Mueller, *Metadevelopment*.

References

Bradley, James W., and Korn, Donald H. "Acquisitions and Mergers: A Shifting Route to Corporate Growth." *Management Review*, March 1979.

Fogg, C. Davis. "New Business Planning: The Acquisition Process." *Industrial Marketing Management*, June 1976.

Levinson, Harry. "A Psychologist Diagnoses Merger Failures." *Harvard Business Review*, March-April 1970.

Mueller, Robert K. *Metadevelopment: Beyond the Bottom Line*. Lexington, Mass.: Lexington Books, D.C. Heath and Company, 1977. (See pp. 123-133.)

O'Connor, Rochelle. *Managing Corporate Development*. New York: Conference Board, 1980.

11 Why Business Combinations Succeed or Fail

Allen H. Seed III

This chapter examines some of the reasons that business combinations succeed or fail and suggests steps that can be taken to improve the success-to-failure ratio in this field of endeavor. The discussion focuses on the ingredients of successful acquisitions and on traps to be avoided. It provides specific comments and insights, particularly on the important personal, managerial, and cultural factors described in chapters 2 and 8.

The grim fact that one divestiture is announced for every two or three acquisitions suggests that corporate combinations—even when undertaken in the best of faith—are hazardous. The aura of good feeling and high expectation that surrounds the closing often gives way to distrust, disappointment, and recrimination. Each case that fell short of expectations obviously looked attractive when proposed, but for one reason or another things did not develop as planned.

Some individuals, such as Royal Little of Textron, Harold Geneen of ITT, and Charles Bluhdorn of Gulf and Western can point to unusual success records. However, for every Textron, ITT, and Gulf and Western, there are scores of companies that share mixed or unhappy experiences as a result of their corporate acquisitions; and even these three giants will admit their mistakes. In fact, the chief executive of a successful acquirer of several businesses confided that "the trick is not to be more aggressive than the next guy, but to simply avoid making mistakes along the way."

The successful acquisitions seem to have several characteristics in common. Not all of these characteristics are present in every acquisition, but the odds of success are enhanced if they are. They include:

1. *Strategic purpose*, resulting in a meaningful fit.
2. *Financial enhancement*, leading to improved earnings and a more desirable financial position.
3. *Personal compatibility* between the managements involved.
4. *Industry knowledge*—a field of business that the acquiring company understands.
5. *Business health*—neither partner is "sick" and seeking an instant cure.
6. *Smooth integration* of the acquired business according to a sensible plan.

7. *Motivated management*—acquired management did not "go fishing" after the deal was closed.
8. *Thorough investigation*, with all the right questions asked prior to acquisition.
9. *Realistic expectations* and proper appraisal of returns, risks, and capital requirements.
10. *Good luck*—subsequent external events favored the combination.

Strategic Purpose

In the conglomerating days of the 1960s, many businesses were acquired with so-called Chinese money. It really did not matter what business the acquired company was in, as long as reported earnings were enhanced. Because stocks selling at "go-go" price-to-earnings (P/E) ratios were used as a medium of exchange, and because the accounting profession did not require that goodwill be amortized, short-term results supported this acquisition binge. After the economy and market turned, this financial "house of cards" of more than one conglomerate collapsed, resulting in many divestitures. All these acquisitions had one characteristic in common: lack of strategic purpose.

Even today, it is easy to succumb to an acquisition opportunity that does not make strategic sense. The proposition looks like a good deal, but it does not fit from a business standpoint. Although the word *synergism* may have been overused, it is still important that an acquired company fit in with the strategic objectives of its parent.

Business strategies can, of course, take different forms in terms of technological development, markets, distribution, manufacturing, and the use of financial leverage and the like. Furthermore, these strategies may be formally and informally articulated to varying degrees in each company. But unless the prospective acquisition contributes to the achievement of a strategic purpose, the odds are that very little synergism will result.

Strategic purpose should not be confused with *strategic rationalization*. Also during the 1960s, several large manufacturing and forest-product companies rationalized entering the land-development and home-building business. This rationalization was based on their extensive capital resources, mass-production skills, and land holdings. Nevertheless, many of these companies subsequently found that the management and financial requirements of home building and land development are quite different from those of manufacturing and paper making. The style of management of each business was different, and mass-production skills do not lend themselves to home building. The building-product interests and land holdings of certain forest-product companies were not compatible with the needs of the builder. The capital of one business could not be used for the other; and when the 1970 credit crunch arrived, in many cases the capital requirements of the acquired company even conflicted with those of the parent.

Management can rationalize almost any course of action it decides to take; the financial community is full of "stories," and the marketing world is laden with "concepts." Some of these stories and concepts are very real and have constructively changed the direction of certain businesses. These usually result from enlightened, imaginative, and hard-nosed strategic planning. In such cases the acquisition is simply a step toward implementing this plan.

Financial Enhancement

There is an old saying in the corporate-development field that two and two must equal five; and indeed, from a financial standpoint, this should be an underlying prerequisite of any acquisition. Unless the projected earnings, market values, and cash flows per share with the acquisition exceed those without it, the acquisition will not make financial sense. Furthermore, the combined companies should reflect a more desirable commitment of financial resources after the acquisition than before.

The projected-earnings calculation is rather straightforward. Projected earnings are divided by the average common shares outstanding with and without the acquisition. The trick in this exercise, of course, is reasonably to project just what these earnings will be. Unfortunately, many five- and ten-year projections call for ever improving results, whereas in the real world results tend to fluctuate from year to year.

Determining prospective financial-market values and cash flows is admittedly a much more difficult task than projecting earnings per share, because even more variables are involved. Market values change depending on stock-market performance and on how the market "perceives" the effect of the combination. Prospective cash flows are based on the future dividend stream as well as on market values. Valuations are based on the present value of these often elusive flows. (These concepts have been discussed fully in chapter 7.)

It should be emphasized that a "more desirable" financial position is not necessarily a "stronger" financial position, as many companies have underutilized financial resources. Rather, it represents a "balanced" position, wherein financial resources are utilized fully without undue risk or strain. Principal potential pitfalls in this area are the excessive use of financial leverage and capital requirements that increase, rather than reduce, the cyclical financial requirements of the business.

Personal Compatibility

The partner in charge of acquisitions for a leading New York investment-banking firm has stated that the ingredient he would put at the top of the list of reasons that combinations succeed or fail would be "people." He said that 80 percent of his time is spent in solving personality problems. It is particularly important, he said, for the principals involved to like each other, because usually they must work with each other for a long time.

Beyond individual personalities, however, each company has its own distinct corporate personality. This personality is often a reflection of the personality, background, and business attitudes of the size of the business, its stage of development, and the industry involved.

Large companies are usually professionally managed and tend to operate in a highly structured fashion. They disperse responsibility for decision making; they employ money specialists; they move slowly and use formal planning, budget, performance evaluation, salary administration, and other techniques. Smaller companies, on the other hand, are generally entrepreneurial in their orientation. They are run by a few key people; they move quickly; and they have few staff specialists, little overhead, and few formalized record-keeping systems. Few small businesses can afford the staff specialization and detailed planning and control procedures that are common to larger companies. Many of the planning and control concepts used by larger businesses could be adapted for smaller businesses, but many acquirers try to install their ways of doing business without modification.

Other personality factors must be considered as well. Some businesses are run by young "hard chargers" who would be uncomfortable in a restrictive, conservative environment. The president of a small Midwestern electronics company, recently expressed concern about the cultural differences between the organization and a Japanese company that was attempting to acquire it.

Pay and employment practices vary widely among businesses. Businesses with relatively high compensation levels cannot afford to absorb businesses that pay close to the minimum wage and offer few fringe benefits.

Ethical standards also vary, as do approaches toward research, product quality, and pricing. The important point is not that these differences exist, but rather the extent to which they can be overcome without jeopardizing success of the business combination.

Industry Knowledge

One fundamental truism, often learned the hard way, is that each industry is unique. Although common organizational, management, planning, control, and financial principles may be applied widely, each field of endeavor has its own special sales, marketing, and technical characteristics that are critical to success.

Even apparently similar businesses are often quite different from one another. Apparel is different from textiles; hobbies and crafts are different from toys and games; irrigation equipment is different from farm machinery; and retail financing is different from commercial financing. Apparel is merchandising oriented, whereas textiles are production oriented. Hobbies and crafts have a creative tilt; toys and games are largely promotional. Irrigation equipment is customized by irrigation specialists, whereas farm machinery is sold through farm-machinery dealers. Retail financing serves the mass market, whereas commercial financing is quite specialized. Other characteristics are often quite subtle, reflecting unique customs, trade practices, and customer buying habits that have evolved over a number of years.

Successful managers in each industry understand these characteristics and are attuned to the culture of the industry. As a result of many years of experience, they know intuitively what motivates their customers and what can and cannot be accomplished within the framework of this culture. They are able to respond intelligently to changing circumstances.

Often, when one company is acquired by another, the acquiring company tries to force its practices onto the company that is acquired. Sometimes a fresh point of view is needed, and many skills are indeed transferable. However, too frequently the management of the acquiring company misses the mark simply because they do not understand the characteristics and culture of the industry that they have entered.

Business Health

A solid, profitable company is not necessarily a well-managed company. It is rather a company with an accepted line of useful products or services, a leading market position, and a history of financial success. Often such companies are managed by caretakers, under-motivated founding-family members, or by others who are not in a position to capitalize on the potentials involved. But such companies *do* generally offer high-quality products, acceptance in the trade, decently maintained manufacturing facilities, conservative accounting practices, and a history of "black numbers." In such cases—and there are many contemporary examples—the acquiring company provides the spark, the capital, and the management momentum needed to help an underachiever realize its full potential. Underachievers can, therefore, provide some of the most promising corporate-acquisition opportunities.

Nevertheless, an important distinction should be made between "underachievers" and "sick situations." There is a fine line between these two types of companies, and the location of this line is often elusive.

Companies for sale are usually in worse shape than the seller would have one believe—even worse, often, than one's preacquisition investigation would indicate. Thus a company that seems to be slightly ill is probably quite ill, and one that seems to be moderately ill is probably dying. Moreover, declining situations develop a momentum that is difficult to arrest and turn around.

Some individuals and firms are "business doctors" who specialize in acquiring and "turning around" sick situations. However, most successful operating-oriented company managers do a very poor job of this. The skills and operating methods that work in successful companies generally do not apply to sick companies.

Most successful managers are business builders. They do not like to fire people and cut back the organization; they do not want to work twelve hours a day, seven days a week; they like to pay their bills when due and do not like stalling their creditors; they do not like disposing of unused capacity and inventory at fire-sale prices. In short, saving a sick situation is an incompatible and unpleasant undertaking that offers only long odds of success for most organizations.

The acquiring company may also be seeking a cure for its own internal illnesses by buying a healthy partner. Sometimes this approach seems to make sense. The buyer may have a large unutilized tax-loss carryforward to offer or may be willing to relinquish management control to the seller. In such cases the combination better utilizes the resources of the component parts.

All too often companies are acquired in order to show continued growth, to dress up a balance sheet, or to divert attention from internal problems. Changes in the accounting rules have eliminated several old abuses, but the practice still continues with generally sour results.

Hard experience, therefore, dictates that healthy businesses have the best chance of success and that combinations should usually be avoided if either party is a sick situation in search of an instant cure. Sick sellers tend to get sicker, and potential buyers that have serious difficulties usually should avoid making acquisitions until they have straightened out their own internal problems.

Smooth Integration

It is important to develop an integration plan for a new acquisition before the deal is closed. The acquired management should know to whom they report in the combined organization; exactly what matters require approval of the parent; and what information will be required, in what form, and on what schedule. Most sellers do not expect to report to the chief executive officer if they are a small business and the buyer is a large one; they do not expect blank checks; and they are prepared to provide business plans, budgets, and monthly financial statements. A typical list of matters requiring parent-company approval is shown in table 11-1. These are usually regarded as reasonable requirements.

An unfortunate aftermath of many corporate combinations, however, is the conquering-army syndrome, which usually involves middle managers and staff personnel, rather than top managers. It goes something like this: "We bought you so we are better than you are . . . our ways of doing business are better than yours, and our systems are better than yours . . we know best. . . ."

Some managers give orders, make requests, and take actions with little concern for the reaction involved. In their eagerness to exercise their responsibilities, they demoralize the acquired organization, distract it from

Table 11-1
Typical List of Matters Requiring Parent-Company Approval

Plans and budgets
  Business plans
  Marketing plans
  Financial budgets
  Capital-expenditure budgets

Financial matters
  New-product-development expenditures in excess of $_____
  Capital expenditures or dispositions in excess of $_____
  Corporate commitments involving in excess of $_____
  Nonbudgeted projects and capital expenditures requiring disbursements in excess of
    $_____
  Licenses
  New long-term leases
  Contractual obligations in excess of $_____

Employment matters
  Additions and terminations of key personnel
  Changes in salaries and compensation of key personnel
  Bonus plans
  Sales-compensation plans
  New-employment-benefit plans
  Employment contracts

Other matters
  Changes in sales terms and discounts
  Changes in distribution methods
  Changes in accounting methods
  Changes in corporate structure
  Settlement of legal claims

the work of "running the store," and ignore all the reasons that the company was an attractive acquisition in the first place.

Our advice is: "Be sensitive, go slow, have a plan." Remember that the management of the acquired company is generally under great stress. Acquired-company management hopes for the best, but fears the worst. Insecurity prevails; every memo, contact, phone call, innocent question, and request is gleaned for clues and hidden meanings and magnified out of proportion.

Integration problems are magnified when a U.S. company acquires an overseas company or vice versa. Not only are substantial geographical distances and differences in language, laws, and currency involved; but, most importantly, there are often immense differences in cultural backgrounds and management techniques, as referred to earlier in this chapter. Under these circumstances, particular sensitivity is required.

Most experienced acquirers minimize their contacts with the newly acquired company. Those changes that are inevitable are made slowly, carefully, and deliberately. Unimportant changes (such as conforming administrative and reporting procedures) are postponed. The disposition to "help" is avoided unless it is clearly called for. The consequences of a clumsy integration—demoralized management, the departure of key personnel, and lost momentum—should by all means be avoided.

Motivated Management

How does one motivate millionaires? This, of course, is one of the perennial challenges of the art of management. It is also a common result of corporate matchmaking, as the owners of the acquired business are often made rich by the transaction. They may have had good incomes beforehand, but now they have something to put in the bank. They do not *have* to work.

This change in the personal financial position of the former owners of a business can change their working habits. Before the sale they may have devoted long hours each day to the business. Now there is a tendency to take time off, relax, and enjoy some of the benefits of the sale, at the expense of the old entrepreneurial spirit. The key to dealing with this problem successfully is to understand the people involved and to fashion incentives that will keep the former owners motivated as managers.

Some former owners will lose their motivation regardless of what they say before the closing or of what incentives the buyer offers. If this was their real reason for selling in the first place, then nothing the buyer can do will change the situation constructively. Although there is no cure for this problem, it should be recognized early as part of the evaluation process and provided for as part of the integration plan.

Other former owners really want to continue to build the business. They are often workaholics by nature, and they do not change their life-styles after the sale. In fact, they often are eager to be part of a well-known larger business. The key to motivating this type of individual is to provide a continued challenge, recognition, and an opportunity to achieve the gratification associated with success. These behavioral needs do not change just because there is money in the bank.

An employment contract is important, usually, only from a psychological point of view—as a signal to the former owner that the acquirer values his talent. Incentives, likewise, are important not so much in terms of what they mean in after-tax dollars, but rather as a form of recognition. Such incentives, of course, should be related to the achievement of specific strategic and profitability goals and should be competitive with amounts paid to comparable managers elsewhere.

Notwithstanding the importance of incentives, often the most important motivating force for successful former owners is freedom and lack of unnecessary interference. Personality differences, as opposed to inadequate compensation, are almost always responsible when acquired managers leave a combined company. Successful managers need the freedom to achieve their goals.

Thorough Investigation

Many corporate-development opportunities have been lost as a result of dilatory decision making. The seller generally knows a great deal more about what he has to sell than the buyer knows about what he is buying. Thus, even under the best of circumstances, the seller has a substantial advantage over the buyer. The buyer, of course, can investigate the company he is buying. Too often, however, his investigation is limited in order to maintain confidentiality or he does not allow enough time to do a thorough job. More importantly, the thoroughness of an investigation is not so much a product of the amount of data gathered as of an ability to identify the key issues and ask the right questions.

Acquisition checklists are useful in ensuring that all the necessary routine information is obtained, but are generally of little help in identifying the soft spots, risks, and possible unexploited opportunities associated with each acquisition candidate. Nor do such checklists help in sorting out the critical factors on which the future success of the business depends.

Answers to these critical questions usually are most effectively obtained from the trade and from others in the industry. Knowledgeable people in the trade (generally at the day-to-day buying level) usually can provide a fairly realistic appraisal of the condition of an acquisition candidate's product line, level of service, competitive position, and quality of sales management and field personnel. They also know what technological changes are taking place and what competition is doing. Each industry has a grapevine, and people usually like to be interviewed. A competitor will often tell you more about a company than will the principals of the company itself.

Because a company is often more affected by external forces than by its internal actions, a thorough investigation will be industry oriented and will focus on the strategic issues involved. A dramatic case in point is the impact of OPEC price increases on oil-company earnings. Too often, however, an evaluation of an acquisition candidate is directed toward the company itself rather than toward the dynamics of the marketing and competitive environment in which the company is operating. As a result, the acquirer often develops a very complete picture of the company but only a sketchy picture of its prospects, because he lacks information about what is going on in the marketplace and what the competition is doing.

Realistic Expectations

It is very easy to become enamored of a deal, as many executives have found. One is attracted to all the virtues of the prospect and tends to overlook, or to explain away, the faults. In the course of courting and selling the candidate, it is natural to identify with him. He becomes a friend, and one shares his hopes and aspirations.

Moreover, each prospective acquisition usually has a sponsor within the acquiring company, whose responsibility it becomes to make the deal attractive to his associates. This individual therefore functions as an advocate rather than as an objective analyst. Consequently, the tendency is often to accept overoptimistic sales and earnings forecasts and to underestimate the problems associated with integrating the business and achieving the forecasts.

We have found, therefore, that as a general rule all projections should be discounted. Future returns will probably be lower than projected, future results will take longer to achieve, and capital requirements will be higher than planned. If realistic expectations are established in the first place, one is less likely to be disappointed with subsequent results.

One way to obtain realistic expectations is to provide a "devil's advocate," logically the chief financial executive, for each potential acquisition candidate. This avoids placing the candidate's sponsor in the schizophrenic position of having both to "sell the deal" and to evaluate the plans and projections that are prepared.

Good Luck

Chance and the element of business risk play a major role in all corporate acquisitions. Despite careful planning, thorough investigation, and realistic analysis, even the best-laid plans can fall apart as a result of unforeseen circumstances. The energy crisis severely curtails prospects for recreational-vehicle manufacturers; droughts crumble the hopes of farm-machinery companies and spark sales for irrigation-equipment manufacturers; and a money crunch raises havoc in the home-building or consumer-finance business.

There is a strong element of luck in corporate acquisitions. Some acquisitions would have worked out had not such and such happened. Others worked out because it did. Some say that men of vision are able to foresee the impact of uncontrollable factors. Perhaps this is so; but, as previously noted, even the most successful acquirers will admit to being wrong a certain percentage of the time.

The point is that risk permeates the acquisition process and that the rules of chance have a strong bearing on the results achieved. Corporate acquisitions are not for the fainthearted. Acquisition is not the easy road to success. Once the road is embarked on, however, the odds of success are enhanced if the characteristics discussed herein are present.

12

Buying Back One's Own Stock as an Alternative to Acquisition

Background and Objectives

This chapter reviews and summarizes a number of issues concerning the repurchase of a corporation's own stock as an alternative to acquisition or internal development. Many corporations are still reluctant to take the buy-back step in lieu of acquisition, in part because sales, total income, asset growth, diversification, and other corporate objectives are not met. In addition, some managements may feel they would be cast in a poor light for failure to develop attractive external- or internal-investment opportunities.

Although the main focus of this book is toward acquisition as a means of achieving corporate growth and diversification, both stockholder and corporate interests can sometimes be better served by a stock-repurchase plan. For corporations with excess cash, buying back one's own stock may, under certain circumstances, be an attractive alternative to a major acquisition program or to large-scale capital expenditures in the business. Although stock repurchases are relatively common, in our view they are not usually considered an alternative to acquisition, but are carried out for other reasons, including the perception that a stock is currently undervalued. (This "undervaluation" concept may on the surface appear to contradict the efficient-market hypothesis of modern financial-economics theory. However, an undervaluation may exist if one assumes, for example, a difference in the time horizons between the passive investor and the active corporation (see chapters 2 and 7)).

Rationale for Stock Repurchase

Reasons sometimes advanced for a stock-repurchase program, beyond the perception that the stock is currently undervalued, are as follows:

1. Increase reported earnings per share and achieve a higher market price for the stock by reducing the number of shares outstanding.
2. Provide income to selling stockholders as capital gains rather than as dividends at ordinary income rates. (Tax advice should be sought here to ensure that capital-gains treatment will be attained.)

3. Change the corporation's capital structure by reducing equity.
4. Effect a change in capital structure by exchanging another class of security for some of the outstanding common.
5. Acquire stock for later use in conjunction with acquisitions or an employee stock-purchase plan.
6. Carry out a defensive strategy to remove shares held by "marginal stockholders" who might sell out to a potential acquirer; that is, improve control.
7. Take out the small stockholder who may be costly to service.
8. Remove a large block of stock held by an institutional seller who wishes to sell without affecting the market adversely.
9. Shift from public to private ownership. (The issues here are beyond the scope and intent of this chapter.)
10. Create greater values for the corporation and/or the remaining shareholders than are possible through acquisition or internal investment.

While all of the foregoing can be valid reasons for initiating a repurchase plan, and all except no. 9 are discussed later on, our emphasis will be on presenting a case for consideration of the last reason as a possible alternative to acquisition as being in the best interest of the corporation and its stockholders.

Methods of Carrying Out a Buy-Back Program

Repurchase can be accomplished by three means. Open-market purchase can be carried out over time where relatively modest percentages of the outstanding stock are involved. As discussed later, this is a common practice. Direct negotiation is possible where substantial blocks are involved and where the purchase is at approximate market value. It is important that this be carried out so that other stockholders are not injured by not being afforded the opportunity to sell their stock to the corporation and that applicable SEC and other regulations are followed. Finally, a tender offer to all stockholders, usually at a premium above market, is an effective and often used tool to repurchase subtantial quantities of stock within a short period of time. Specific disclosure requirements apply to tender offers and open-market repurchases.

Recent Practice

We have not tabulated the number of companies repurchasing their own stock, but it is subtantial. A published study in 1975 indicated that more than 25 percent of the companies listed on the New York Stock Exchange have been engaged in repurchase activities. This practice was particularly common when stocks were selling at low prices compared to book value—for example, in the 1973-1975 period. In the late 1970s one of the most massive stock repurchases, in dollar terms, was that of IBM, although less than 5 percent of the outstanding common was involved.

Currently a substantial number of corporations are or have recently been engaged in a repurchase program. A small sample of these is shown in table 12-1, to illustrate size, types of repurchase, and stated reasons for doing so. Many of these have been carried out through the cash-tender route; in some cases, the dollar amounts involved have been substantial.

In most cases a combination of reasons seems to dictate repurchase. Only in a few instances can we detect a clear-cut decision not to reinvest or not to consider an acquisition at any one point in time in favor of a stock repurchase. However, the lack of better alternatives for corporate assets is a part of some decisions to repurchase.

Discussion of Conventional Repurchase Rationale

Increase Earnings per Share and Sometimes Book Value per Share as Well as Achieve a Rise in Market Price; Provide Nondividend Cash Income to Stockholders (1, 2). [Numbers in parentheses refer to items in the list earlier in this chapter.] Shares repurchased and held as treasury stock, like stock repurchased and cancelled, are not credited with earnings or book value, which apply only to outstanding common stock or stock equivalents. Thus earnings per share of the remaining stock outstanding are increased by the percentage of the stock repurchased. For example, if 10 percent of the outstanding stock is repurchased, then earnings per share are increased 10 percent. Since stockholders' equity is reduced by the cost of the reacquired shares, the book value of the remaining stock outstanding is affected. The precise book-value change is dependent on the price at which the stock was reacquired. If the stock is reacquired below book value, then a book-value increase applies to the remaining shares.

Importantly, if the outlook for the corporation is not changed, and the same price-to-earnings ratio is in effect, then the fewer remaining shares with higher per-share earnings should, in theory, have a greater per-share value. Sale by stockholders above their cost basis may be subject to capital-gains treatment, rather than to treatment as ordinary income. Companies with a sudden spurt of earnings and/or a heavy cash position may want to use a stock-repurchase plan as an alternative to dividend payments, when they are uncertain of being able to maintain a higher dividend rate. Thus they may be able effectively to offer the stockholder a payment at capital-gains rates in place of dividends.

Table 12-1
Selected Examples of Stock Repurchase

Company	Rates of Repurchase	Form of Repurchase	Number of Shares Repurchased and Percentage of Outstanding Stock	Price per Share of Tender Offer	Approximate Dollar Value of Repurchase	State or Apparent Reason for Repurchase
Bundy Corporation	Announced 4/4/80	Open market	500,000 shares 12.2% of outstanding common	—	$4.4 million at 4/80 price	To accumulate treasury shares for general corporate purposes
Continental Corporation	Announced 10/19/79	Open market and negotiated transaction	3 million shaers 5.6% of outstanding common	—	$75.7 million at 10/79 price	Undervaluation of stock
Esmark, Inc.	Announced 7/6/80	Tender	10 million shares 49.5% of outstanding common	$30 per share plus subordinated debenture with a $40 undiscounted value for each share	$400 million at $40/share	Part of company's reorganization program. Repurchase will also utilize the large credit to 1980 income created by Esmark's sale of Vickers Energy.
Hilton Hotels	11/14/77	Tender	1,838,195 shares 13.9% of outstanding common	$22 per share	$40.4 million	Stock was undervalued relative to fair market value.
Saxon Industries	2/8/80	Tender/negotiated transactions	766,700 shares 11.0% of outstanding common	$10.50 per share	$8.1 million	Strengthen control (purchased shares from group of shareholders, including Icahn & Co. and Carl Icahn)
Spencer Companies	Announced 8/8/80	Negotiated transaction	269,000 shares 15.7% of outstanding common	—	$2.4 million	Repurchase by Spencer of holdings including Initio Inc.'s. Prior to repurchase, Initio acquired 110,000 shares and simultaneously proposed a joint venture with Spencer in the mail-order business.
Syntex Corporation	8/11/80	Open market	2.0 million shares 10.7% of outstanding common	—	$58 million	Undervaluation of stock

Company	Date	Method	Shares	Price	Amount	Purpose
Texaco Inc.	Announced 4/4/80	Open market	3 million shares 1.1% of outstanding common	—	$106.1 million at 4/80 price	To provide shares in anticipation of conversion by holders of certain convertible debt of subsidiary companies
Tyler Corporation	Announced 2/29/80	Tender offer	Shareholders owning less than 100 shares as of 2/19/80	$17 per share or closing market price on date of receipt plus $25 transaction fee	—	To weed out small shareholders
United Brands	Announced 1/19/80	Open market	1.0 million shares 9.1% of outstanding common	—	$12 million	Corporate purposes; stock-option plans for company executives

The long-range market-price effect of repurchase programs remains somewhat muddled, in our view. Since repurchase may be construed as a lack of alternative opportunities or as a partial liquidation of the corporation, the purchase may not materially affect market price, at least from a reduced-supply standpoint. However, the fact that management believes the stock is undervalued with respect to its true longer-term future prospects, as evidenced by a repurchase program, or the fact that a company can reacquire its stock below book value, can be philosophically attractive to the corporation in periods of low stock prices. Some studies have indicated that stock-repurchase plans generally do not affect stock prices favorably in relation to the overall market, at least over the near term. But other observers have come to a different conclusion. The perceived prospects for individual companies, the state and direction of the market at the time, and other similar considerations make any overall conclusion on this issue difficult.

Change the Company's Capital Structure by Reducing Equity (3,4). Some companies may find themselves in a heavy cash position, believe their equity as a percentage of total capital is too high, and be content to live with more leverage. This could be the case in a relatively mature industry or where changes in technology or other aspects of the business will require less equity capital in the future than they did in the past. The effect of a major stock-repurchase program is immediately to reduce cash and equity and to increase earnings per share. This argument has been used to explain, for example, some of the stock repurchase by well-capitalized bank holding companies in the early 1970s. Similarly, other classes of securities could be exchanged for common to effect a change in capital structure.

Purchase of Stock for Later Use in Conjunction with an Acquisition or a Stock-Purchase Plan (5). Although under current economic and financial conditions cash is often preferred over stock for acquisitions, the use of stock still continues. Stock-for-stock transactions have been at various periods of time in the past—and probably will be again at some point in the future—the prevalent mechanism for achieving acquisitions. Repurchasing stock for later use in acquisitions, as opposed to issuing new stock, can allow, in effect, an advantageous exchange of stock equivalent to a cash-for-stock deal. A similar argument can be made with respect to employee stock-purchase plans. A number of companies publicly state these two reasons for repurchase.

Repurchase as a Defensive Strategy (6). Repurchase, particularly if it involves a tender offer above market, has been advanced as a strategy to remove shares held by marginal stockholders who might be amenable to a sellout via a tender offer from an acquirer. More generally, one can view

repurchases, if in reasonable volumes, as a step to improve control of the corporation by management.

Remove Selected Stockholders from the Market (7,8). An institution or other investor may have a substantial block of stock that it desires to dispose of. As a sale to other outsiders, however, it might adversely affect the market or control of the corporation. In such cases, sale of that stock directly to the corporation under a repurchase scheme in direct negotiation may well be appropriate. A related device is a stock-purchase plan designed to remove the small stockholder who is costly to service.

**Repurchase as an Alternative to Acquisition or
Major Reinvestment in the Corporation's
Existing Business**

As previously mentioned, corporations and others have used a variety of reasons to explain stock-repurchase plans. These often center around the belief that the corporation's stock is selling at "too low a price" or that the corporation should reserve shares for future acquisitions or stock-purchase plans. However, repurchase may be interpreted under the "step doctrine" as being part of a merger plan and might interfere with a later tax-free exchange (see chapter 8).

The argument advanced in this section is that corporations should consider directly the question of repurchase of stock as an alternative to acquisitions (and internal reinvestment). Some comments and principles are set forth.

Acquisition-evaluation techniques have been treated in chapter 7. In summary, the majority of large corporations generally analyze acquisition and other investment opportunities based on discounted cash-flow techniques. This recognizes the time value of money and a minimum rate of return or hurdle rate based on the cost of capital and other factors. The required rates of return are often adjusted for the varying risk factors of the proposed acquisition or investment. Short-term earnings-per-share effects, pay-back period, and other measures also clearly come into play.

An analysis similar to that for an acquisition is appropriate for stock repurchase. We conclude that the buy-back alternative should be considered more often by firms with liquidity in excess of operating needs, and where present major acquisition or reinvestment opportunities to the corporation yield returns no higher than its cost of capital. In addition, of course, the indicated returns from a buy-back proposal should be above both the cost of capital and that of available investment alternatives. Some of the questions to be considered, including that of insider information, are presented in table 12-2.

Table 12-2
Some Issues to Be Considered in Repurchase Transactions Carried Out in Lieu of Acquisition or Internal Investment

From the Corporation's Viewpoint	From the Passive Investor's Standpoint
1. Is the indicated return favorable, and is it clearly above both the cost of capital and that of other investment alternatives?	1. If analysis favors the sale: 　a. Does the corporation know something the investor does not that will soon be reflected in the market price? 　b. Is too short-term a view being taken?
2. Have all costs been considered, including, where appropriate, the opportunity cost of capital and interest costs on any borrowed funds used for repurchase?	2. Are dividends and/or earnings likely to increase and, if so, would the investor be better off holding his stock?
3. Could repurchase be considered part of a "step transaction" and, therefore, interfere with a nontaxable acquisition situation? Is it otherwise a problem because of statutory restrictions or loan covenants (net-worth tests)?	3. Have all tax consequences been considered?
4. Have earnings-per-share and book-value effects been carefully reviewed? Would a change in dividend policy be preferable to repurchase?	4. Does the investor have better alternatives for the funds received from the sale?
5. Are assumptions about present stock undervaluation and future prospects supportable?	5. Is the effect of the repurchase likely to impair the liquidity in the market for the stock?
6. What are the overall efects from repurchase on the capital structure?	
7. Are the present holdings of management and the size of repurchase program such a large percentage of the stock outstanding that management versus stockholder control becomes an issue? What effects will these have on the market price of the stock? On listing the stock?	
8. Is the repurchase program likely to impair liquidity in the market for the stock such that the cost of equity capital will be higher subsequently?	
9. Is there anything about the transaction that implies improper use of insider information?	

Note: Tax issues for stock repurchases from both the shareholder and corporate viewpoints are complex. In this table and accompanying discussions we have made the simplifying assumption that the repurchase will be treated as a sale and not as a dividend. This will not necessarily be true in all cases, however.

Illustrative Example: Valuation Disparities

To show some of the issues involved, we have considered company "Cash Rich." Basic data are shown in table 12-3. The company can be further classified as a firm in a relatively mature business sector, which has recently added to productive capacity that is not expected to be fully utilized for several years. The market has not reflected the relatively favorable long-range prospects for the company. No large-scale acquisition or other investment opportunities currently present themselves at a yield above the company's present cost of capital, as perceived by the corporation.

The viewpoints of both the corporation and the stockholder need to be considered. As indicated, the repurchase may be attractive to one party and not the other under certain assumptions.

Simplified Analysis from the Corporation's Viewpoint. If a buy-back could be achieved at or close to the current market price of $50 per share, then the excess corporate assets of $20 million would be equivalent to 400,000 shares or 20 percent of the outstanding common stock. With the

Table 12-3
Data for Company "Cash Rich"

Before repurchase	
Excess corporate liquidity	$20 million
Weighted average cost of capital perceived by the firm.	13%
Estimated range of returns (IRR) for major acquisition and re-investment projects available to the company today	10-12%
Number of shares presently outstanding	2 million
After-tax earnings	$12 million
Net income per share	$6.00
Dividends per share	$4.00
Book value	$120 million
Book value per share	$60.00
Market price per share	$50.00
After repurchase of 400,000 or 20 percent of outstanding shares at $50 per share	
Number of shares now outstanding	1.6 million
After-tax earnings	$12 million
Net income per share	$7.50
Dividends per share (same before repurchase)	$4.00
Book value	$100 million
Book value per share	$62.50

present dividend rate being maintained, $1.6 million of annual after-tax income now paid in dividends would be saved by the corporation for a one-time cost of $20 million. We further assume that the stock could be resold to the public or used for an acquisition or other purposes five years from now when better opportunities are expected to present themselves. At the equivalent of today's price of $50 per share, what is the return to the corporation from such a repurchase plan? What if future earnings are higher than those of today, as management projects, and for this or other reasons management is convinced the stock could be sold later at a higher price?

An after-tax-income stream of $1.6 million (the overall dividend savings to the corporation) on an investment value of $20 million (the present market value) represents an after-tax rate of return of 8 percent, well below the company's opportunity cost of capital. In such circumstances a buy-back does not appear to be a viable alternative from the corporation's standpoint. However, a 15-percent return from a discounted cash-flow calculation is indicated under the assumption that the terminal value is $30 million for the shares five years in the future. This higher value might be anticipated because projected improved corporate earnings (and dividends) are expected to be reflected in a greater maket value or because of changed market conditions, different prospects for the company, or other factors. Under these latter circumstances, a repurchase may well be warranted if these and other assumptions stand up to detailed analysis. It should also be noted that whereas the book value of the company as a whole declines by the amount of the cash purchase, the per-share book value of the remaining shares increased in this example.

The point to be made is that more corporations should consider buy-backs, particularly in the face of poor investment/acquisition alternatives, high liquidity, and perceived low market price for their stock. Such considerations, however, should not be focused on an expected recovery of stock price, but rather on an overall comparison of alternatives, which may include forecasted effects from market forces on earnings and dividend changes.

Simplified Example from a Stockholder's Point of View. The position of company "Cash Rich" is the same as before. Stockholder A's cost basis is $25 per share and the shares have been held for at least twelve months. Dividends are $4 per share. The stockholder tenders 200 of his shares at $50 and receives $10,000. His capital gain is $5,000, which is taxed at 25 percent. (In this example, we are assuming that the profit on the sale of the stock would not be treated as a dividend.)

Under our assumptions for company "Cash Rich," the same per-share dividend is maintained; but because of the company's repurchase of 200 shares, stockholder A's annual dividends are reduced by $800. Thus he receives a $10,000 pretax payment and incurs $1,250 in capital-gains taxes. The investor gives up $800 per year of future dividends. In the case of the dividends, we assume that they would be taxed at a 50-percent rate, making the after-tax dividend income $400 per year. How attractive is this repurchase from the stockholder's point of view?

Pretax Basis. Assume a short two-year time horizon of the investor and a 20-percent pretax return objective. Ten thousand dollars is received from the sale of 200 shares. At a 20-percent discount rate, the present value of the annual dividend given up, plus the present value of the market price two years in the future (assuming no change in the $50-per-share price), is $8,166. This is $1,834 less than the investor receives from the sale under the repurchase plan.

Under these specific circumstances the investor is better off from the sale. Rather than an annual return of 8 percent from dividends, he achieves a total return of over 20 percent from the immediate gain on the sale.

After-Tax Basis. Assume the same two-year time horizon, but with a 10-percent annual after-tax-return requirement. Proceeds from the sale of stock on an after-tax basis at the long-term capital-gains rate would be $8,750. The after-tax proceeds on the annual dividend of $800 would be $400 at a 50-percent tax rate.

Here also the repurchase plan favors the investor selling rather than holding his stock. His after-tax receipts of $8,750 would compare to a present value of future dividends of $694 and a present value of $7,231 for the investment itself, a total of $7,925. In fact, under the foregoing assumptions the investor would have to receive annual dividends of about $875 ($4.38 per share) after taxes to make holding the stock equivalent to sale under the repurchase plan. Alternatively, an increase in future market value could have the same effect.

Cautionary Comments.* The preceding illustrative example is clearly over-simplified. For example, the corporation's increased earnings—not only from the repurchase, but also from overall growth in earnings—might well be reflected in a growing dividend rate and increasing stock price. Arguments can be made for different time horizons. Also, the corporation presumably would lose interest on the "excess cash" used to effect the purchase or would incur interest charges if it were borrowed. Additionally, the likely future price of the stock is a key variable; and reducing the shares outstanding may affect market value. Other related issues include per-share

---

Note that we have followed the general accounting practice of treating repurchased shares as a reduction of assets and equity. However, an argument can be made for carrying reacquired stock as an asset when these shares are intended for later use as part of an employee compensation plan or possibly for merger/acquisition and other purposes. Where such shares are carried as an asset, no net worth or per-share book value effects would normally occur. However, regardless of how treated, repurchased shares are not entitled to dividends, have no voting rights, and are excluded from earnings per share calculations. In addition, any applicable state or Securities Exchange regulations, or restrictions imposed by creditors, must be observed, for example regarding changes in assets or equity from repurchase transactions.

book-value changes and the effects of different investor tax rates and cost bases for the stock.

Concluding Note

The cash repurchase of a portion of a company's common stock shrinks total assets and net worth. (However, under the usual circumstances it increases both the remaining per-share earnings and book value.) The buy-back of a corporation's own stock can be viewed as a "temporizing" move consistent with the different time horizon and disparities in valuation between the corporation and the passive investor.

References

Boczar, Gregory E., and Rice, R. Michael. "Stock Repurchases by Bank Holding Companies." *Magazine of Bank Administration*, February 1979.

Brigham, Eugene F. *Financial Management*. Hinsdale, Ill.: Dryden Press, 1977. (See pp. 693-697.)

Coates, C. Robert, and Fredman, Albert J. "Price Behavior Associated with Tender Offers to Repurchase Common Stock." *Financial Executive*, April 1976.

Ellis, Charles D., and Young, Allan E. *The Repurchase of Common Stock*. New York: The Ronald Press, 1971.

Ferris, Kenneth R.; McInik, Arie; and Rappaport, Alfred. "Factors Influencing the Pricing of Stock Repurchase Tenders." *Quarterly Journal of Economics and Business* 18 (Spring 1978):31-39.

Lee, Steven James. "Why Some Companies Buy-Back Stock—and Some Don't." *Nation's Business*, August 1975.

LeMaster, Richard Y. "The Effect of a Stock Repurchase Upon Earnings and Profits of a Public Corporation." *Journal of Corporate Taxation*, Winter 1976, pp. 476-500.

Merjos, Anna. "Well-Timed Repurchases." *Barrons*, 8 January 1979.

Petty, J. William, and Pinkerton, John M. "The Stock Purchase Decision: A Market Perspective." *Journal of Accounting, Auditing and Finance*, Winter 1978.

Stewart, Samuel S., Jr. "Should a Corporation Repurchase its Own Stock?" *Journal of Finance*, June 1976.

Wittebort, Suzanne. "The New Boom in Stock Repurchases," *Institutional Investor*, August 1980.
Young, Allan E. "Accounting for Treasury Stock." *Journal of Accounting, Auditing and Finance*, Spring 1978.

Index

Index

About the Authors

James W. Bradley is a senior management consultant for Arthur D. Little, Inc., with major responsibility for the Financial Industries Group's acquisition practice. He is also active in corporate planning, capital investment decision making, and company valuation projects, as well as new-venture consulting and financing. Clients have included the managements of financial, manufacturing, and service industries. Mr. Bradley was a founding diector and an officer of a small manufacturing concern; is author and coauthor of publications dealing with acquisition and corporate-development topics; and is active in professional groups. He received the A.B. from Lafayette College and the M.B.A. from Cornell University

Donald H. Korn, a senior management consultant, directs the Investment Analysis Unit in the Financial Industries Group of Arthur D. Little, Inc. His focus includes corporate and institutional investment strategies and policies appropriate to a rapidly changing business, technological, and regulatory environment. His work includes industry studies, valuations of acquisitions, and new-venture financing, for private industry and government. He is a chartered financial analyst and director of the Boston Security Analysts Society. He received the B.S. and M.S. degrees in engineering from Tulane University and the S.M. degree from the Massachusetts Institute of Technology. Mr. Korn was on the securities research staff with State Street Research and Management Company.